LEGENDARY LOCALS

OF

EL PASO

TEXAS

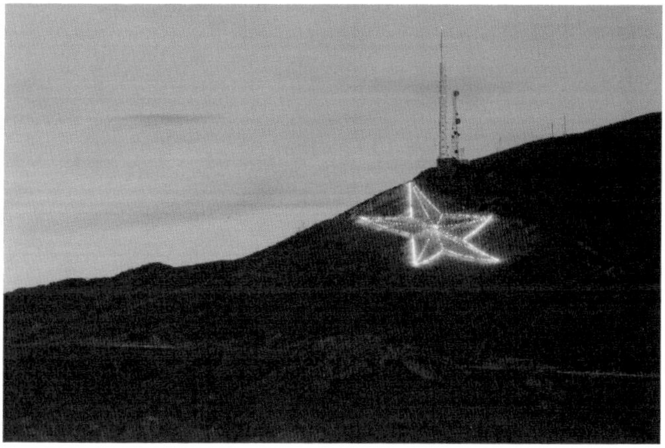

I0805761

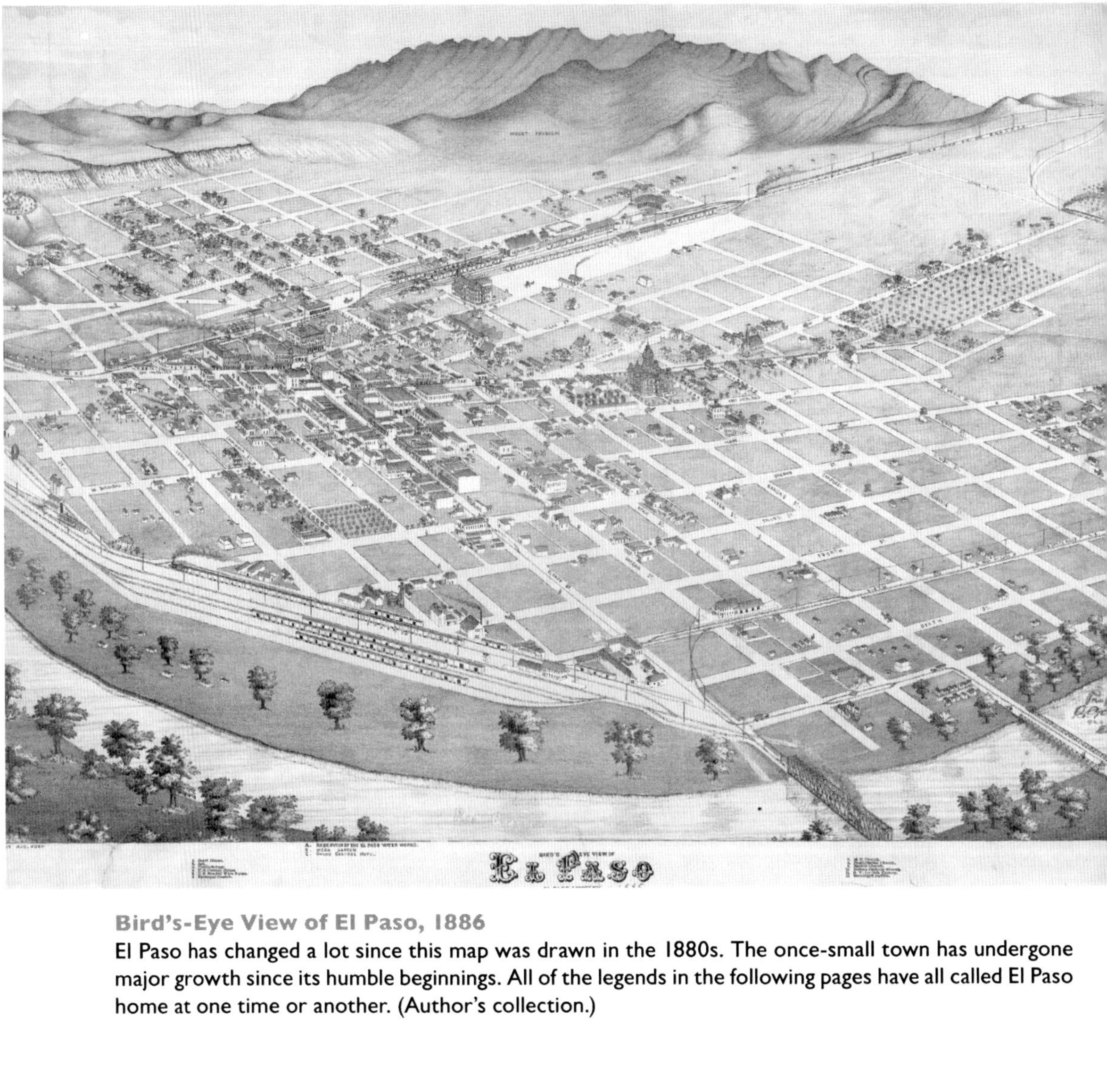

Bird's-Eye View of El Paso, 1886
El Paso has changed a lot since this map was drawn in the 1880s. The once-small town has undergone major growth since its humble beginnings. All of the legends in the following pages have all called El Paso home at one time or another. (Author's collection.)

Page 1: El Paso Star on the Mountain
The star on the mountain is a landmark that is recognized by El Pasoans everywhere. First built in 1940 by El Paso Electric, the local icon has seen upgrades over the years and is lit on a nightly basis. Look for the brightly lit star, and find the way home. (Courtesy of Brian Wacho.)

LEGENDARY LOCALS

OF

EL PASO

TEXAS

DAVID A. BERCHELMANN III

LEGENDARY LOCALS

ISBN 978-1-4671-0187-5

Legendary Locals is an imprint of Arcadia Publishing
Charleston, South Carolina

Printed in the United States of America

Library of Congress Control Number: 2014944081

For all general information, please contact Arcadia Publishing:
Telephone 843-853-2070
Fax 843-853-0044
E-mail sales@arcadiapublishing.com
For customer service and orders:
Toll-Free 1-888-313-2665

Visit us on the Internet at www.arcadiapublishing.com

Dedication

To the people of El Paso, past and present, who have helped make this place one of the most wonderful and unique cities in the great state of Texas and the Southwest.

On the Front Cover: Clockwise from top left:
Felix Martinez, businessman, politician, and diplomat (courtesy of the El Paso Public Library; see page 20), Jim Ward, musician and entrepreneur (courtesy of Lindsey Best; see page 59), Henry Trost, architect (courtesy of Margaret Smith and family; see page 57), Dana Pittard, major general, US Army (courtesy of El Paso Inc.; see page 106), Adair Margo, founder and president of the Tom Lea Institute (courtesy of El Paso Inc.; see page 64), Willie Farah, businessman (courtesy of Jim Farah; see page 26), Joseph Magoffin, El Paso founder (courtesy of El Paso Public Library; see page 14), Diana Natalicio, president of the University of Texas El Paso (courtesy of University of Texas El Paso; see page 76), Tom Lea, artist (courtesy of the Tom Lea Institute; see page 58)

On the Back Cover: From left to right:
Gaspar Enriquez, Chicano artist (courtesy of El Paso Inc.; see page 63), Danny Olivas, US astronaut (courtesy of Danny Olivas; see page 92)

CONTENTS

ACKNOWLEDGMENTS

This project was quite the undertaking, and there were times when I felt overwhelmed and not sure where to go. Fortunately, my wife, Mallory, kept me on track with love, encouragement, and more than a few cups of coffee. To all of my family and friends, I am honored to have you in my life and am excited to share this with all of you.

El Paso is full of so many great people, and there are many more who are forging their legacy right now. I enjoyed listening to the personal stories of the people featured in this book. In everyone's life there has come a time when they faced a fork in the road. The path they chose at that time in their life helped lead to the stories you will read in the following pages.

Many thanks to everyone at the Border Heritage Center of the El Paso Public Library (EPPL BHC), the El Paso County Historical Society, and the University of Texas at El Paso (UTEP) Special Collections Department. Their assistance in locating photographs of early El Pasoans was integral in not only completing this book but lowering my stress levels too. Melody Parra at El Paso Inc. put up with my constant requests for photographs and was always friendly and accommodating. To the families who took the time to speak with me about their relatives and share their stories—thank you. To those who spoke with me and shared their journey, it was an honor.

Finally, thank you to Arcadia Publishing for giving me the opportunity to explore my community and share what I learned.

INTRODUCTION

The first time I visited El Paso I was 16 years old. My dad and I were to take the Amtrak Sunset Limited from San Diego, California, to San Antonio, Texas, but a mistake in the booking changed our plans, and we ended up traveling from El Paso. I vividly remember staying in a motel off of I-10 near the airport and seeing the green shimmering lights of Juarez, Mexico, across the border. We were only in El Paso for a day before we had to board our train at Union Station. Little did I know that my life would lead to this city again when I moved out to the far tip of West Texas in 2008.

Before El Paso was a large metropolitan area at the border of three states and two countries, it was home to Native American tribes. Centuries later, it became a pathway for explorers from the 1500s on. This north-south route came to be called Paso del Norte, or Pass of the North. One of the most well-known Spanish explorers who had a lasting effect on the area was Juan de Oñate. He is locally credited with celebrating the first Thanksgiving in North America in 1598 at a site near present-day San Elizario. A 36-foot-tall bronze tribute to Oñate depicting the explorer on his horse is permanently placed at the entrance to the El Paso International Airport. While Oñate continued north, the area along the Rio Grande continued to become more populated.

The Paso del Norte region became Mexican territory after the country claimed its independence from Spain in 1821. A few years later, Juan María Ponce de León was given a land grant that encompassed much of what is the central area of El Paso today. Americans such as James Magoffin began to make their way into the region to take advantage of the trade routes that stretched from Mexico into the Santa Fe area. From there, growth continued, and small settlements such as Magoffinsville were formed along the Rio Grande. Today, tourists can visit the home that was owned by Joseph Magoffin, James Magoffin's son, who helped El Paso develop from a small town into a thriving city. With the arrival of the railroads, the population grew quickly from just a few hundred people to thousands by the late 1800s. Zach White and other pioneers helped modernize the city by establishing basic utilities such as gas and electricity while creating transportation options that would help link El Paso to Juarez.

In 1909, Mexican president Porfirio Díaz and US president William Howard Taft met in El Paso to discuss diplomatic relations. A year later, the Mexican Revolution began, and Diaz lost power. With the revolution came the rise of Pancho Villa. Villa knew El Paso well and spent time in the city during the years of the revolution. Even with the revolution in full swing across the border, El Paso continued to grow. Industry continued to call the city home, and Fort Bliss continued to be a major influence in the area. The 20th century brought El Pasoans such as artist Tom Lea, the 1949 state champion baseball team from Bowie High School, national championship coach Don Haskins, and many more. At some point during the last few decades of the 20th century, El Paso hit a wall. The city that had been the star of the Southwest began to see its twinkle fade.

After a couple decades of stagnation, El Paso appears to be turning the corner and entering a new period of growth and prosperity. Businessman Paul Foster has played a key role in helping reinvigorate downtown El Paso with renovations of historic buildings and investments in other areas of the city. Fort Bliss has seen a multibillion-dollar investment by the US government to help support the growth with base realignment. The youth of El Paso are choosing to make El Paso home instead of leaving for other cities like their predecessors did in years past. Expatriates are also returning to the Sun City and bringing new ideas to implement in the community. The effects of what is happening right now in El Paso will help write the history books of the future, and that future is bright.

Finally, this book cannot feature everyone; there are many more who have made and are now making a difference in this community. Take a moment, sit back, maybe grab a cup of coffee, and enjoy delving into the lives of people who have had an impact on one of the Southwest's most interesting cities.

CHAPTER ONE

Early Times

Before Europeans came to the area, Native American tribes inhabited what was then an untamed Rio Grande. In the 1500s, European explorers made their way into the area. It is said that Cabeza de Vaca visited the El Paso area as he made his way through Texas, but the first well-known El Paso explorer is Juan de Oñate. After crossing the river, Oñate stopped near present-day San Elizario and celebrated what many locals consider North America's first Thanksgiving.

El Paso would not see significant growth until the 1800s. During that time, people from the East made their way into the area to become some of the first pioneers. James Magoffin and Hugh Stephenson helped establish some of the first permanent settlements in the area while becoming successful merchants and traders.

The town attracted people of all walks of life, and some were of the more violent type. To quell the violence, Dallas Stoudenmire was hired as the town marshal and was immediately thrust into controversy with four dead in a five-second gunfight. His controversy would not end there, as he continued to attempt to impose order in the lawless Southwest. Going up against an establishment that was not particularly fond of law enforcement made for a rough outing no matter who held the top law-enforcement post.

In the early 1880s, the population began to skyrocket after the railroads came through town, and with an increase in population came an increase in basic city needs. Joseph Magoffin, Zach White, and Anson Mills helped transition the city from a small frontier town into a growing and prosperous city. The city hosted President Taft in 1909 during the Taft-Diaz summit. A year later, the Mexican Revolution began, and Pancho Villa would go on to become one of the most romanticized revolutionaries in the Western Hemisphere. These colorful characters of El Paso's past were laying the groundwork for what is now a city of hundreds of thousands; their effect on El Paso is not forgotten.

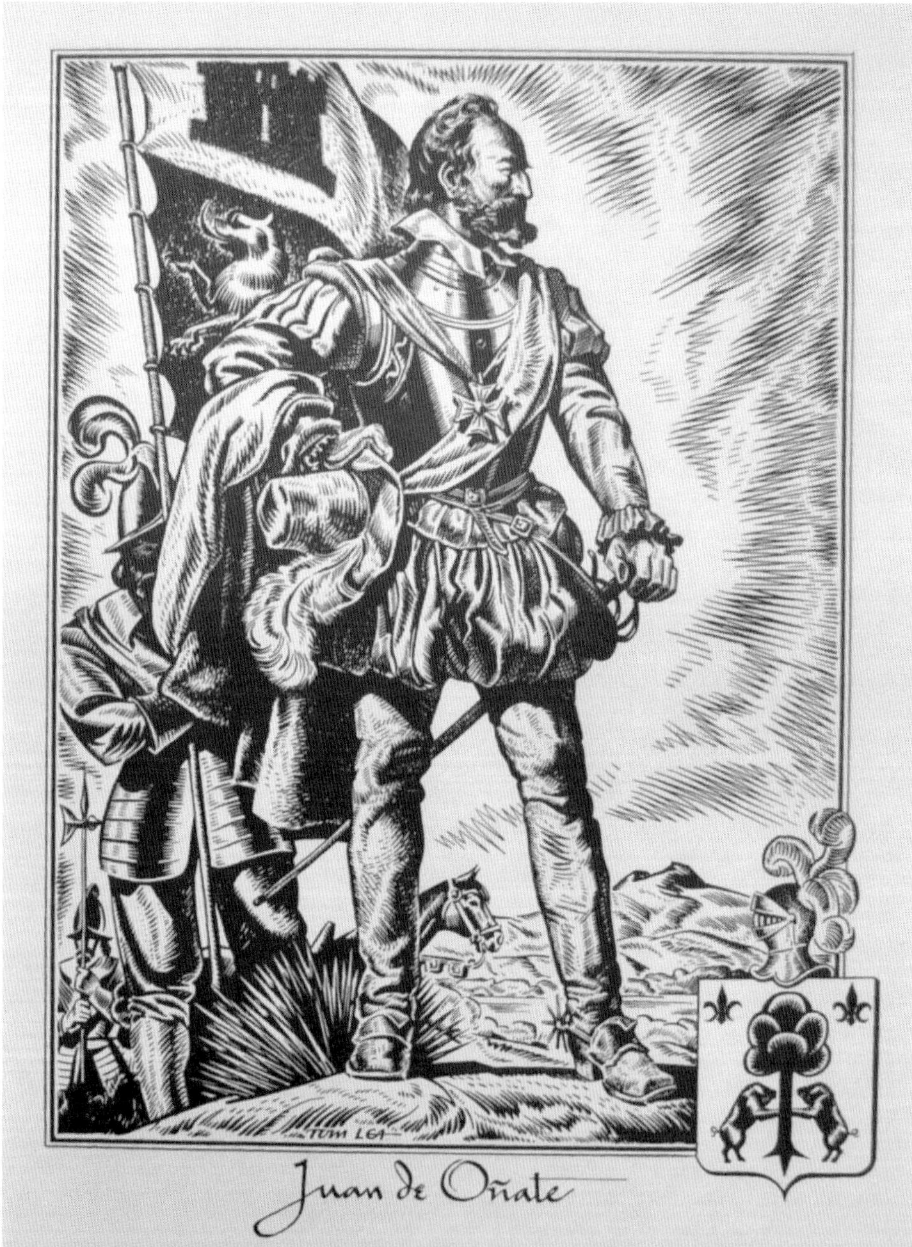

Juan de Oñate

Juan de Oñate was a Spanish conquistador and explorer who is locally credited with celebrating the first Thanksgiving, near present-day San Elizario, in 1598. King Philip of Spain tasked Oñate with exploring the region and spreading Catholicism. Oñate helped establish the first colonies of the Southwest in northern New Mexico. He eventually resigned his position after the colony began to fail, and was recalled back to Mexico City after allegations of his treatment of the native population. Juan de Oñate lived the last years of his life in Spain, where he passed away in the early 1620s. (Courtesy of the Tom Lea Institute.)

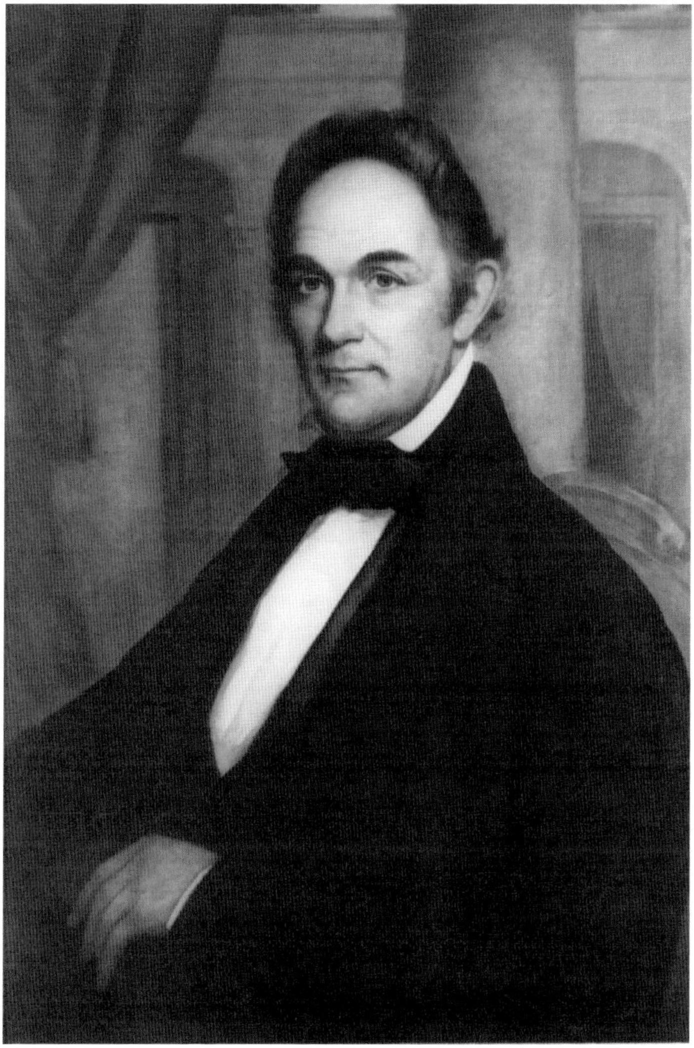

James Wiley Magoffin
The frontier was settled by adventurers, and James Wiley Magoffin can be counted among them. Born in Harrodsburg, Kentucky, in 1799, Magoffin left the Bluegrass State in search of opportunities in Mexico. His travels eventually led him to northern Mexico, where he developed into a successful Santa Fe trader. Wiley met his future wife, María Gertrudis Valdés, in Mexico, and they were married in the 1830s. They had several children, including Joseph Magoffin, who would become a prominent El Paso politician.

After moving to Independence, Missouri, Magoffin was asked by Pres. James K. Polk to be a special envoy to the US Army. He helped negotiate the surrender of Santa Fe in 1846 during the Mexican-American War but was arrested as a spy by the Mexican government several months later while making preparations for the advancing US Army. After his release, Magoffin returned to the Paso del Norte area in 1849 and settled an area that would later become known as Magoffinsville, where Fort Bliss would first be established in the 1850s.

A strong supporter of the Confederacy, James Wiley lost his property holdings in the El Paso area after the Civil War. Never able to reclaim his holdings from the US government, Magoffin ended up moving to San Antonio. He was granted amnesty, and his citizenship was restored in 1866. After suffering from a long bout of dropsy, Magoffin passed away in 1868. (Courtesy of El Paso County Historical Society.)

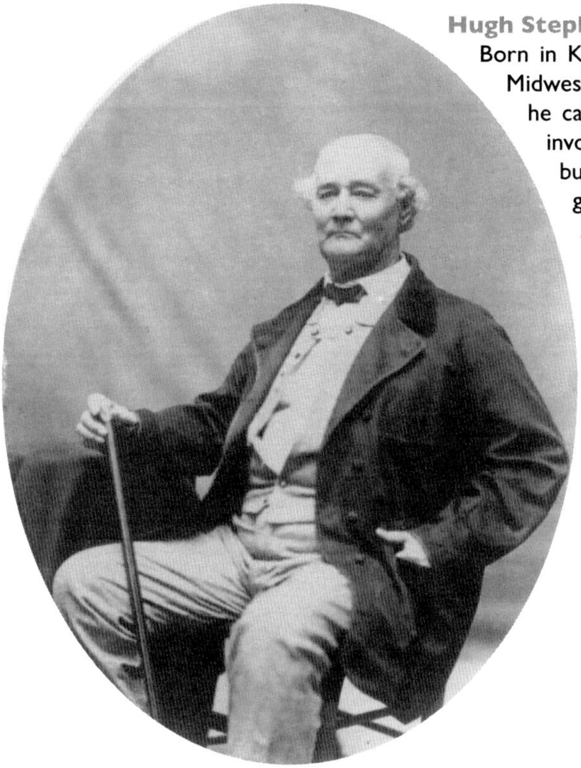

Hugh Stephenson

Born in Kentucky, Hugh Stephenson grew up in the Midwest and mostly worked as a trapper. When he came down to the El Paso area, he became involved in the prospecting and mining business in the Organ Mountains, where he grew his wealth. Stephenson married Juana Azcárate of the prominent Azcárate family. As an early pioneer in the El Paso area, Stephenson created the settlement along the Rio Grande called Concordia. Part of Concordia would eventually become Concordia Cemetery in central El Paso. (Courtesy of the El Paso Public Library Border Heritage Collection.)

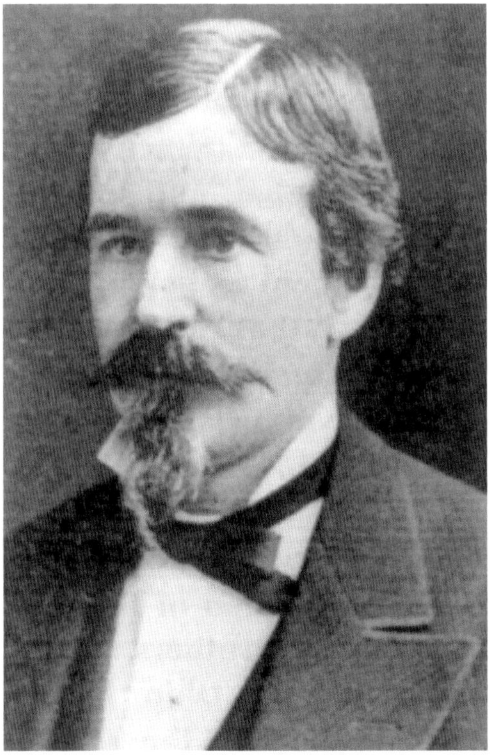

Anson Mills

Anson Mills had an idea for how the small settlement of El Paso should be set up, and he put that vision on paper. The current layout of downtown El Paso is very similar to how Mills envisioned it over 150 years ago. The man who gave El Paso its name also served as an officer in the Army and as the American boundary commissioner. In 1883, Mills built the Grand Central Hotel, which succumbed to a fire years later. In 1911, he worked with Trost & Trost to design one of the largest concrete structures of the time. The Mills Building is still standing today and underwent an extensive renovation after being purchased by Paul Foster. Anson Mills was an integral part of setting up a solid foundation for El Paso, and his legacy can be seen daily in the heart of downtown. (Courtesy of the El Paso County Historical Society.)

James Hague

The railroads had not reached El Paso in 1871 when James Price Hague was appointed the district attorney for the area. Instead of a smooth ride over rail, he had to take a stagecoach. Like many other pioneers in the area, Hague was involved in the community during its early years. He was a proponent of bringing the railroads into the area and also had a prominent law practice. In addition to being district attorney, Hague also served as a district judge, county attorney, and alderman. In 1895, he passed away in San Antonio. (Courtesy of the El Paso County Historical Society.)

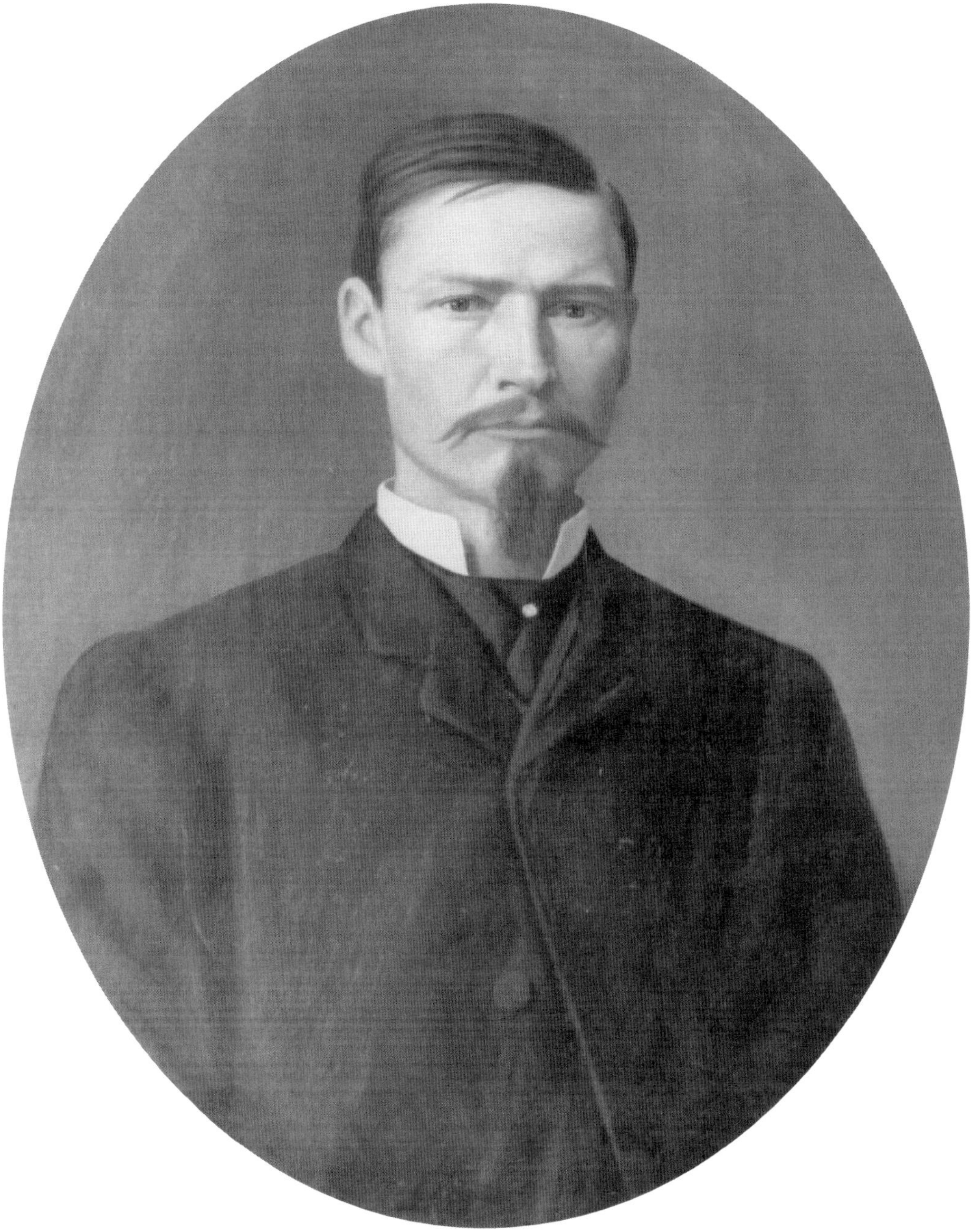

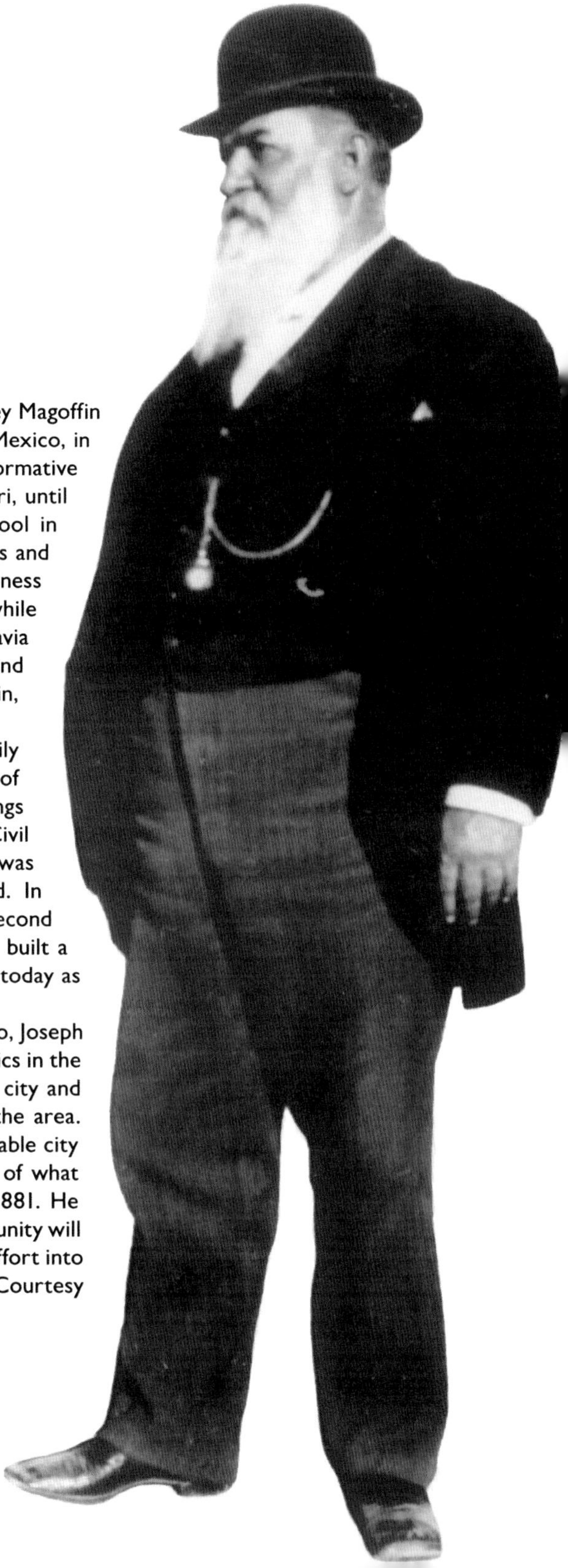

Joseph Magoffin

Joseph Magoffin, the son of pioneer James Wiley Magoffin and María Gertrudis, was born in Chihuahua, Mexico, in 1837. The future mayor of El Paso spent his formative years going to school in Independence, Missouri, until the passing of his mother. After finishing school in St. Louis, Joseph Magoffin moved back to Texas and began helping his father with the mercantile business in Magoffinsville. During the Civil War, while fighting for the Confederacy, Magoffin met Octavia MacGreal in Houston. The two wed in 1864 and welcomed their first child, James Wiley Magoffin, in 1865.

After Joseph's father died in 1868, the family moved to El Paso so he could begin the process of reclaiming ownership of his father's land holdings that had been taken by the Union during the Civil War. After several years of work, the land was reacquired, and the family's wealth increased. In 1873, Joseph and Octavia welcomed their second child, Josephine. Several years later, the family built a home on a portion of their land that is known today as the Magoffin Home and is a state historic site.

As one of the original incorporators of El Paso, Joseph Magoffin played a vital part in business and politics in the area. He helped establish the first bank in the city and was also integral in bringing the railroads to the area. As El Paso grew, there was a need to have a stable city government. Magoffin was elected to his first of what would be four terms as mayor of El Paso in 1881. He passed away in 1923, but his effect on the community will forever be felt as one who put much time and effort into spurring growth and development in the area. (Courtesy of the El Paso County Historical Society.)

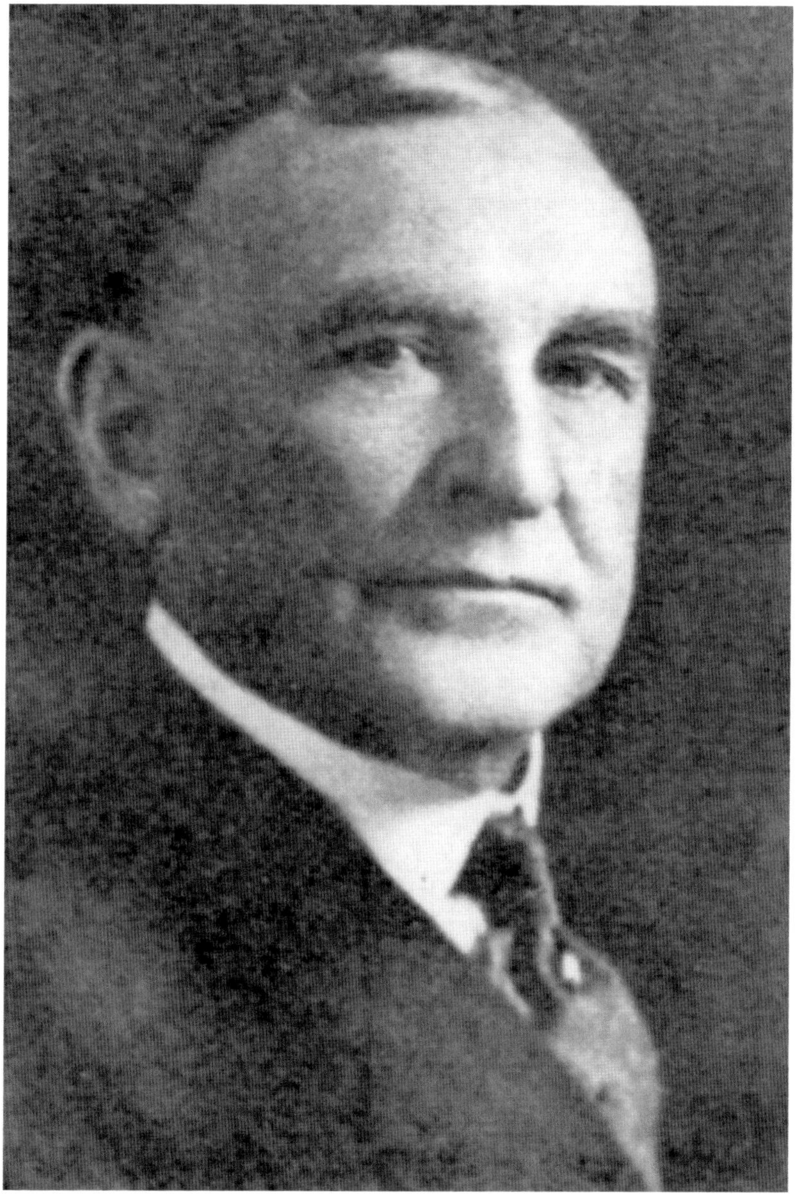

Zach White

One of El Paso's most prominent businessmen at the turn of the 20th century was Zach T. White. Born in 1850 under the Blue Ridge Mountains in Virginia, Zach White knew he wanted to go West from a young age. In 1881, his travels led him to El Paso, where he helped transition the once quiet town into a bustling city. He had many business interests, which ranged from a mercantile store to bringing electricity and gas service to the area. White financed the construction of Hotel Paso del Norte, which was designed by Trost & Trost. The entrepreneur also had a major effect on transportation in the area with the construction of the Santa Fe Street Bridge, and his streetcar service, which was known for Mandy the mule. He also donated a portion of his land in the Upper Valley to help establish a new space for the El Paso Country Club. White, who was married twice, passed away in 1932. (Courtesy of the El Paso County Historical Society.)

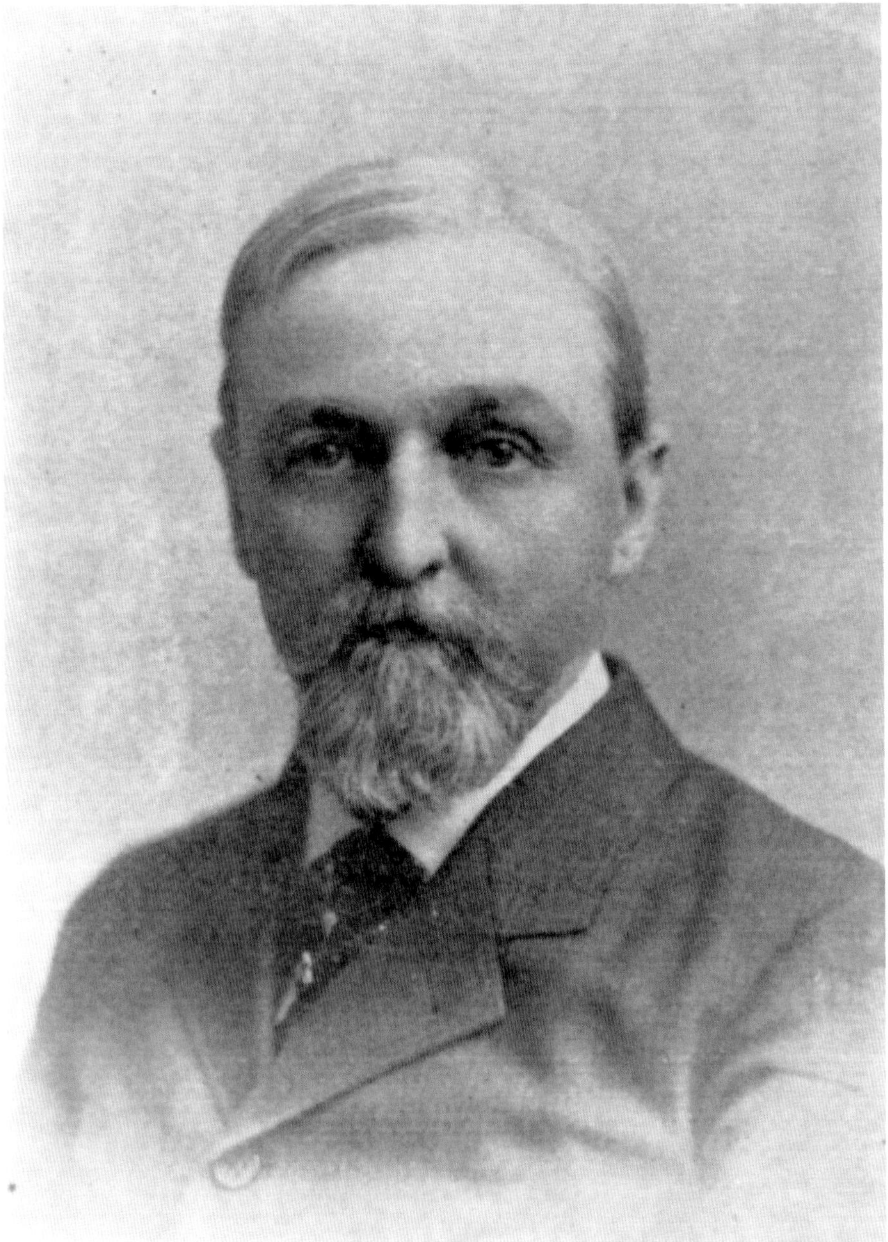

Charles Morehead

Charles Morehead was built for the life of a pioneer. In his early years, he spent time guiding wagon supply trains in the Midwest, where he ended up enduring multiple Indian attacks. Initially brought to El Paso to look at the feasibility of bringing in the railroads, he found himself here permanently in 1881. His leadership skills and smarts made him integral in setting up El Paso's first major bank (State National Bank), and he was also key in establishing the public school system, which he served as chairman. A true entrepreneur, Morehead was involved in multiple businesses in the area. Public service came calling, and the former wagon master went on to win the mayoral seat. Charles Morehead served in that capacity from 1903 to 1905 and passed away in 1921. (Courtesy of the EPPL BHC.)

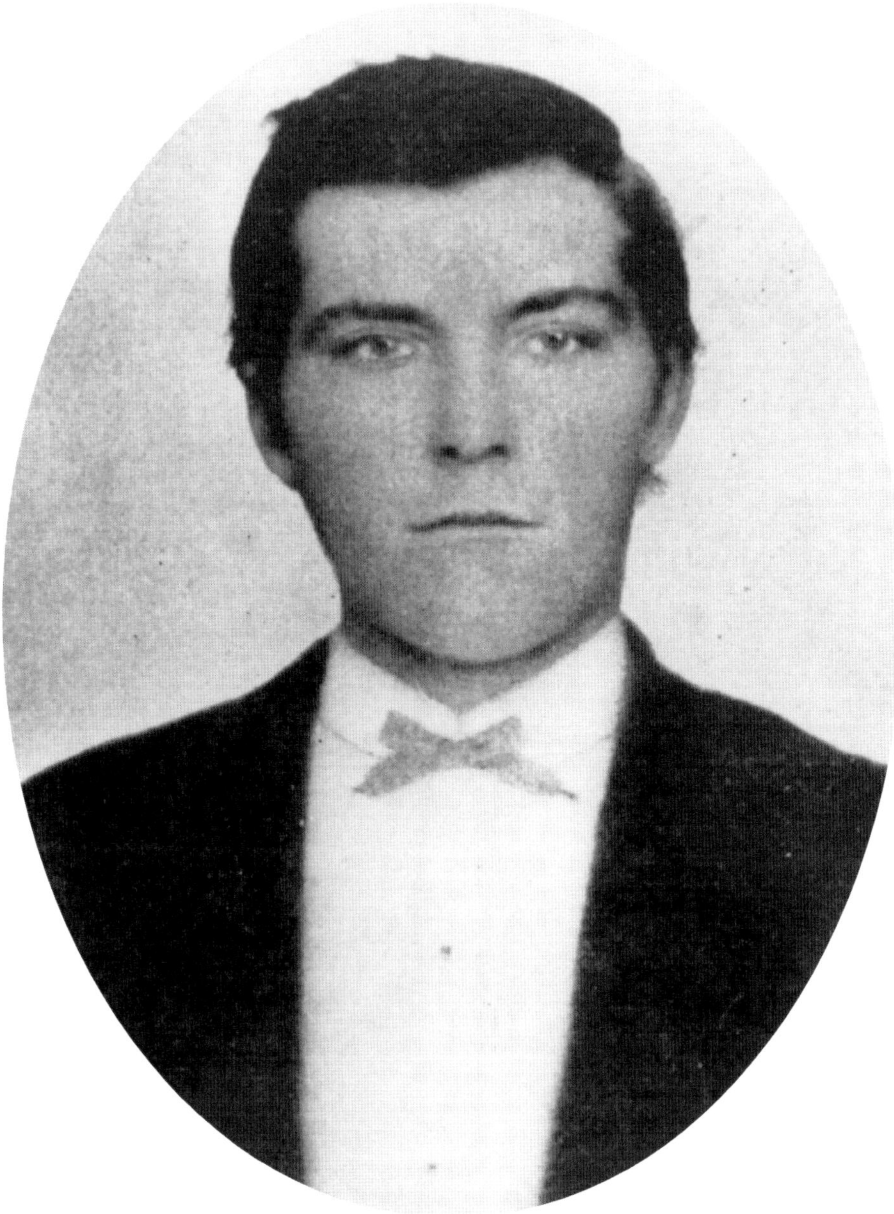

John Wesley Hardin

There were outlaws, and then there was John Wesley Hardin. Deadly accurate, Hardin left a trail of unfortunate souls who had succumbed to the barrel of his gun. It has been debated who would win in a gun fight between Billy the Kid and Hardin. The overwhelming verdict is that while Kid would get the first shot off, he would end up the loser to Hardin's accuracy. Hardin's crimes caught up to him, and he was convicted and served time in Florida, where he spent his days locked away studying law. After being pardoned, he made his way to El Paso to open a law practice. Being a reformed man is not easy, and his old habits came back, which led to him being shot in the back while at the Acme Saloon by constable John Selman in 1895. Buried in Concordia Cemetery, his grave can still be seen today. (Courtesy of the EPPL BHC.)

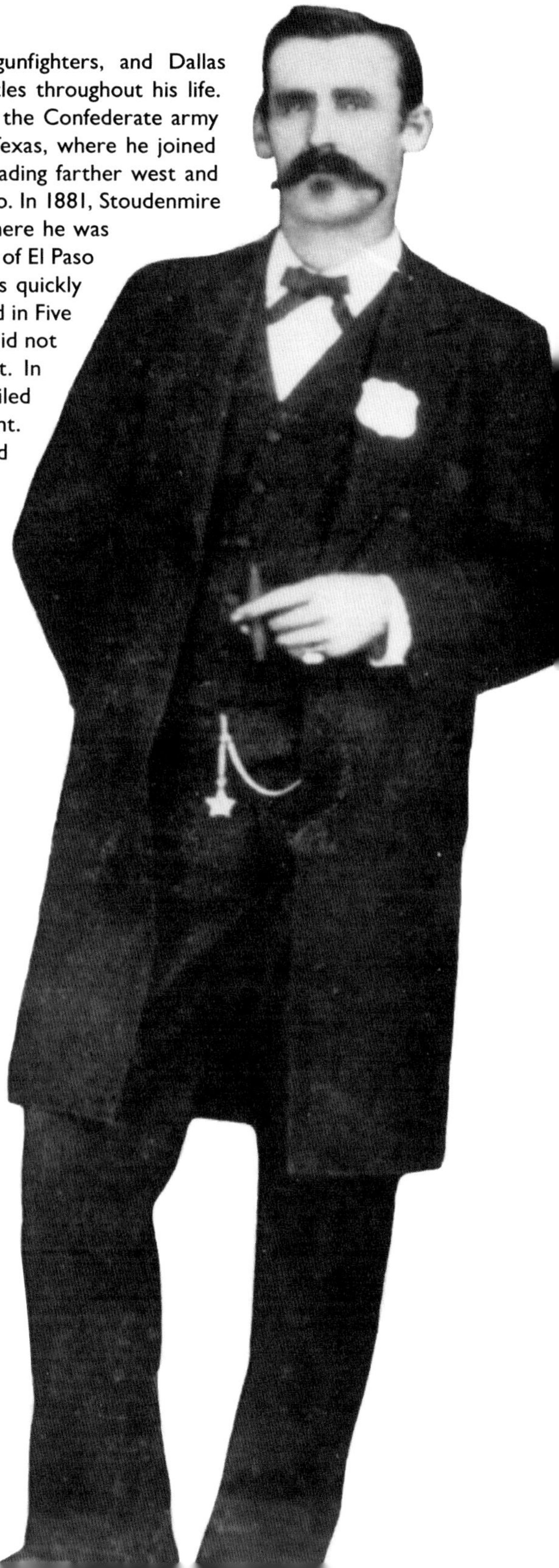

Dallas Stoudenmire

The West is known for its lawmen and gunfighters, and Dallas Stoudenmire was able to lay claim to both titles throughout his life. Born in Alabama in 1845, Stoudenmire joined the Confederate army in 1862. After the war, he made his way to Texas, where he joined the Texas Rangers for a short stint before heading farther west and becoming the marshal for Socorro, New Mexico. In 1881, Stoudenmire made his way south and arrived in El Paso, where he was soon appointed town marshal. The young town of El Paso needed a strong lawman, and Stoudenmire was quickly put in the spotlight with the famous "Four Dead in Five Seconds" gunfight. Life as a lawman in El Paso did not get easier for Stoudenmire after that incident. In 1882, a feud with the local Manning family boiled over, and Stoudenmire was killed in a gunfight. While his time in El Paso was short-lived, he did make a difference in the community and helped bring the city under control. (Courtesy of EPPL BHC.)

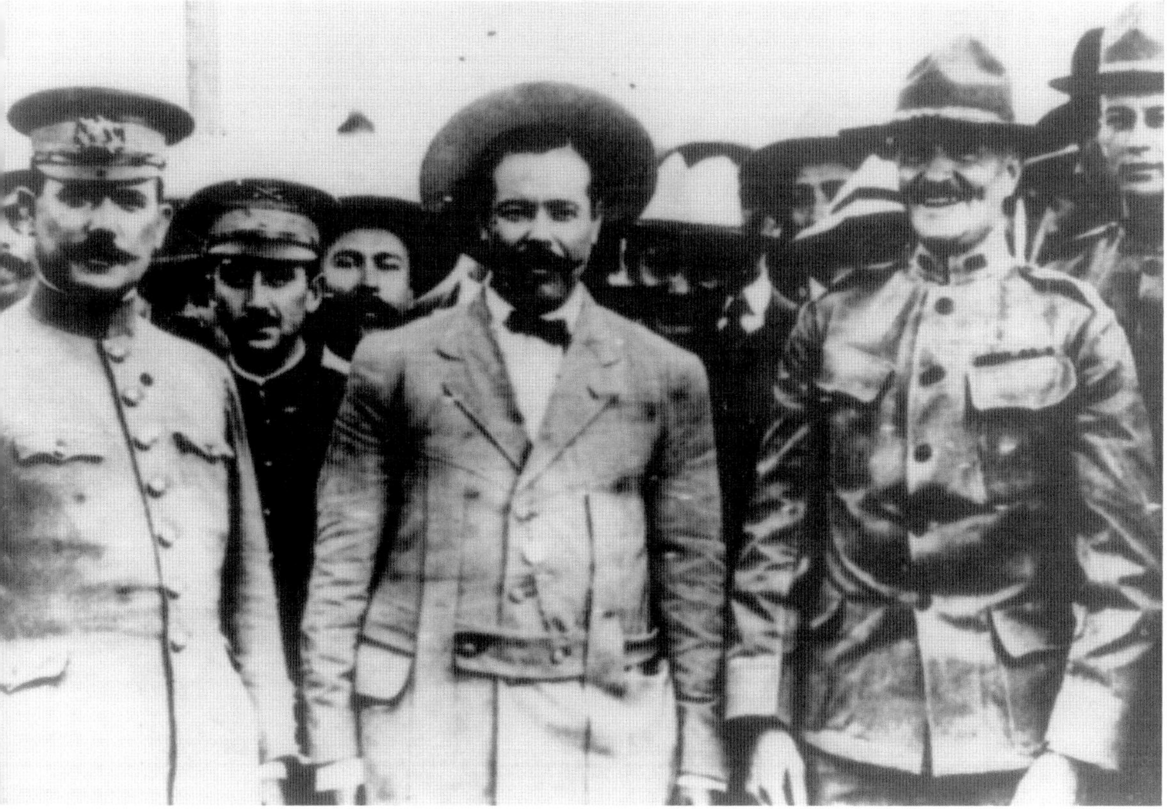

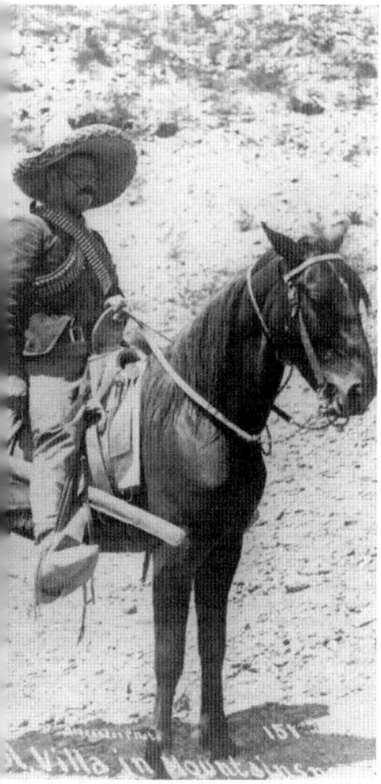

Pancho Villa

One of the Western Hemisphere's most well-known revolutionaries spent a lot of time between El Paso and Juarez during the Mexican Revolution. Doroteo Arango changed his name to Pancho Villa while on the run from authorities living life as a bandit in his early years. In 1910, Villa joined Francisco Madero in the revolution against Mexican president Porfirio Díaz. Madero took over as president of Mexico but was killed in a coup in 1913.

After hearing what happened to Madero, Villa was back in the spotlight as a revolutionary leader, commanding what was known as the Division of the North. Villa spent time on both sides of the border, and not only purchased supplies from El Paso businesses but also enjoyed the occasional taste of sweets from the Elite Confectionary. El Pasoans watched the battles in Juarez as Villa led the fight against opposing forces.

The fighting in Mexico continued, as there was no stable leadership at the top. Villa lost his support from the United States after it decided to back his foe, Venustiano Carranza. Shortly thereafter, Villa attacked the town of Columbus, New Mexico, and was pursued into Mexico by Gen. Jack Pershing, to no avail. In 1920, Villa hung up his guns and left the revolutionary life; three years later, he was assassinated in his vehicle while driving in Parral, Mexico. (Above, courtesy of the El Paso County Historical Society; left, courtesy of the EPPL BHC.)

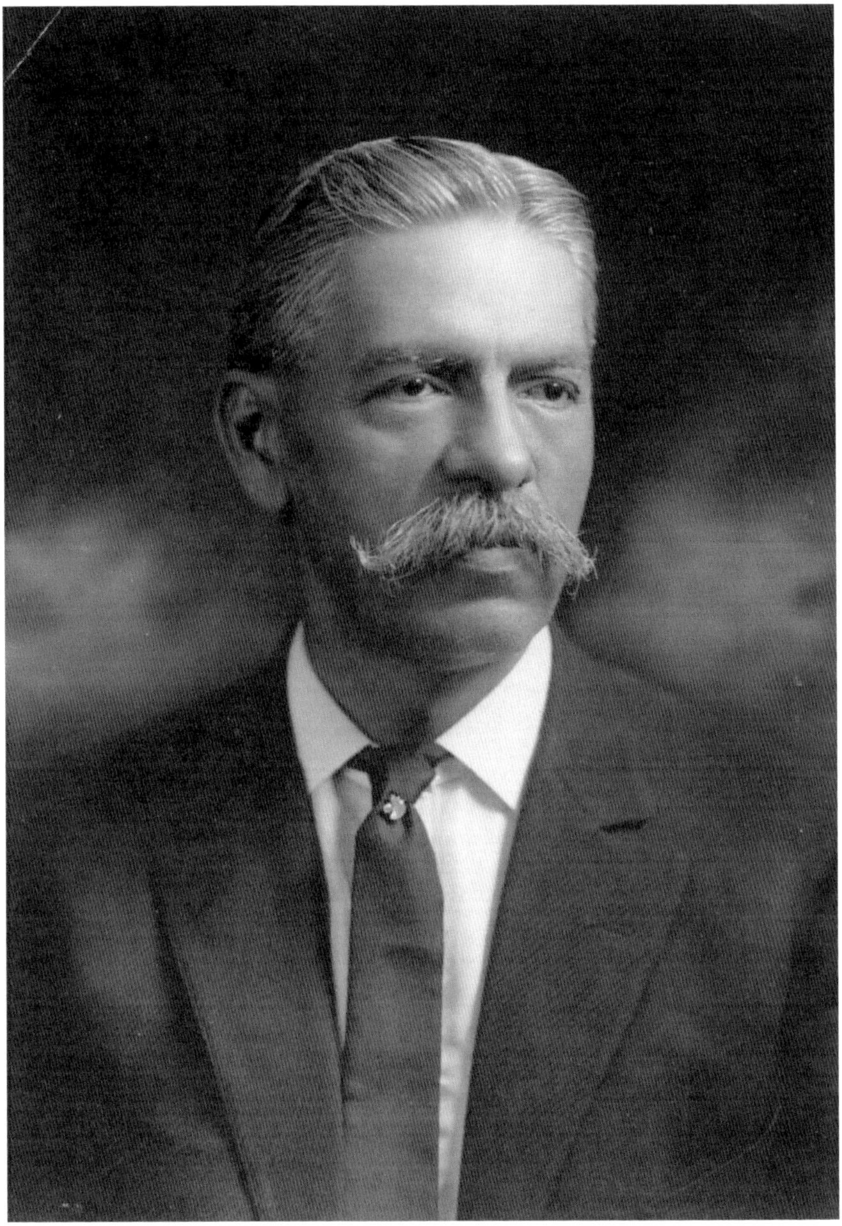

Felix Martinez

A savvy business mind opened up many opportunities for Felix Martinez when he moved to El Paso from New Mexico in 1897. He operated and published the *El Paso Daily News* for 10 years and was involved in other ventures, including the Southwestern Portland Cement Company and numerous building projects in downtown El Paso. Well respected by his peers, Martinez was a driving force in establishing the Elephant Butte Dam so that the areas downstream could have a reliable water source. Martinez had a great reputation and not only served as an original director for the Dallas Federal Reserve Board, but was also the chairman of the Panama-Pacific Exposition in 1912. His work ethic and leadership put El Paso on an upward trajectory that continued for decades. Martinez passed away in 1916. (Courtesy of the EPPL BHC.)

Richard Burgess

The El Paso Historical Society's current home was once the residence of attorney Richard Burgess. In 1892, Burgess moved to El Paso and opened his own law practice. He fought against gambling, helped establish the first city charter, and served two terms in the state legislature. Like other early pioneers of El Paso, Burgess was a proponent of and key backer behind the Elephant Butte project. When World War I broke out, Burgess organized Company B of the Texas National Guard, which was rolled into the 36th Infantry Division. After fighting in the Meuse-Argonne Offensive, Burgess was awarded the Croix de Guerre for his heroic service. Richard Burgess passed away in 1946. (Courtesy of the El Paso County Historical Society.)

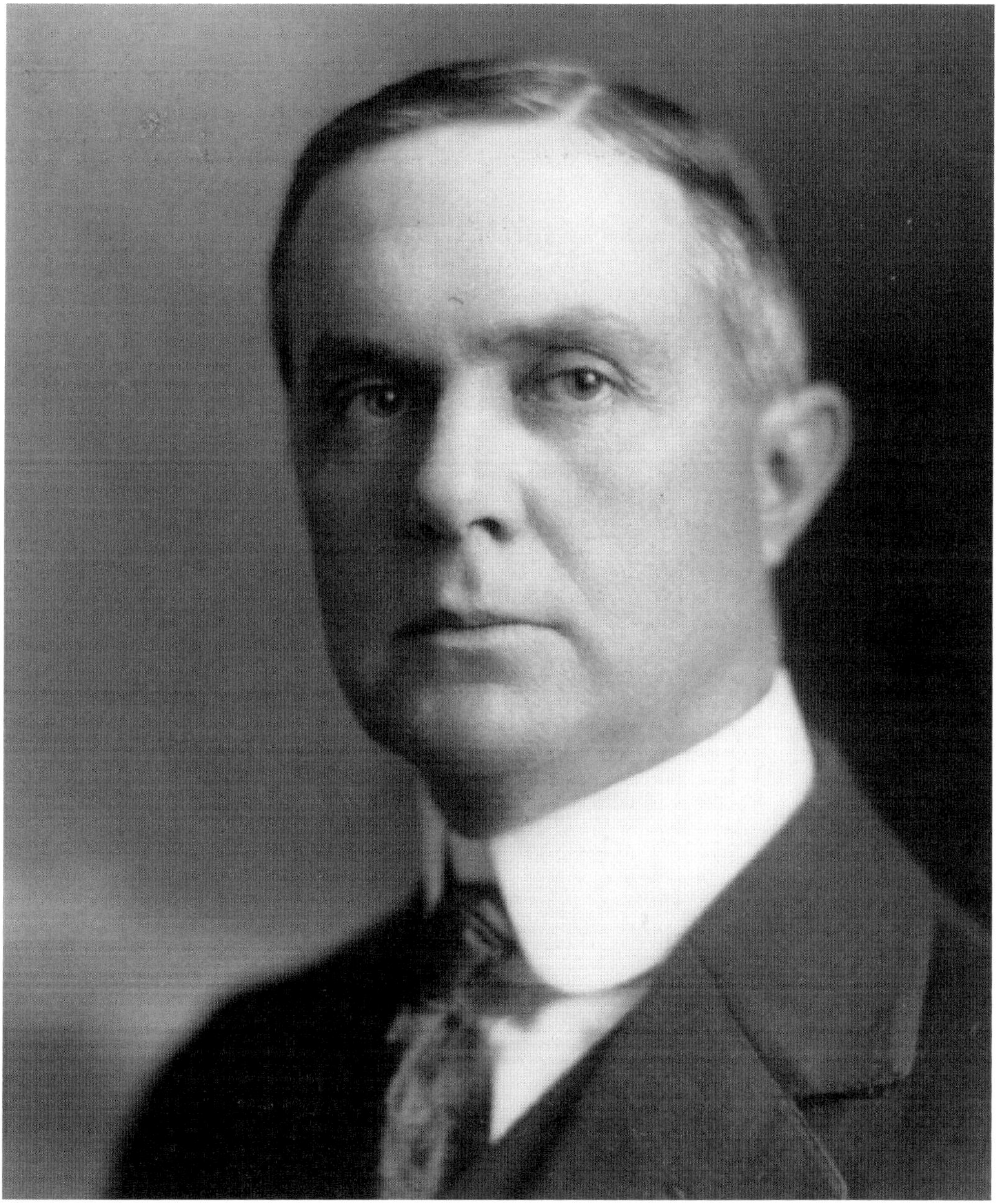

Mary Stanton

The El Paso Public Library can trace its beginnings back to Mary Stanton. After following family to El Paso, she found a job teaching third grade. Her teaching led her to offer a collection of 600 of her own books to the local students for a reading club. This led to the formation of the Public Library Association a year later, in 1895. Four years later, there were over 2,000 books available. With a growing collection, Stanton helped secure funds for the city's first independent library building. Mary Stanton passed away in 1946, but her effect on education in the city continues to be felt to this day. (Courtesy of the EPPL BHC.)

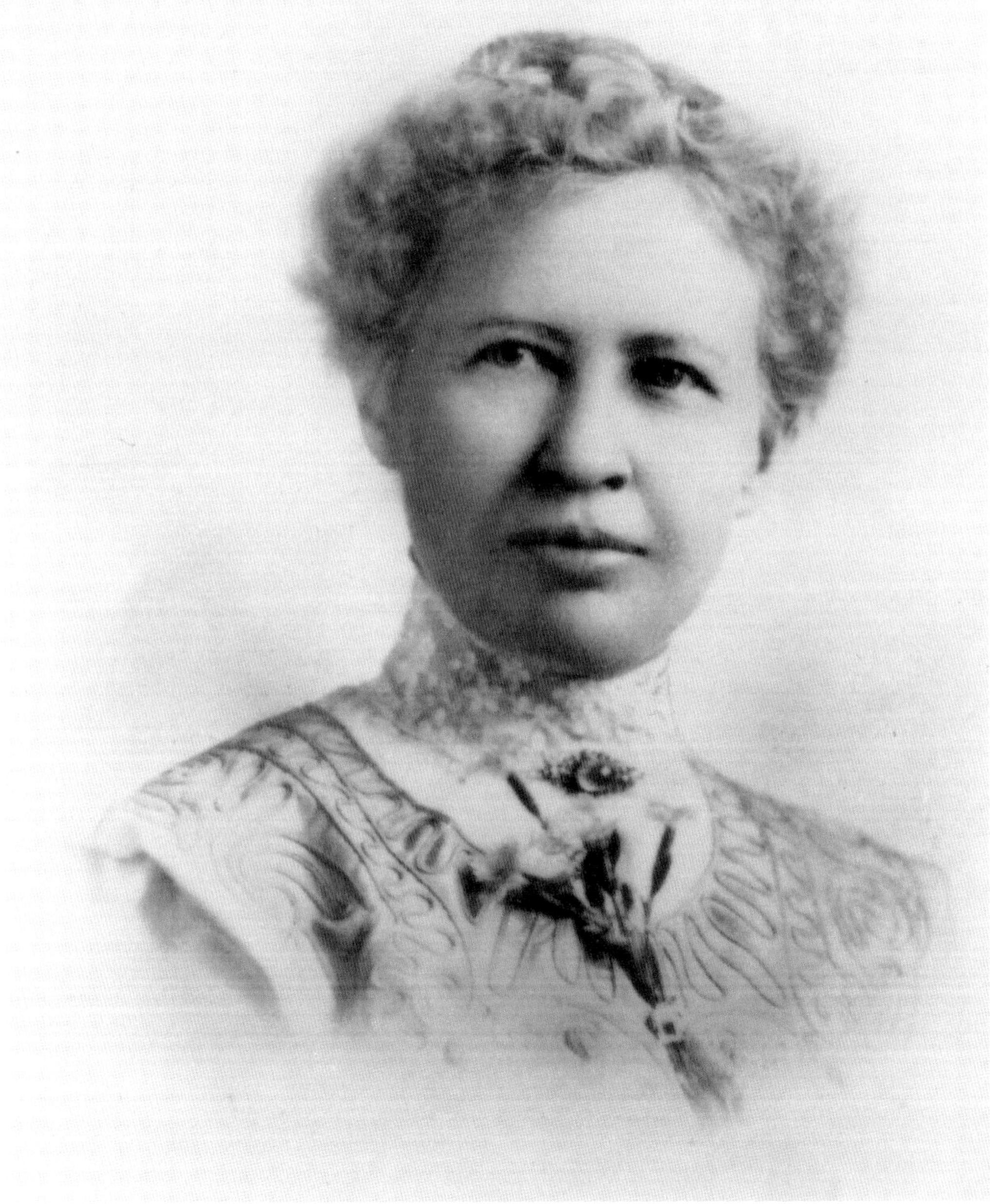

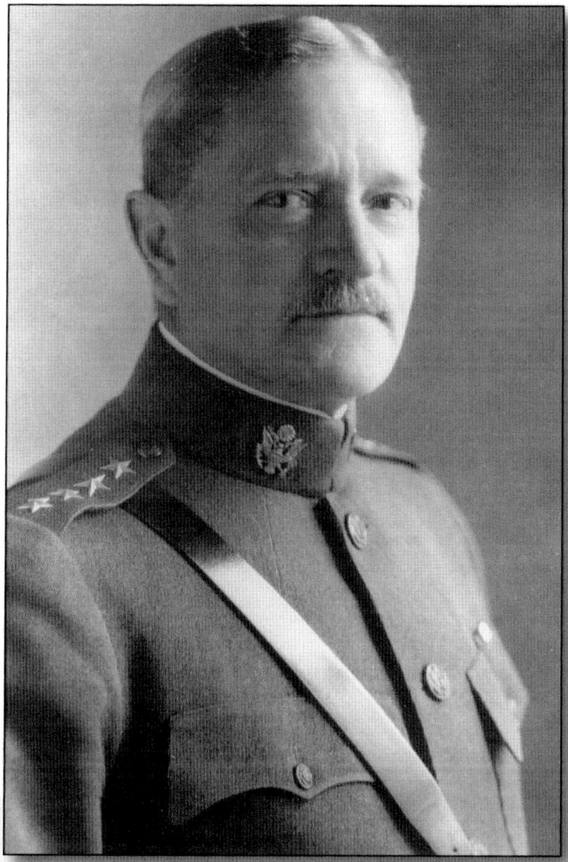

Gen. John "Blackjack" Pershing
One of the early 20th century's most well-recognized generals spent a number of years as the commander of Fort Bliss during the Mexican Revolution. General Pershing had already seen duty at the Battle of Wounded Knee and the Spanish-American War before making his way to El Paso in 1914. While in command at Fort Bliss, Pershing pursued Pancho Villa into Mexico after Villa's attack on Columbus, New Mexico, in 1916. Pershing's expedition did not result in the capture of the famed revolutionary, and in 1917, Pershing was reassigned to Fort Sam in San Antonio as the United States entered World War I. Pershing went on to lead American forces in Europe and attain the title of General of the Armies. He passed away in 1948. (Courtesy of the El Paso County Historical Society.)

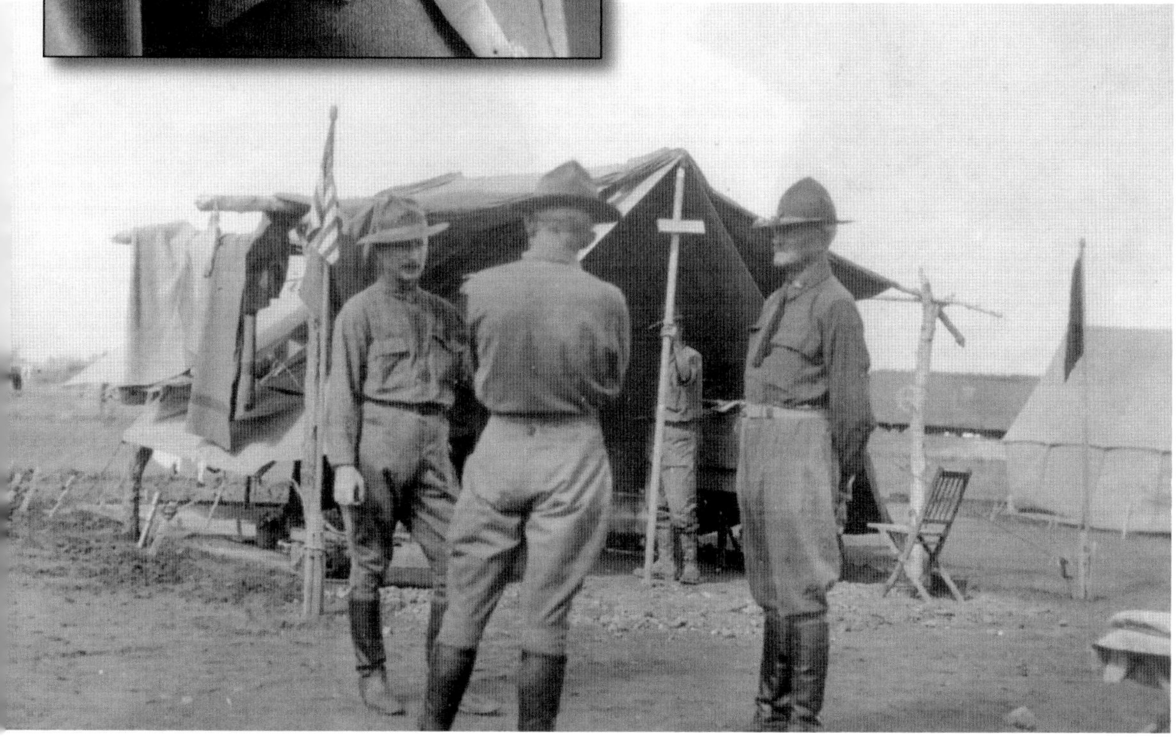

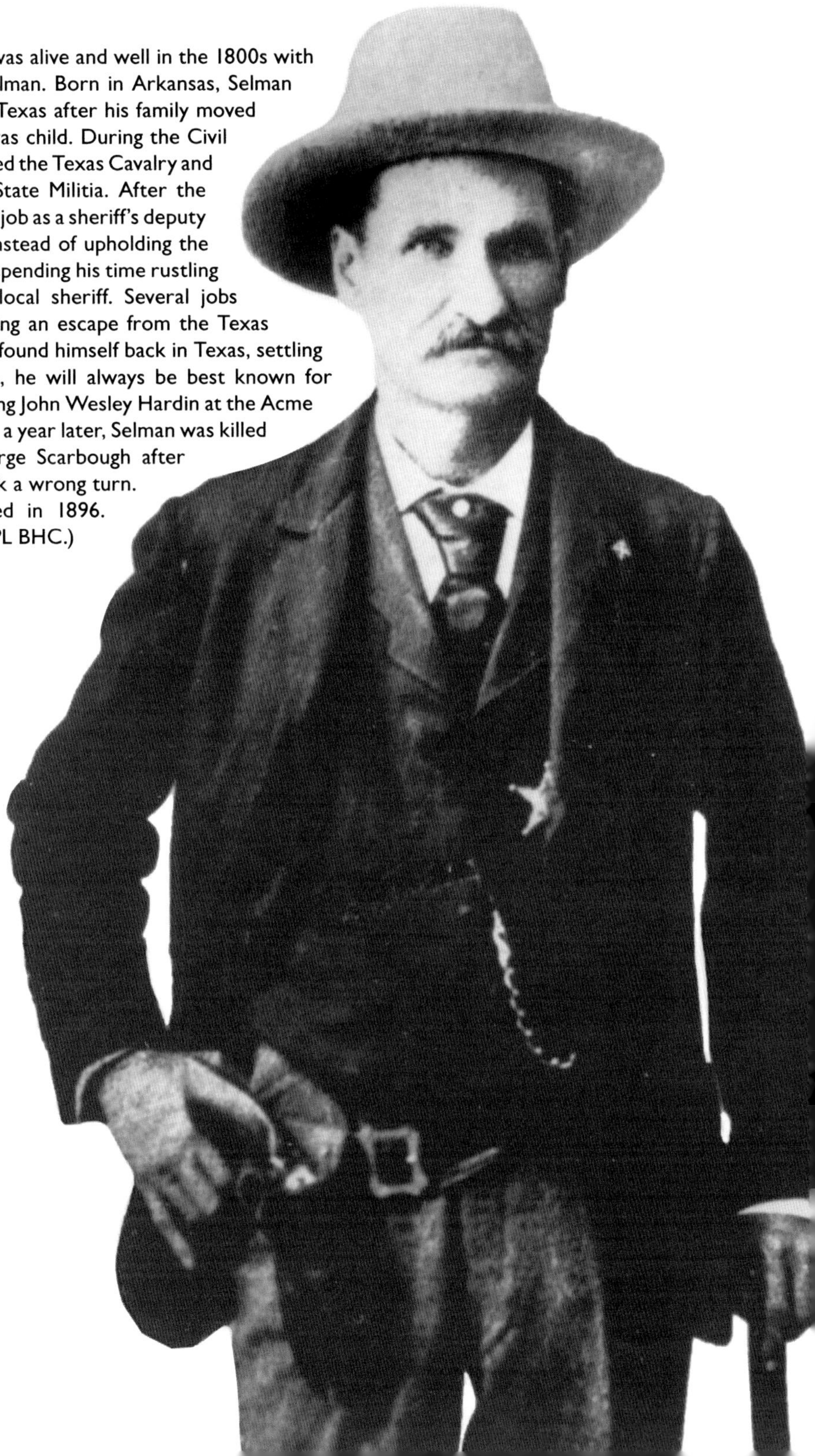

John Selman

The Wild West was alive and well in the 1800s with men like John Selman. Born in Arkansas, Selman found himself in Texas after his family moved there when he was child. During the Civil War, Selman joined the Texas Cavalry and then the Texas State Militia. After the war, he secured a job as a sheriff's deputy in Fort Griffin. Instead of upholding the law, Selman was spending his time rustling cattle with the local sheriff. Several jobs later, and following an escape from the Texas Rangers, Selman found himself back in Texas, settling in El Paso. Here, he will always be best known for shooting and killing John Wesley Hardin at the Acme Saloon. Less than a year later, Selman was killed by Marshal George Scarbough after an argument took a wrong turn. John Selman died in 1896. (Courtesy of EPPL BHC.)

CHAPTER TWO

Movers and Shakers

A city's prosperity can be measured by the quality of its economy and the unemployment rate. Businesses are the life blood of any city, and the following pages share stories from those who have had a hand in helping push El Paso forward. Some are nonprofit leaders like Salvador Balcotre, who runs La Fe. Others, like Paul Foster, are known for leading companies that are listed on the New York Stock Exchange.

Before them, there were successful businessmen like Felix Martinez, who was involved in multiple industries in the early 1900s. Edward Schwartz Jr. ran the Popular, a store that all El Pasoans visited at one time or another before it closed in 1995.

Every day, El Pasoans get up, walk out the door, and head to their jobs across the city. For a period of time, many of them held jobs in the manufacturing sector. Companies like Farah Manufacturing and Tony Llama boots are still household names today. Behind every successful company is a successful advertising campaign, and Bob Wingo is helping companies achieve just that with a business he has been involved with for decades.

As El Paso grows, the need for housing has grown as well, and the Driggers family has been a part of the real estate industry in El Paso since the 1970s—watching it transform over the years. Business owners have been and will continue to be an important pillar of the community who drive the economic engine here in the borderland.

William "Willie" Farah

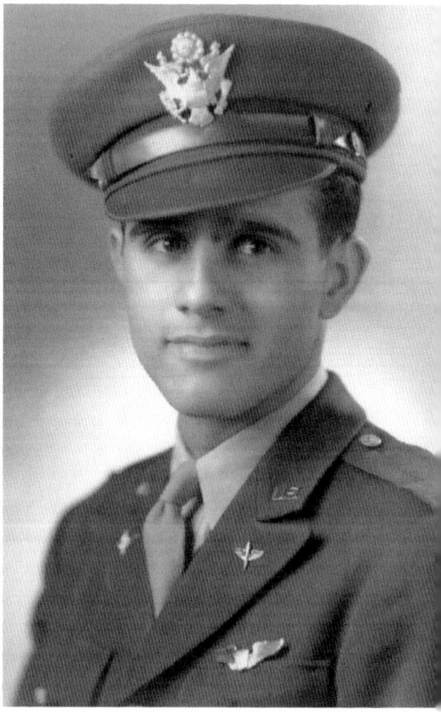

Farah Incorporated traces its beginning to 1920, when Mansour Farah opened a small shop off San Francisco Street. Mansour was a beacon of strength and influence to his two sons, but he unfortunately passed away in the mid-1930s. After graduating from school, Willie joined the Army Air Corps and piloted a B-26 bomber. After the war he returned to El Paso, where he joined his brother at Farah Inc. Their personalities worked well together, and they formed a strong team as they managed the growth of the company while being financially sound. After Jimmy Farah passed away in 1964, Willie Farah stepped up to lead the company.

Farah Inc. underwent explosive growth under his leadership. From jeans to leisure suits, the Farah name became a leader in the garment industry. The company became involved in a well-known labor dispute that eventually led to the unionization of its 2,000 employees in El Paso. Farah remained with the company up until his resignation in 1989. Outside of the company, he maintained his love of flying and was also involved with the cancer treatment board. Willie Farah, one of the great clothing icons, passed away in 1998 at the age of 78. (Both, courtesy of Jim Farah.)

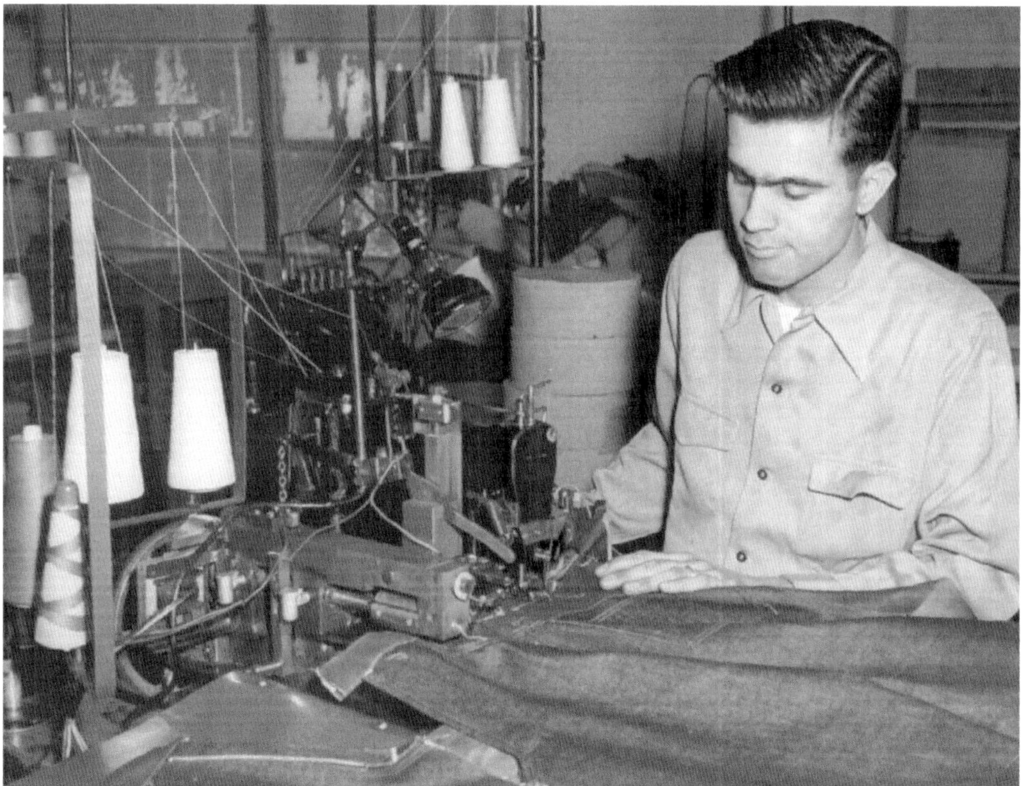

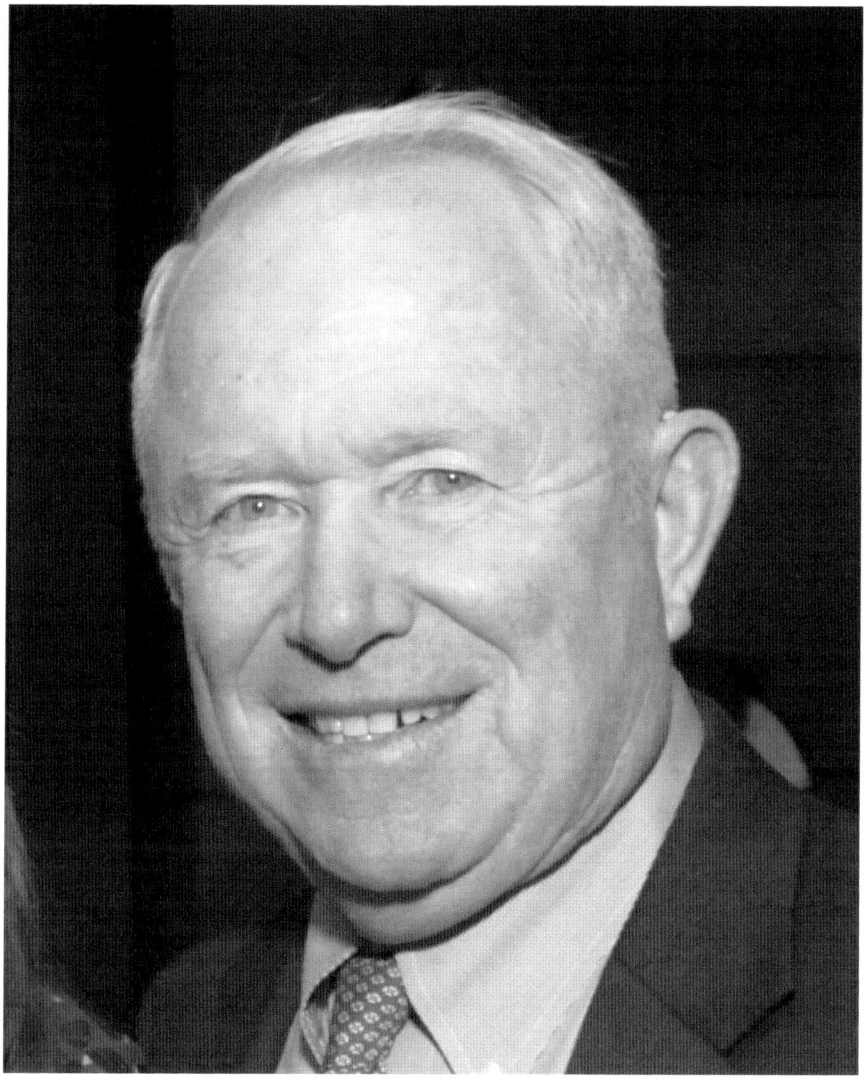

Bill Sanders

A good businessperson looks for opportunities in the marketplace where needs are currently being underserved or where processes can be refined and improved. A great businessperson finds those opportunities before their competitors. El Pasoan Bill Sanders found his opportunity in the real estate world. After growing up in the borderland and attending El Paso High, Sanders went to college at Cornell and graduated in 1964. After some time in a Peace Corps–style program in Honduras, Sanders returned to El Paso and saw a need for a different type of real estate company. Shortly thereafter, he started International Development Corporation. When an opportunity arose in Chicago, he moved the company there and renamed it LaSalle Partners.

Their unique approach to the real estate market was very successful, and Sanders sold the company in 1990. Always looking for a niche in the market, Sanders saw one and started Security Capital Group. The company was heavily involved in developing real estate investment trusts across the nation, and Sanders again saw much success. After selling the company to GE Capital in 2002, Sanders made his way back to El Paso, where he now runs Strategic Growth Bank. Bill Sanders was a pioneer in the commercial real estate world, and his influence continues to be felt to this day. (Courtesy of Bill Sanders.)

Paul Foster

A sound business mind, great work ethic, and perseverance are just some of the qualities of Paul Foster. His philanthropic ways have affected El Paso and the state of Texas and will be felt for generations to come. Born in Snyder, Texas, Foster spent most of his childhood in Lovington, New Mexico. His father served as a key influence early in his life, and watching him as he worked set the example for how Foster himself approached his career. As a child, he worked as many jobs as he could, from paper routes to sacking groceries at Piggly Wiggly. When it was time for college, he made his way to Baylor University in Waco.

After realizing that pre-medical studies were not for him, Foster went into the business school. When he lost his scholarship in his freshman year, he picked up two jobs to help pay for school, including driving school buses. The experience instilled in him the value of hard work.

After college, Foster worked in multiple fields, learning the ins and outs of business. Eventually, he found himself back in El Paso working for El Paso Refining. When the business went bankrupt a year later, Foster put together a plan to oversee and manage the assets and presented it to the bank. Knowing the business could do well, Foster decided to purchase the company, which had been renamed Western Refining. It was not easy, but after going to over 150 banks to raise capital and being told no, he was able to close the deal.

After going public, Foster wondered, "How can I make the most meaningful large investment in this community that will have a profound impact on quality of life on both sides of the border?" His answer was to give $50 million to establish a medical school through Texas Tech in El Paso. The giving has not stopped, and his philanthropy can be found in renovations of key downtown buildings and other numerous charitable causes. He, his wife, Alejandra, and the Hunt family have helped bring affiliated baseball back to El Paso with the Chihuahuas, and Foster also is current chairman of the University of Texas System Board of Regents. His hopes for El Paso are bright, and for those looking for their own path, Foster advises, "Do what you enjoy doing in life, chase your dreams, and don't give up." (Courtesy of Paul Foster.)

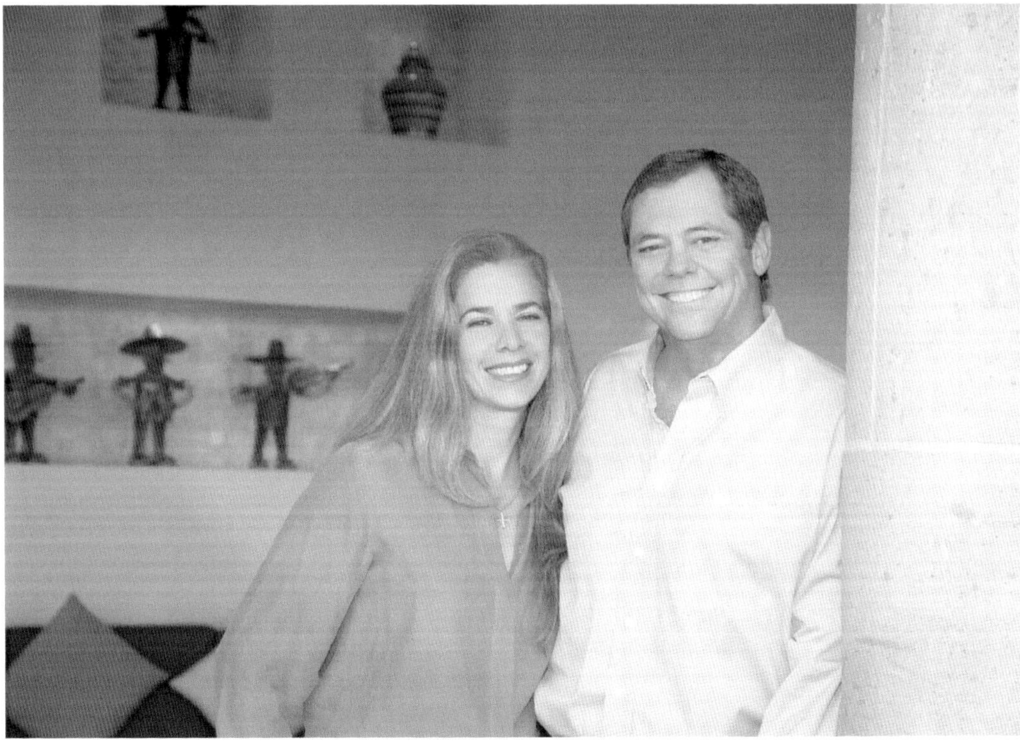

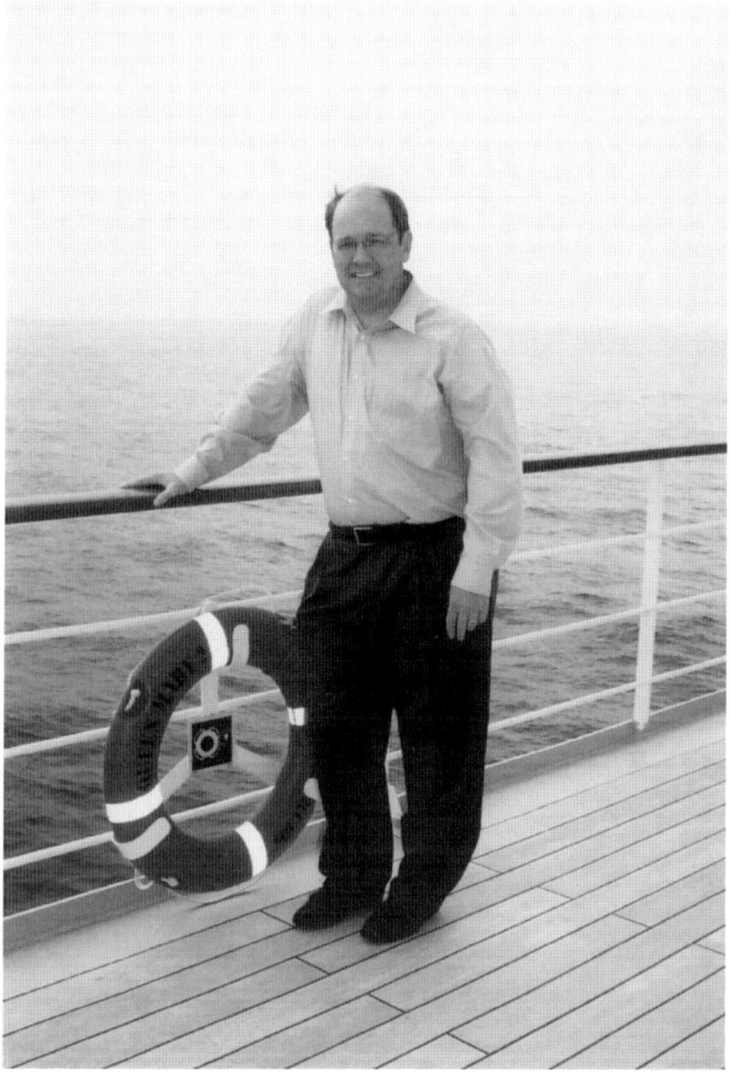

A.R. Driggers
A.R. "Randy" Driggers is a natural-born entrepreneur. At 12 years old, Driggers dug ditches to install sprinkler systems he sold to the clients of his realtor parents. Once he was legally old enough to work at McDonald's, he kept his sprinkler business by outsourcing the ditch digging to other friends.

After graduating from Eastwood High School, he went on to obtain his real estate license at age 18 before heading off to Baylor University, where he planned to study medicine.

One summer home from Baylor, he sold $2 million in real estate and grossed $50,000 in commissions in just three months. He paid his tuition with what he made that summer, but he questioned his career path. After graduating with a biology degree, he chose not to go to medical school and instead quietly bought Century 21 APD Associates, the first national real estate franchise in El Paso, from his father.

Driggers believes in the concept of teamwork, and his leadership style is one of giving all the credit to others. He would never say this of himself, but many others would say that he is the genius behind what was the longest-running and most successful marketing campaign between a real estate company and one of the most productive local home builders in El Paso. That success created a roadmap that many other brokers have followed since. (Courtesy of the Driggers family.)

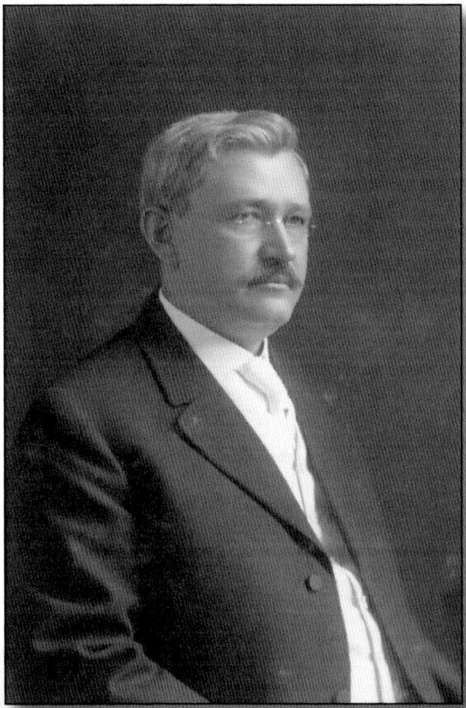

The Schwartz Family

Adolph Schwartz and his nephew Maurice opened the Popular Dry Goods Store in 1902. Known for its nice selection of clothing and house wares, the company became a household name to generations of El Pasoans. During the Mexican Revolution, it was said that Pancho Villa visited the store a number of times. The business was a family affair, and many relatives were involved in its operation throughout its history. As El Paso evolved, so did the store. It employed multiple generations of families throughout El Paso until its closing in 1995. Locals still recount their trips down to the Popular, and many have lamented its closing as they see downtown El Paso being revitalized. (Both, courtesy of the UTEP Special Collections.)

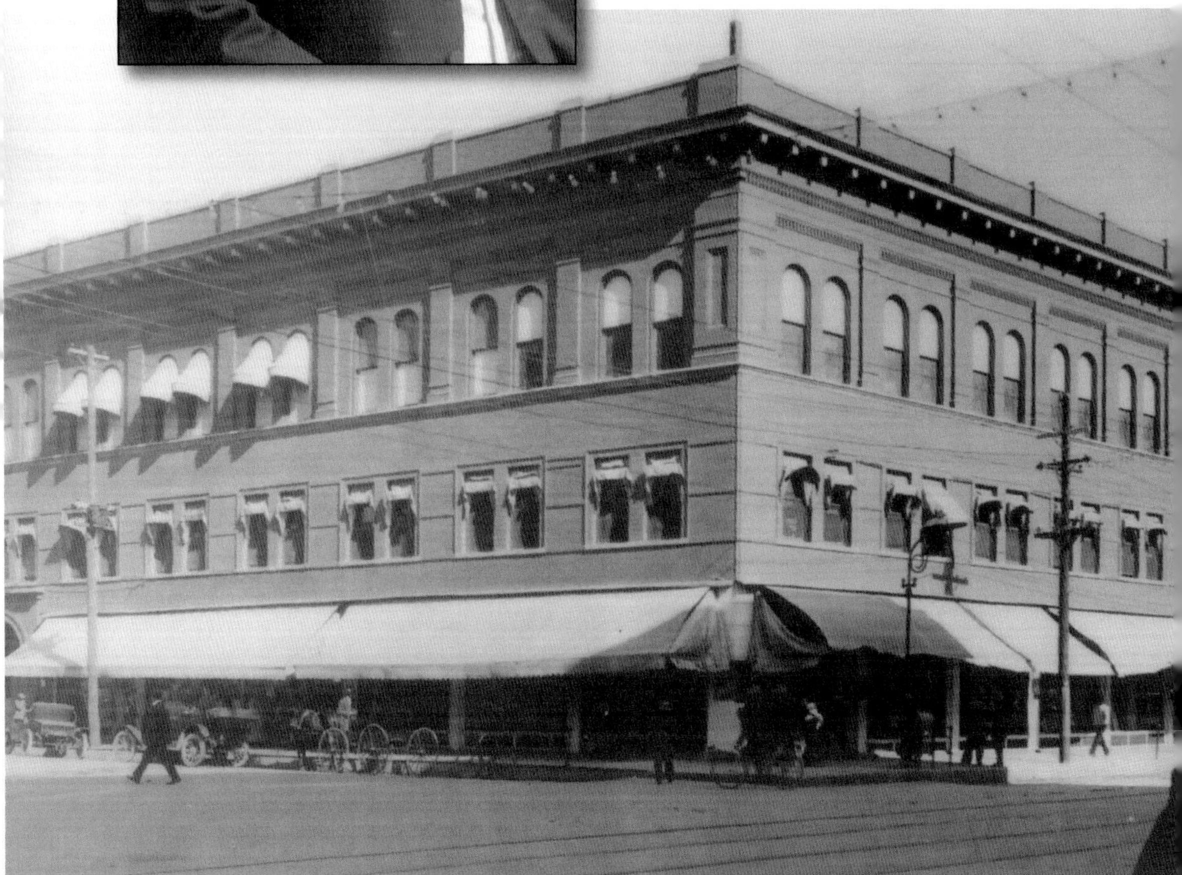

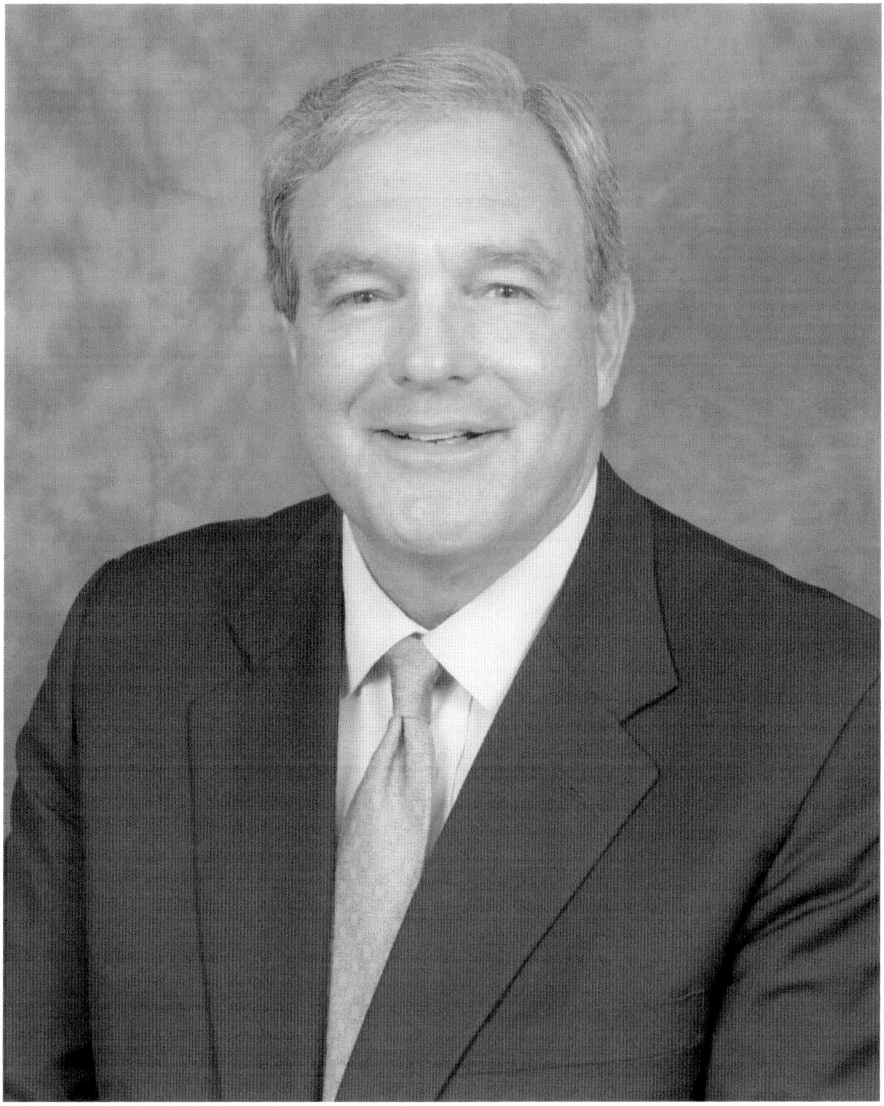

Dee Margo
Some of El Paso's most active citizens were not born in the Sun City but came here later in life. Born in Oklahoma City, Oklahoma, in 1952, Dee Margo married El Pasoan Adair Margo in 1976. A college football player and graduate of Vanderbilt University, Dee began working for the El Paso–based John D. Williams Company in 1977. He worked his way up and eventually became the president of JDW. When asked about the greatest life lesson he has learned in his career, he stated: "You are who you are. One does not separate their business life from their personal life—how you conduct yourself in one will ultimately be the same in the other."

Dee has been a supporter of numerous civic and philanthropic organizations. His work with Operation Noel has helped distribute over 19,000 coats to children throughout the region, while he and his company's involvement with the Border Fund helped raise and donate over $26 million to the community from 1993 to 2006. Dee also served in the Texas House of Representatives from 2011 to 2012, representing District 78. He also served as the president of the EPISD Board of Managers. Dee and Adair have two children, William and Don, and two granddaughters. (Courtesy of Dee Margo.)

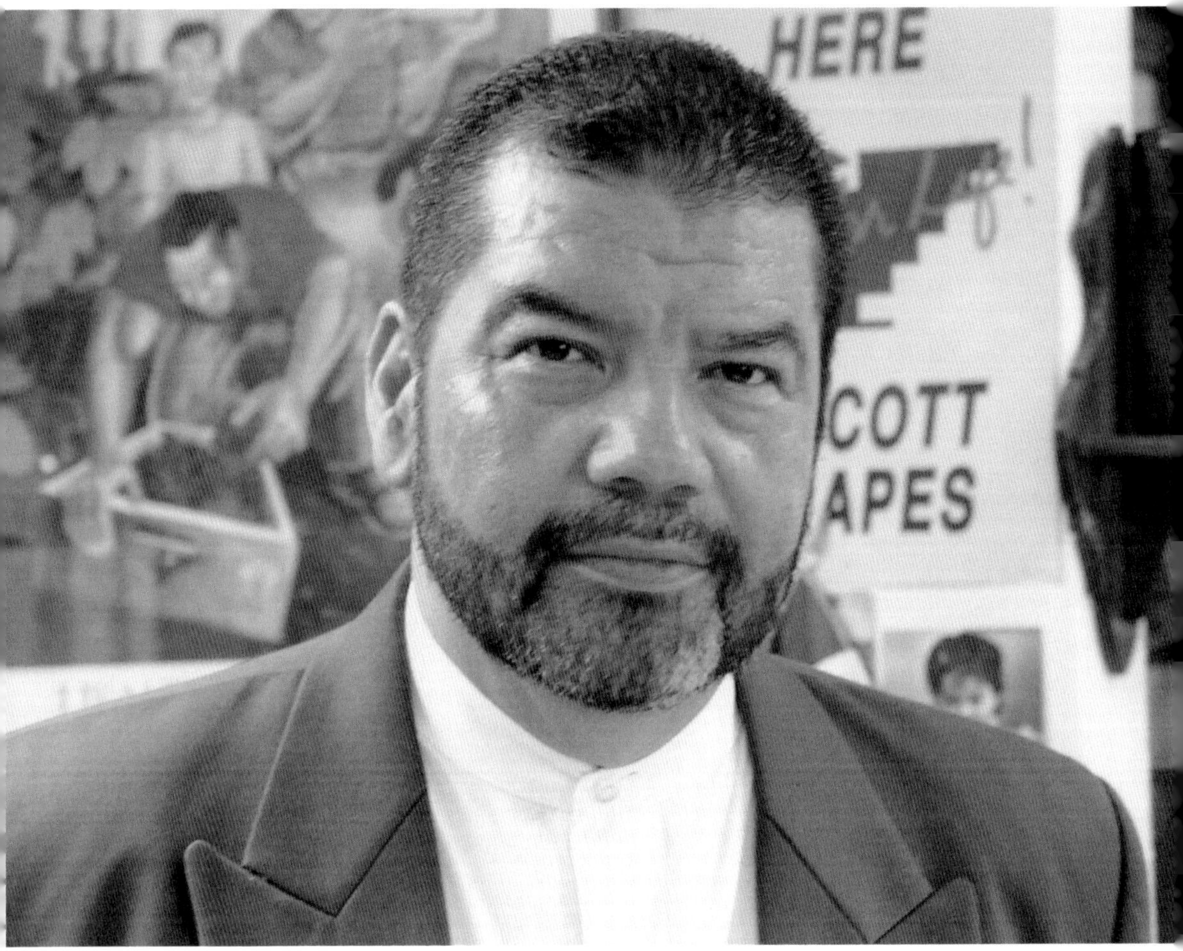

Salvador Balcorta

Segundo Barrio is a tradition-rich community that also is one of the country's poorest neighborhoods. Growing up in a small apartment that lacked proper plumbing and heating, Salvador Balcorta had a tough path to escape the endless circle of poverty, drugs, and violence. Balcorta had a plan and knew from the age of 14 that he and others in the community deserved more. An activist from almost the beginning, the young boy from Segundo Barrio made it a point to improve his community's quality of life through basic services like healthcare, education, and violence prevention. Balcorta attend UTEP and received a degree in social work and then went to the University of Texas at Austin and obtained his master's degree.

After working in leadership positions at several not-for-profits, he was offered the job as the executive director of La Fe. He has transformed the organization from a small clinic into a communitywide comprehensive health- and human-service organization. In 2007, La Fe Preparatory School opened to serve the needs of the children in the Segundo Barrio area. La Fe and Balcorta have also been working on providing more affordable housing in the area. Balcorta has been the recipient of numerous awards and sits on many community boards, but his passion for social justice and being a leader for those struggling will always be a priority. (Courtesy of Centro de Salud Familiar La Fe Inc.)

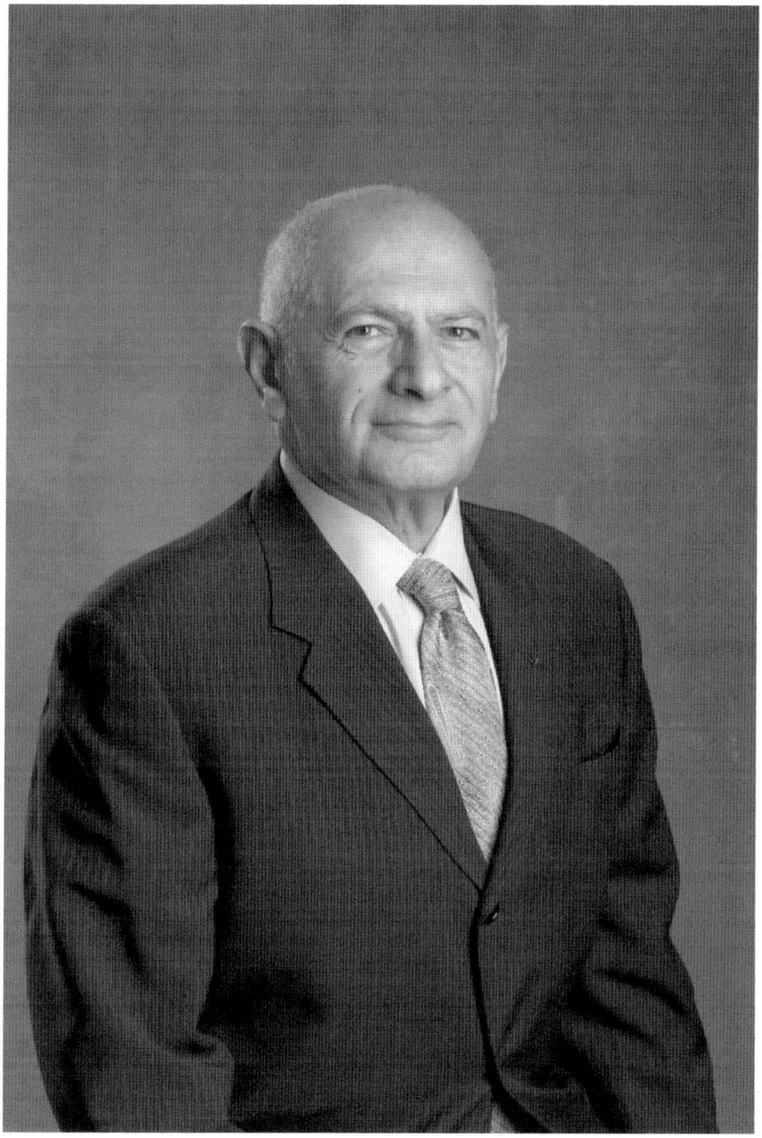

Richard Dayoub
Over the last 14 years, El Paso has seen a resurgence of hope and growth. A key component behind this transformation has been the El Paso Chamber of Commerce and its CEO, Richard Dayoub. Born in 1947 in Arnold, Pennsylvania, the foundation of a strong work ethic was forged as Dayoub watched his father work during the day at the local steel mill and moonlight as a mechanic to provide for the family. After running a successful travel agency for many years, Dayoub became the CEO of the El Paso Chamber of Commerce in 2003.

The chamber's involvement in advocating for the survival of Fort Bliss in the last base realignment and closure process round was critical, and the base ended up seeing an expanded mission. Dayoub and the chamber were also integral in pushing for and seeing the creation of the designated commuter lane at the Stanton Street International Bridge that helped drivers avoid long wait lines. For the future, he hopes to see the chamber in a new facility that houses several business organizations as it "becomes the model for collaboration and unity of purpose." (Courtesy of El Paso Chamber of Commerce.)

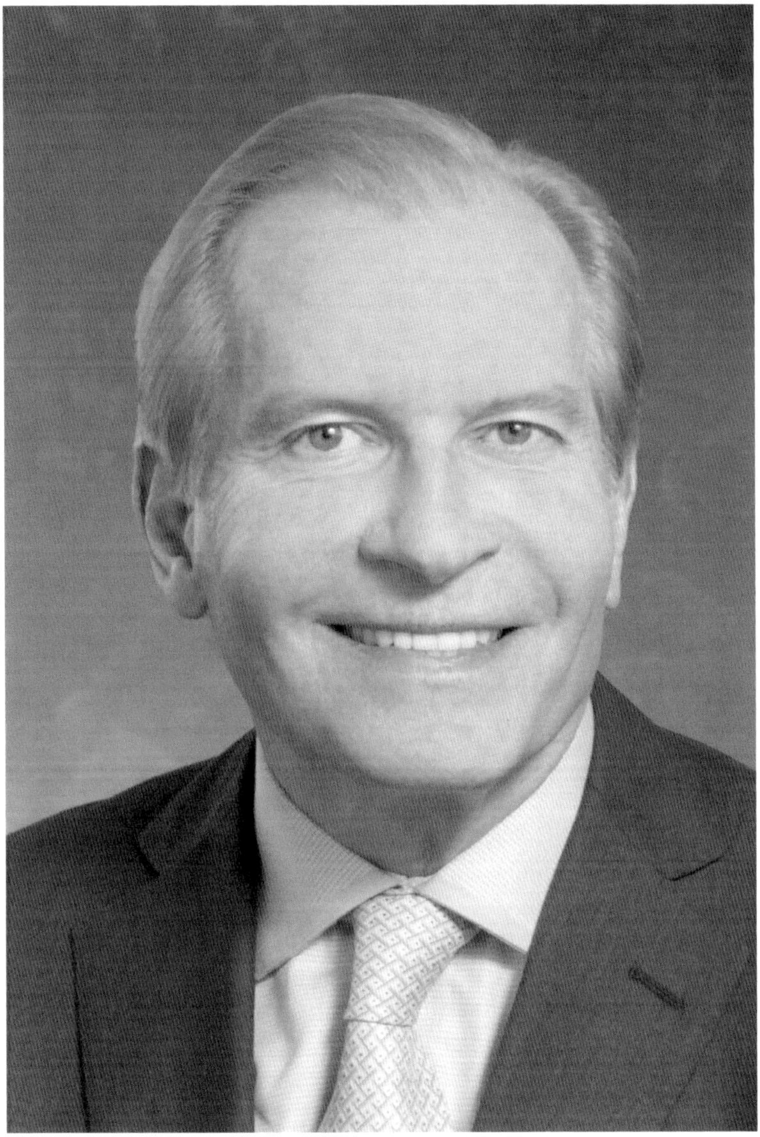

Woody Hunt
Growing up in the lower valley, Woody Hunt was not sure what he wanted to do when he grew up. Both of his parents had business degrees and influenced his life. After graduating from high school at age 16, Hunt made his way to UT Austin, where he obtained his undergraduate and graduate degrees in finance. Hunt Companies was started in 1927 as a retail and wholesale building supply company. After returning to El Paso in 1968, Hunt began to expand the geographic footprint of the company and slowly advanced it from a local presence to national significance.

El Paso is home, and Hunt has worked with other business and political leaders throughout the community to help El Paso rebound as a city. "You don't want to lose your competitiveness. It's easy to lose it and it is hard to gain it back" is one of Hunt's pieces of advice for the future of El Paso. He believes that focus on education and recruitment of top talent will make El Paso competitive again. There is no denying his passion for El Paso and seeing it return to its status as one of the top cities in the Southwest. (Courtesy of Hunt Companies Inc.)

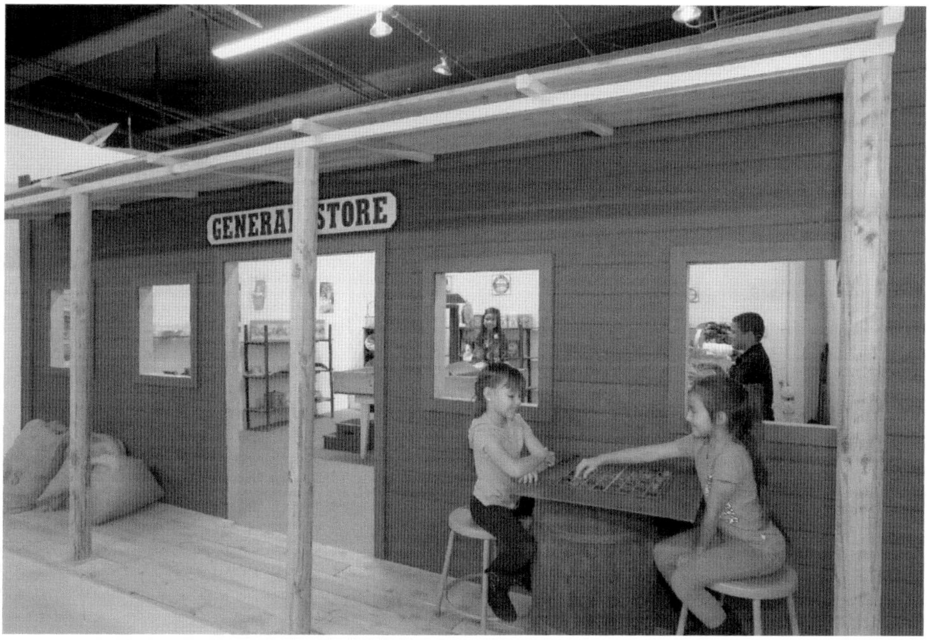

El Paso Exploreum

Laurie Paternoster and her husband, Mike Churchman, started a nonprofit children's museum in downtown El Paso called Lynx Exhibits. The museum transitioned to the El Paso Exploreum, and the facility now has over 14,000 square feet of space for fun and interactive exhibits that children of all ages enjoy. The museum has filled a void in El Paso, and its success has led to increases in attendance every year. The Exploreum has a board called the Youth Explorers that is comprised of children ages eight to 16 who oversee all aspects of the museum except the budget and personnel. The board is integral in what new exhibits will be featured in the Exploreum's space. (Both, courtesy of the El Paso Exploreum.)

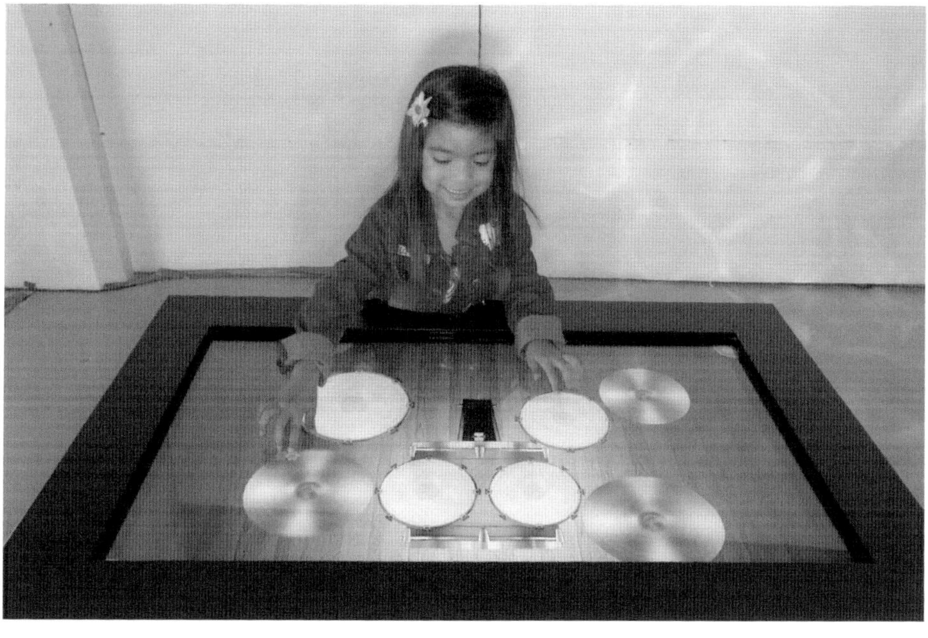

Bob Wingo

With offices in Austin and New York, Sanders\Wingo advertising agency has grown through an aggressive strategy that has seen national success. Wingo grew up in El Paso and went to UTEP. After graduation, he took a job at the Billy the Kid Apparel company. After moving up the ranks, he joined Dave Sanders at his advertising agency. The business has continued to grow and land national brands as clients. For Wingo, life is not all business, and giving back to the community through boards like the Martin Luther King Memorial Foundation and the UTEP Business Advisory Council is extremely important. (Courtesy of Sanders\Wingo.)

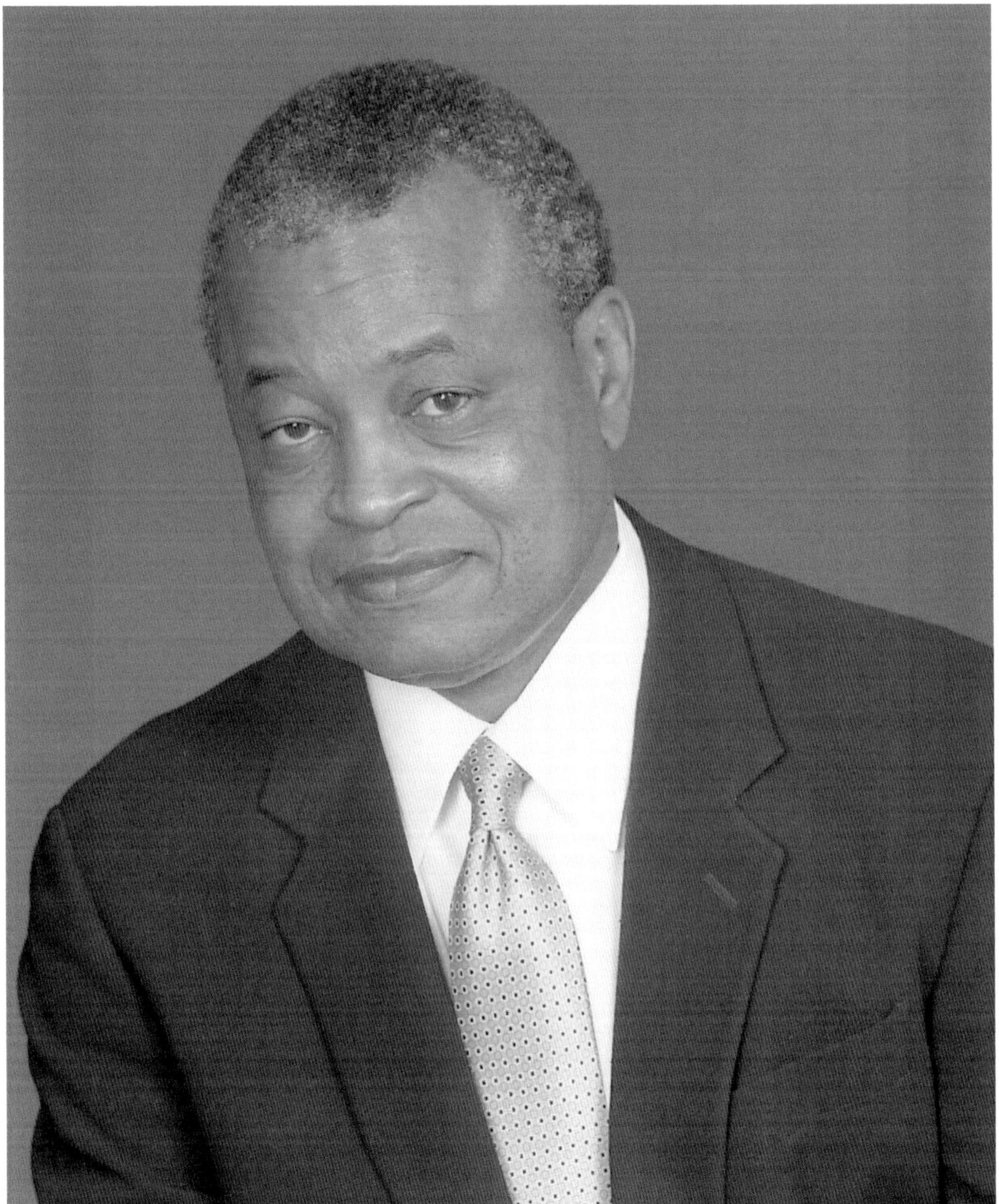

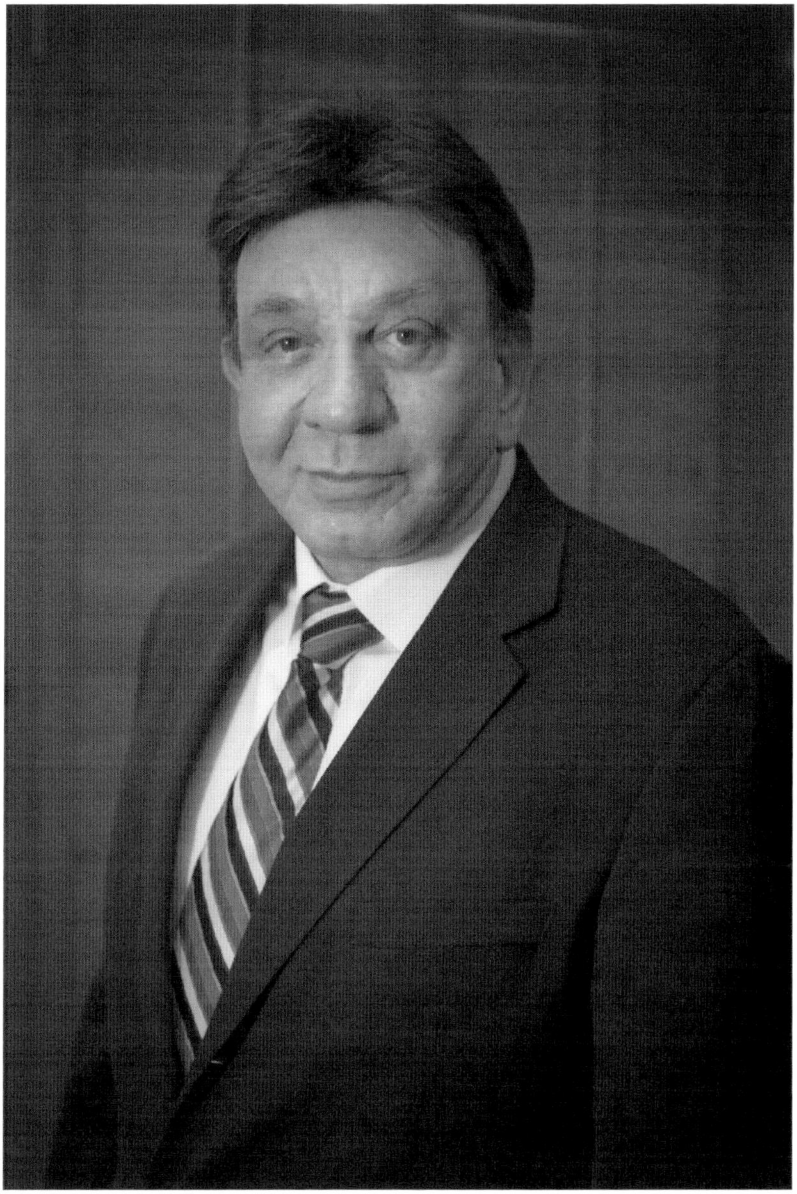

Richard Castro

Richard Castro embodies the mantra that anything is possible with hard work, discipline, and defined goals. As a student at Texas State, he worked as a short-order cook to make ends meet. Fast forward to today, and he is the largest Hispanic operator of McDonald's franchises in the country, initiated the HACER scholarship program that has donated over $21 million to recipients all over, and helped the El Paso community in countless other ways. Castro did not start out as businessman. He began his life as a schoolteacher before becoming city manager of Del Rio, Texas. In 1983, he was awarded his first McDonald's franchise, and since then, it has grown to 23 restaurants and over 1,000 employees in the El Paso and West Texas area. Over his lifetime, he has made it a point to give back to the community and continues to do so through civic involvement and philanthropic endeavors. (Courtesy of Richard Castro.)

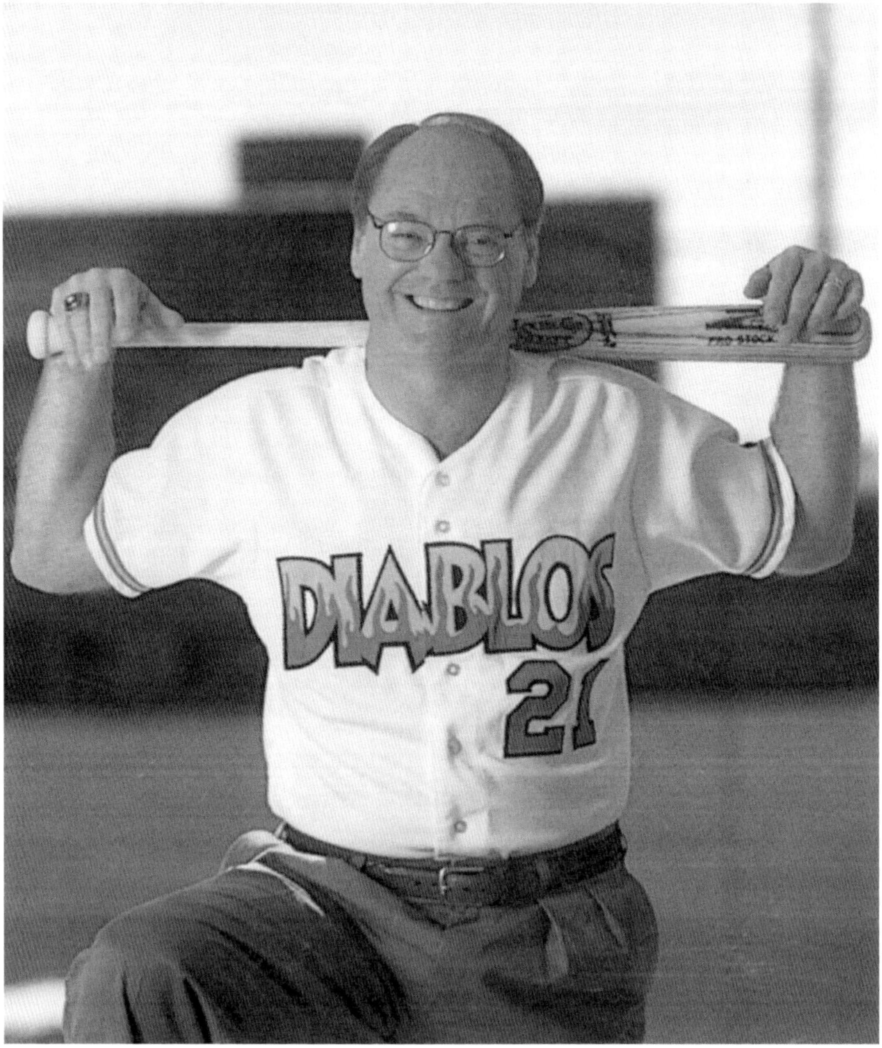

Jim Paul

Minor league baseball has transformed over the decades. As far as game-day experience, much of that can be attributed to Jim Paul and the changes he enacted as the owner of the El Paso Diablos. The Vietnam veteran came to own the team after being brought back to be the Diablos' general manager. When Paul first took over, he would give his credit card to the team manager to charge all transportation, food, and lodging for their seven-day road trips. When they got back, Paul would pay off the card from the revenue brought in from the home stands.

In their first season, the team finished 18 games out of first place but broke all the attendance records. In the 1970s, organ music was played between the innings of baseball games. To excite patrons, the Diablos had the Diamond Girls, who danced on the dugouts to popular music. "I would go record music at home on a cassette player that I bought at Radio Shack. Then on game day, we would put the recorder next to the microphone and use that as our sound system. Our organ had been repossessed." With interest from other teams in Paul's success in providing a fun fan experience, he started an annual seminar that grew to over 300 people, including representatives from Notre Dame, LSU, the Houston Astros, and the Texas Rangers. Paul sold the team in 1996, but he left a legacy in the minor leagues that continues to this day in game-day experiences across the country. (Courtesy of Jim Paul.)

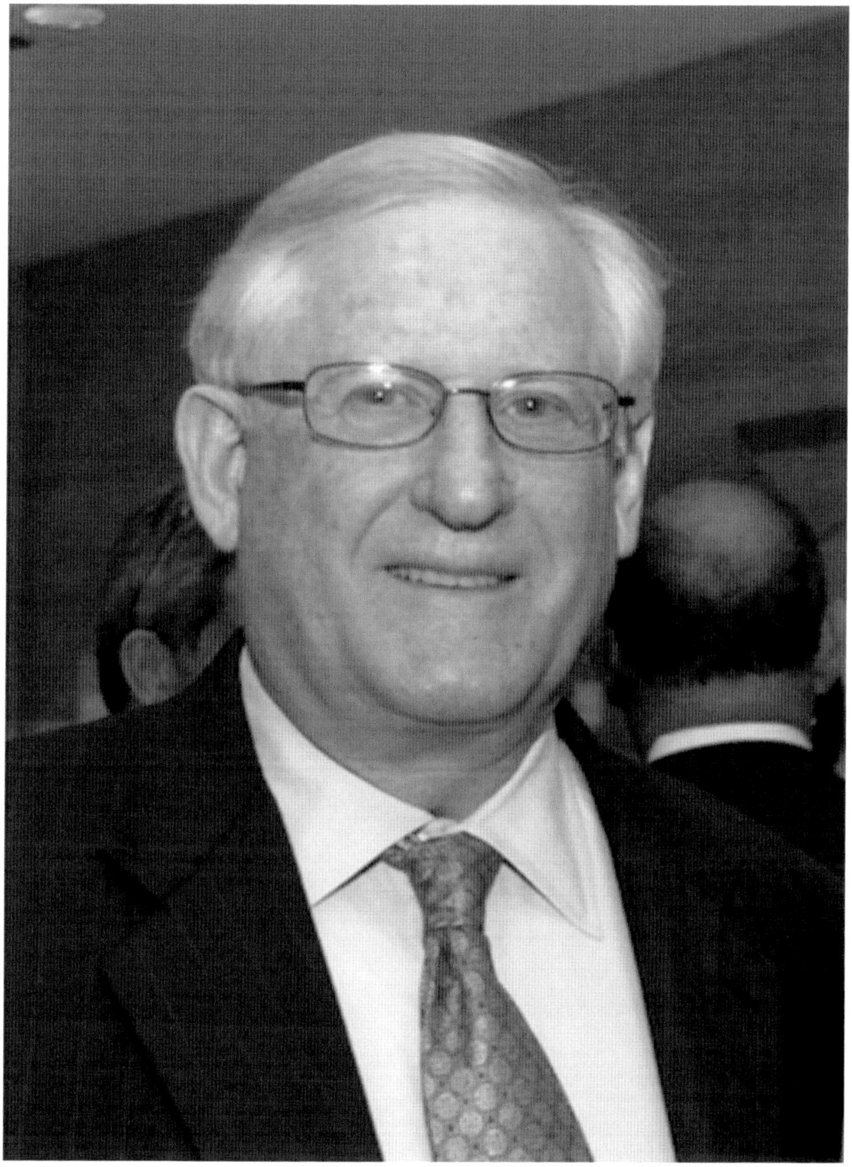

Gerald Rubin

One of the most successful businesses in El Paso over the last several decades has been Helen of Troy. The publicly traded company founded by Gerald Rubin started off small but has grown exponentially since its founding in 1968. Originally a wig shop, Rubin transitioned the company over the years to sell everything from brand-name hair-care products like Bedhead to household products like Oxo. With the corporate headquarters located in El Paso, Helen of Troy has also been one of the most important employers in the area. Rubin departed Helen of Troy in 2014 and has now focused his efforts on his other venture, River Oaks Properties, a shopping-center developer. In addition to his business prowess, Rubin has always been engaged civically. In 2004, the annual Sun Bowl game was without a title sponsor. Rubin and Helen of Troy stepped up and provided corporate title sponsorship of the game through the 2009 bowl season, which helped maintain one of El Paso's most treasured holiday traditions. (Courtesy of El Paso Inc.)

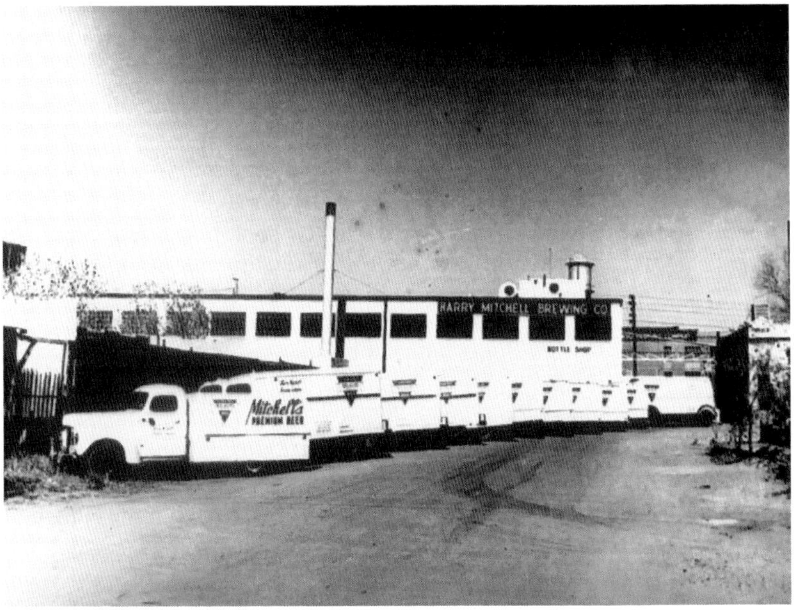

Harry Mitchell
During Prohibition, El Paso's close proximity to Juarez made it a popular destination for those looking to have a sip of whisky or drink a cold beer. In 1912, Harry Mitchell made his way from England to El Paso, where he attained his US citizenship after serving in World War I in the US Army. A bartender by trade, Mitchell worked at the Paso del Norte Hotel before heading to Juarez during Prohibition and opening up the Mint Café. When Prohibition ended, Mitchell returned to El Paso, and he and some partners opened Harry Mitchell Brewing Company. Mitchell sold the brewery in 1951, and from there it changed hands several times before finally shutting its doors in 1967. The building still stands today on North Stevens Street. (Both, courtesy of the El Paso County Historical Society.)

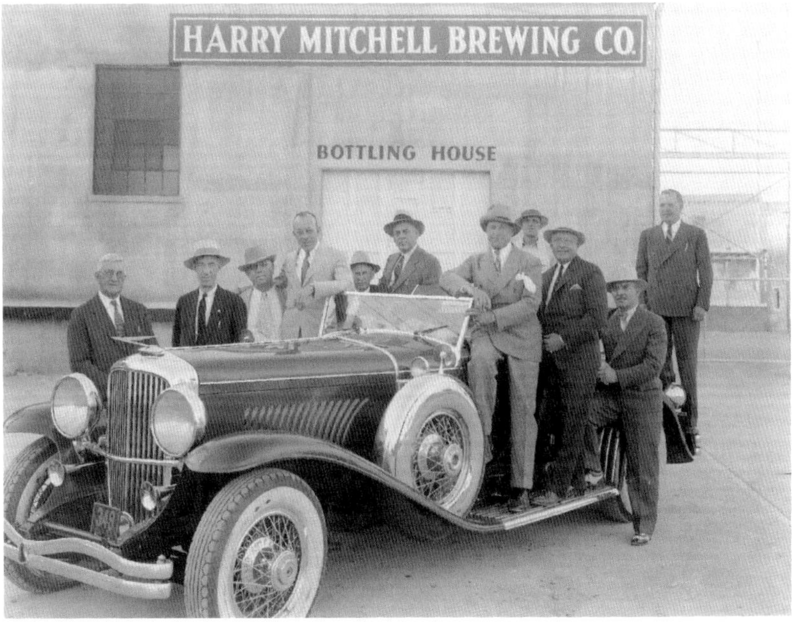

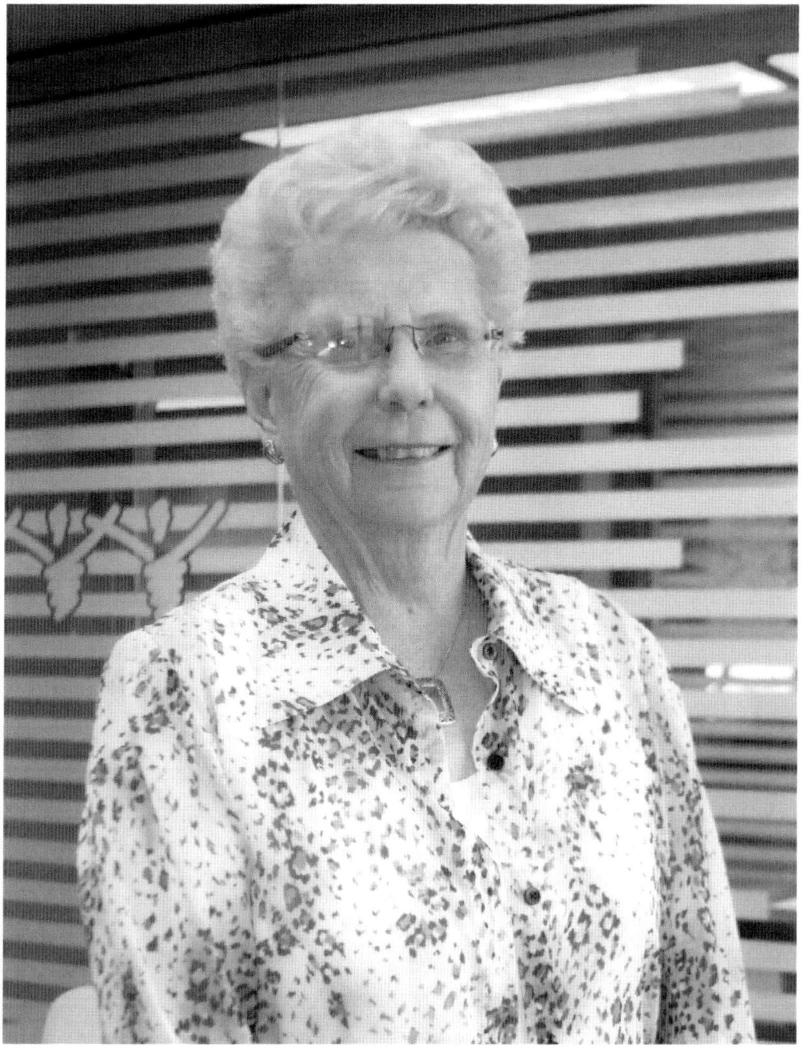

Myrna Deckert
One of the largest and most successful YWCAs in the nation is here in El Paso and was spearheaded by Myrna Deckert and the team she established while she was the executive director. Born in Kansas, Deckert arrived here with her husband after he was assigned to Fort Bliss. After he got out of the Army, the couple moved back to California, but they quickly realized how much they loved El Paso and were back within six months. Looking for a job, Deckert answered an advertisement for the YWCA and accepted a position as the teenage program director. Six years later, she was asked to become the associate executive director, a role she held for over a year before becoming the executive director in 1969. Deckert recalled: "Because of the YWCA mission, I learned so much about racism and discrimination. I feel that we all must fight judging people by their race or ethnicity, financial circumstances, gender, and age."

After 38 years there, the former executive director took on a position as the COO of the newly formed Paso del Norte Group and helped get it off the ground. Today, she serves as the CEO of Paso del Norte Health Foundation, whose mission is to improve health in the region. Over her career, Deckert has provided strong community leadership, and her love and commitment to the El Paso region will always be remembered. (Courtesy of El Paso Inc.)

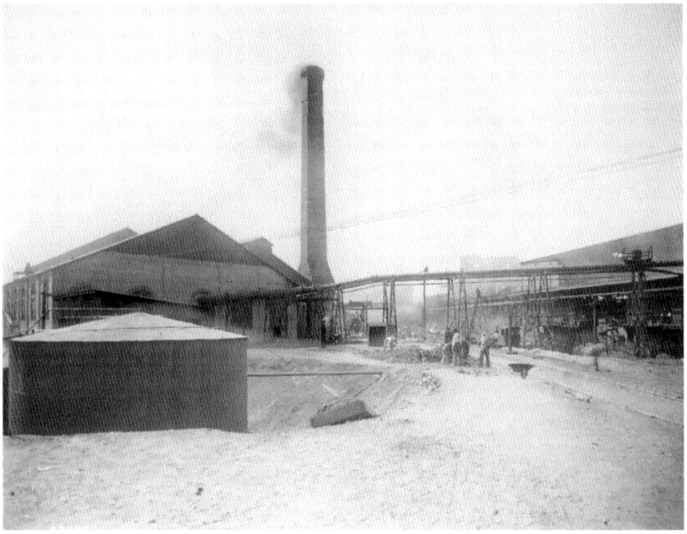

ASARCO

One of the most well known El Paso economic generators was copper-smelter operator ASARCO. ASARCO was formed by Robert Towne in the late 1880s and grew from 250 employees to over 1,000 by the end of the 20th century. The smelting operation saw El Paso grow from a small town to a modern city, and while it was an important economic generator for the city, it was not without its own controversy. The operation was putting out high levels of pollutants, and the city had the highest air levels of lead concentration in Texas in the 1960s.

The lead concentrations in the air and soil led to the closing of Smeltertown, a company town next to ASARCO where multiple generations of families who worked nearby grew up. The facility closed in 1999 due to low copper prices. It tried to get a permit to restart the blast furnaces, but failed due to heavy opposition from the concerned community.

Now all remnants of the ASARCO operation have been demolished, including the iconic smoke stacks that were built in the 1950s and 1960s. While the land's future is unknown, the history of the smelter, its effect on the El Paso economy, and the families who worked there will not be forgotten. (Courtesy of the EPPL BHC.)

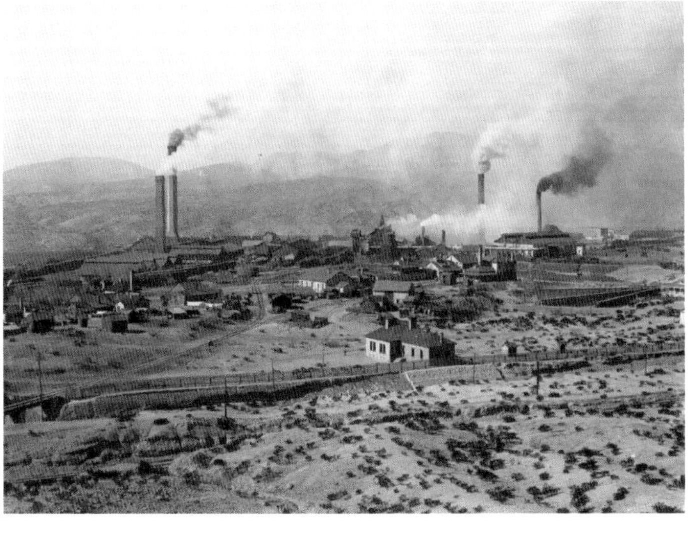

CHAPTER THREE

Groups

Sometimes change in a city is not caused by one, but by many. Throughout the history of El Paso, different groups have helped shape the city. Some have been around since the beginning, like Fort Bliss. The post has been a part of El Paso in some form since the 1840s. It has moved around a few times, but the soldiers and families from the installation have all been a part of El Paso history.

Those who brought and built the railroad helped transform El Paso from a town into a city; the transcontinental railroad had lasting effects on the area. Many of the rail workers were Chinese immigrants, and after the railroad was complete, they settled in El Paso, creating El Paso's own Chinatown of eateries, shops, and goods. Downtown was a focal point for many El Pasoans, and two groups have made it a point to help improve the area. The El Paso Community Foundation played a role in saving the historic Plaza Theatre and helped raise the money to see the theater renovated. That theater is now home to the Plaza Classic Film Festival, which has seen stars like Al Pacino grace the stage to give preshow talks.

Seeing a renewed interest in the city center, Chalk the Block was formed to allow artists not only to showcase their work on sidewalks and streets across downtown but also as a fun event for families to attend. Covering events like Chalk the Block and restoration of the Plaza Theatre have always fallen on the shoulders of the newspaper. The *El Paso Times* has been around since the 1880s, and it is the last surviving print paper in the city—the *El Paso Herald-Post* went out of business in 1997.

There are groups like Project Bravo whose main goal is to help those who are economically disadvantaged and assist them with achieving a better qualify of life. When it comes to philanthropy, the Hunt Foundation has been there to give funds to entities all over El Paso who are helping the community.

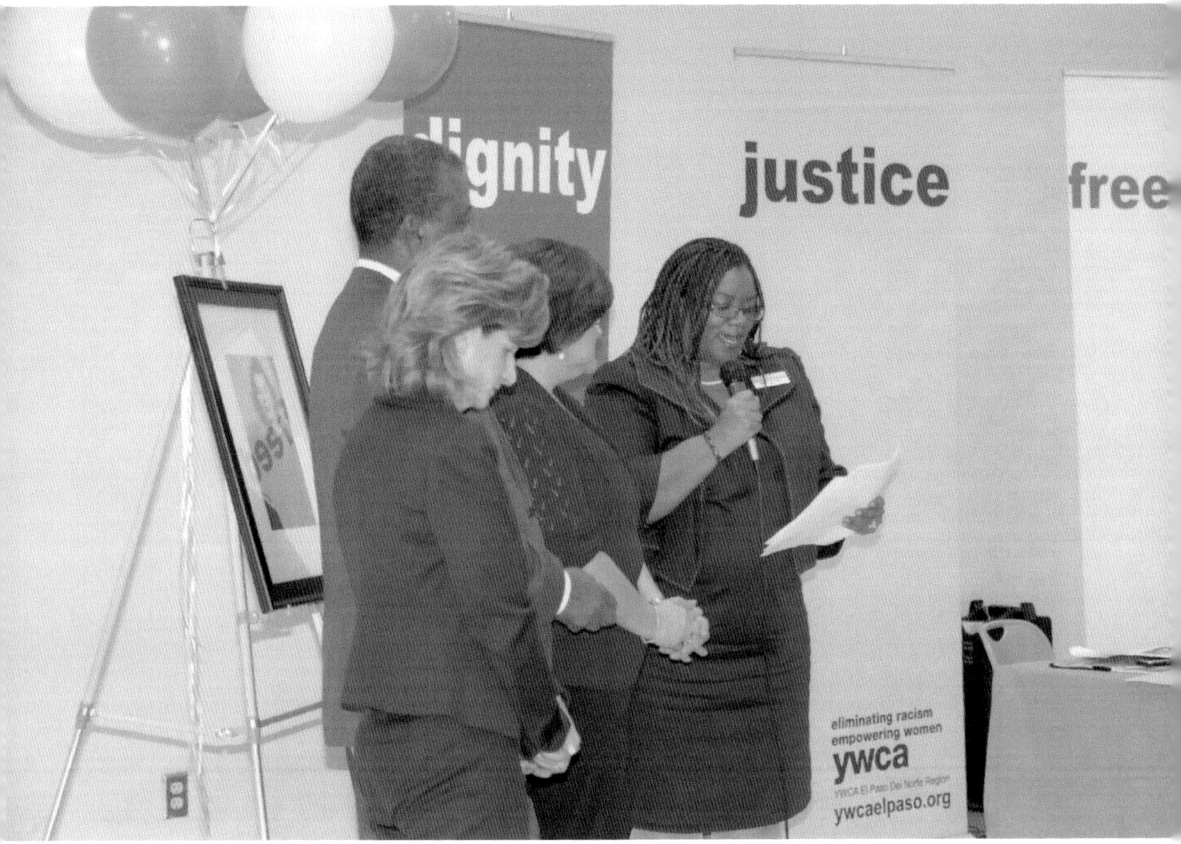

YWCA

The YWCA in El Paso received its charter in 1909 and has benefited from great leaders like Myrna Deckert and Sandra Braham. Shortly thereafter, the association opened up a 52-bed residence for young women and a gymnasium where health classes where taught. Throughout its history in El Paso, the YWCA has found many ways to make a positive difference in the El Paso community through offering afterschool programs for children, summer camps, or transitional housing with programs to empower women to become more independent. The El Paso Chapter of the YWCA is one of the largest in the country, and the association continues to support generation after generation of El Pasoans. (Courtesy of the Hunt Family Foundation.)

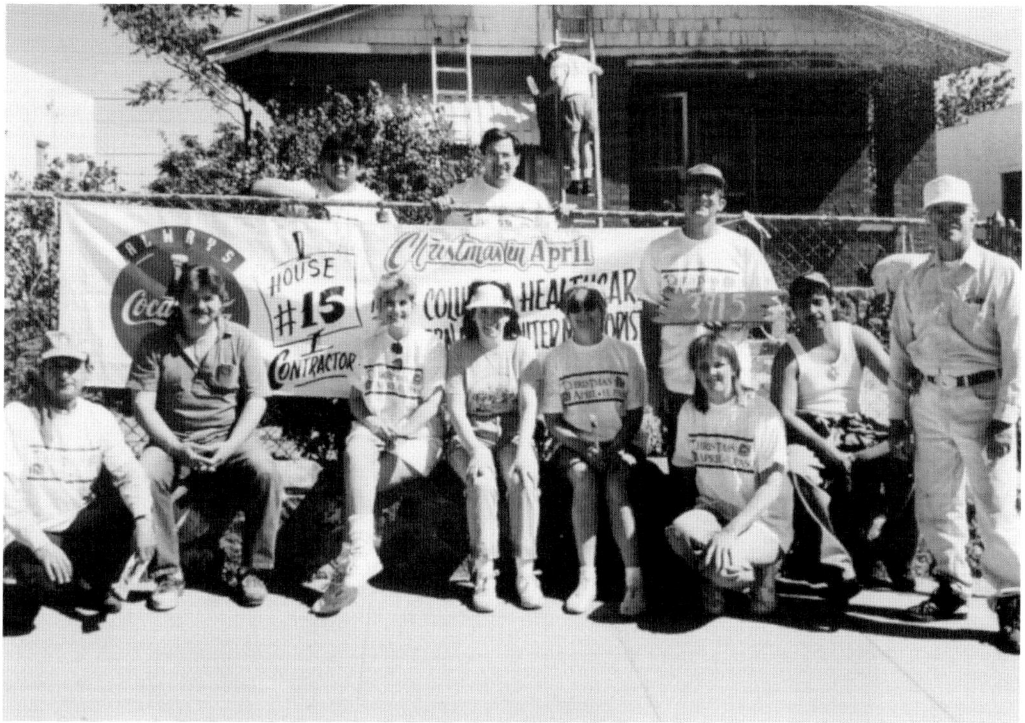

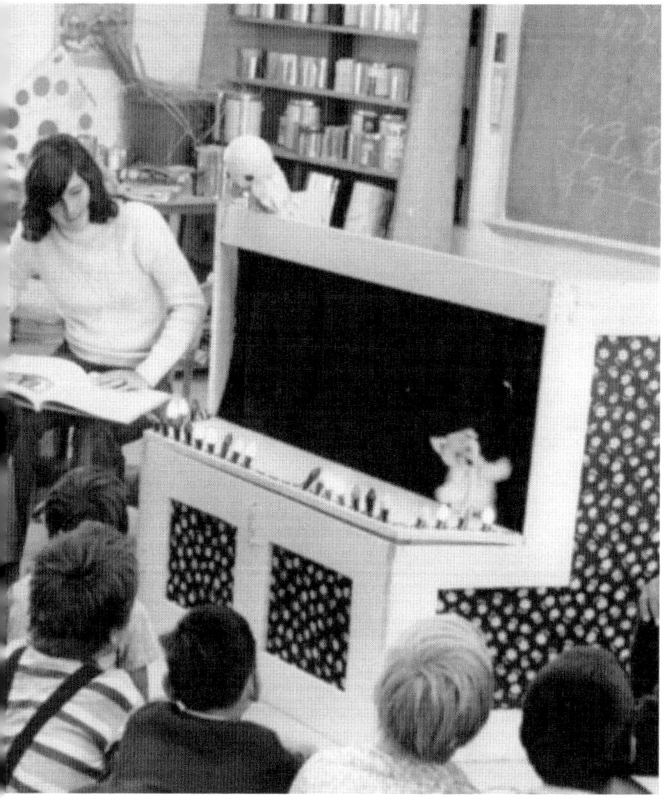

El Paso Junior League

Volunteering is an integral part of all communities. In 1930, twelve El Paso women, including Patricia Ainsa and Ruth Rawlings, decided to form a Junior Service League. By the end of year, over 80 El Paso women had joined, and the stage was set for an organization that continues to make a difference in the area. Over the years, the El Paso Junior League has contributed to the community through projects like Independence House, A Christmas Fair, El Paso Desert Botanical Garden, and numerous other quality of life projects. Today, the organization continues to thrive in developing new generations of leaders and volunteers who have a positive effect on El Paso and the surrounding area. (Both, courtesy of the El Paso Junior League.)

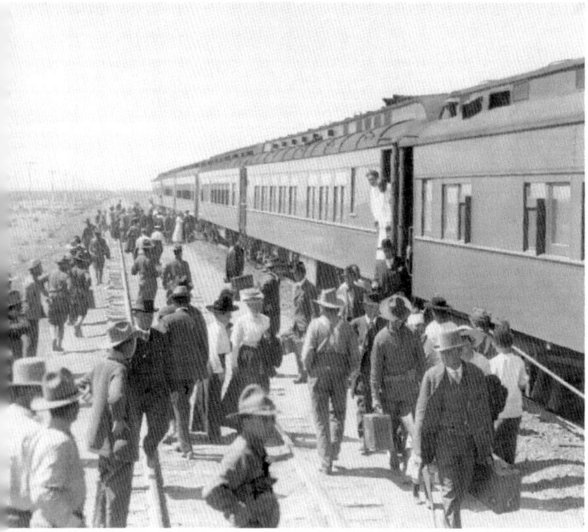

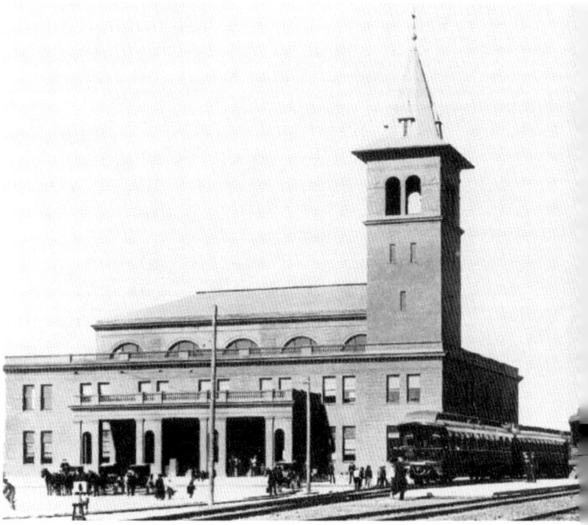

Railroads

When the railroad made its way to El Paso in 1881, it turned the city from a small town into a bustling settlement. With rail going through town, El Paso was now an important stop as people traveled to the West. From steam engines to diesel locomotives, the rail industry has maintained an important presence in El Paso. El Paso's Union Station, designed by Trost & Trost, is a marvel in its own right and serves as a reminder of El Paso's deep connection with the railroad. Today, both Union Pacific and Burlington Northern Santa Fe are important employers in the area. While companies like Union Pacific have gotten much from the city, they have also been steadfast in giving back to multiple organizations like the El Paso Museum of History. (Left, courtesy of EPPL BHC; right, courtesy of the El Paso County Historical Society.)

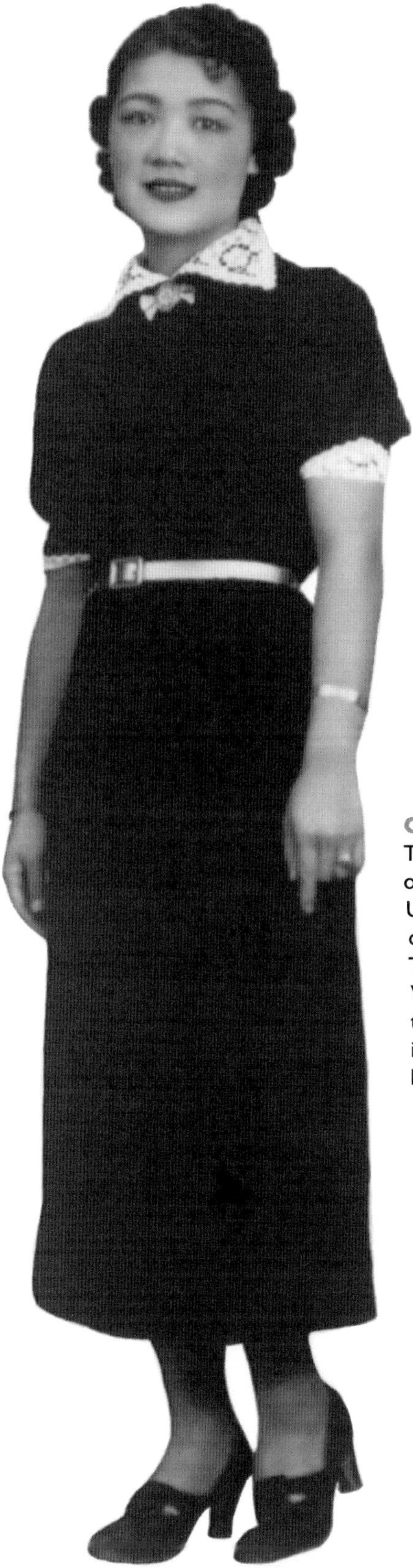

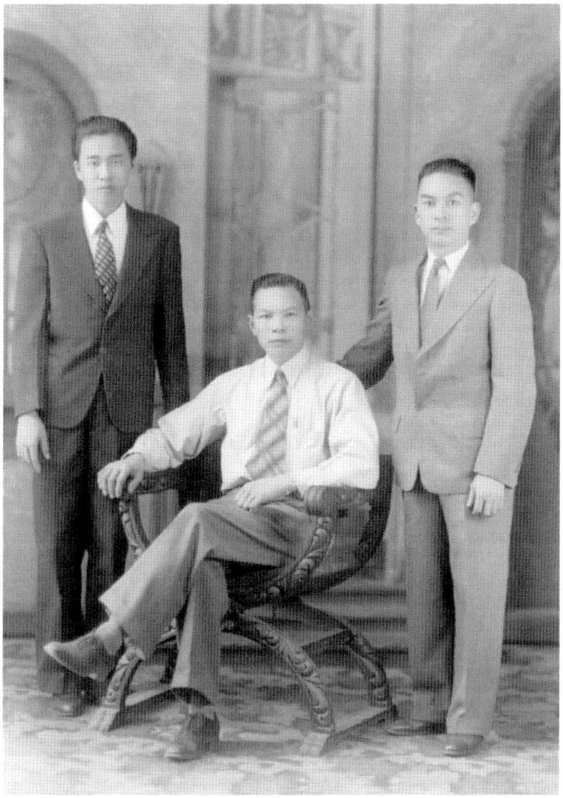

Chinese Immigrants

The railroads in El Paso were built in large part by the labor of Chinese immigrants who had made their way to the United States for a new life. El Paso had a flourishing Chinese community in the early 1900s and even had a bustling China Town in South El Paso before it began to fade in the 1940s. While the Chinese community has declined in population, the community remains an important pillar of El Paso. Many in the current generation serve as doctors, attorneys, and business owners. (Courtesy of UTEP Special Collections.)

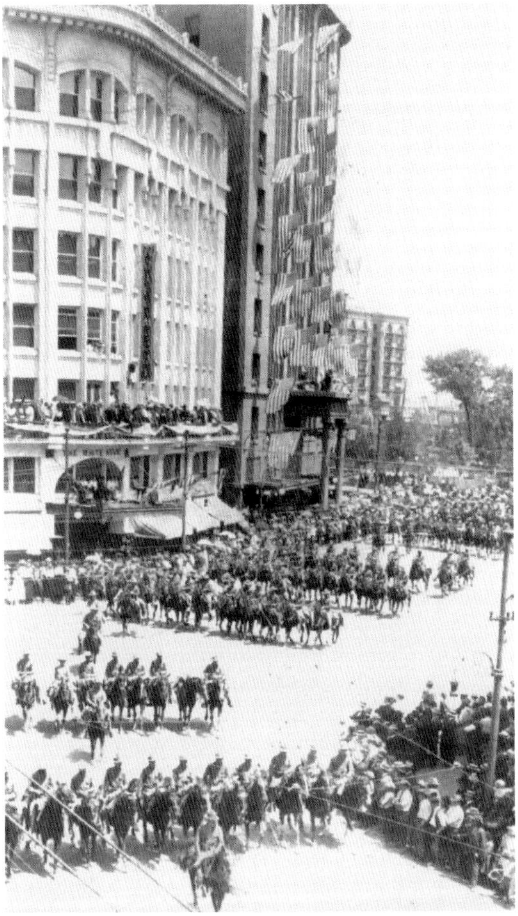

Fort Bliss

Fort Bliss has been in a few locations since its initial formation in 1848 after the Mexican-American War. In 1854, Fort Bliss was officially christened, named after officer William Wallace Bliss. After moving to several locations, Fort Bliss found its final location in 1893. Since then, it has trained and sent multiple generations of soldiers to war. The post has grown in size over time and is now one of largest military installations in the United States. It recently underwent a multibillion-dollar transformation, and over 30,000 troops and their families call it and El Paso home. Fort Bliss has been woven into the fabric of El Paso history, and it will hopefully be a part of the area for many decades to come. (Both, courtesy of El Paso County Historical Society.)

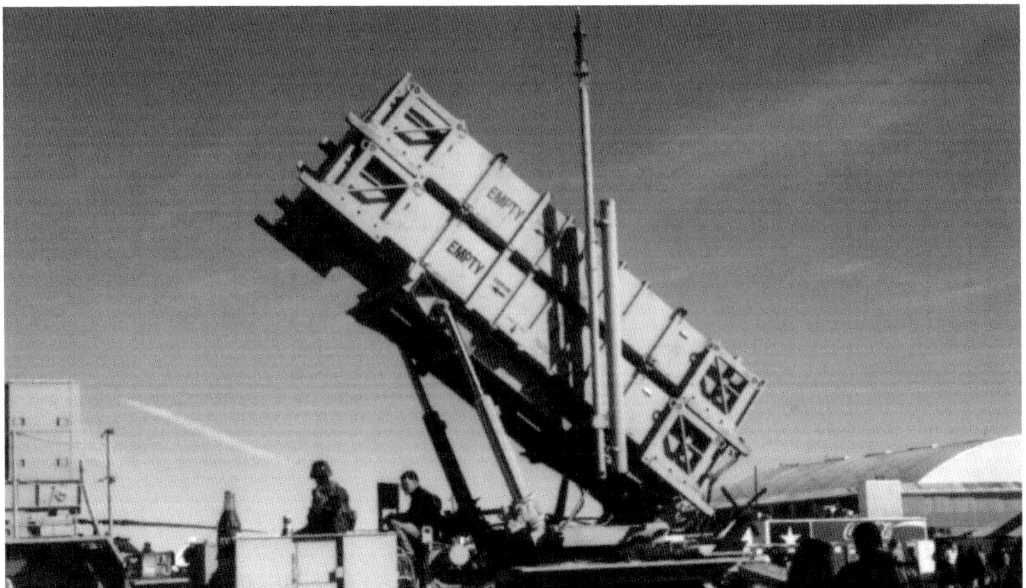

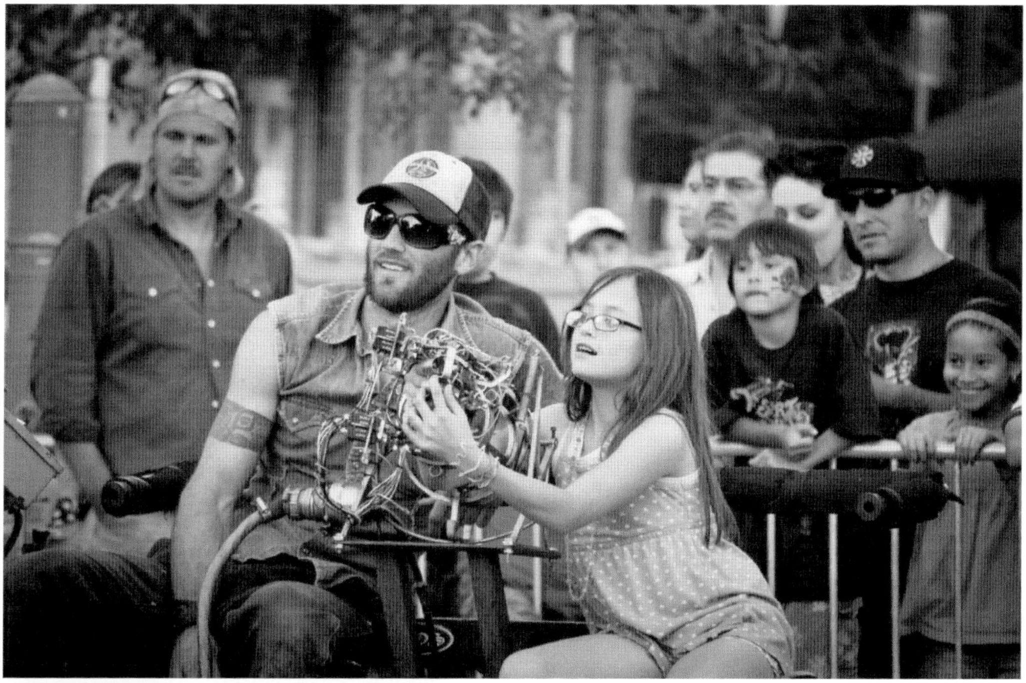

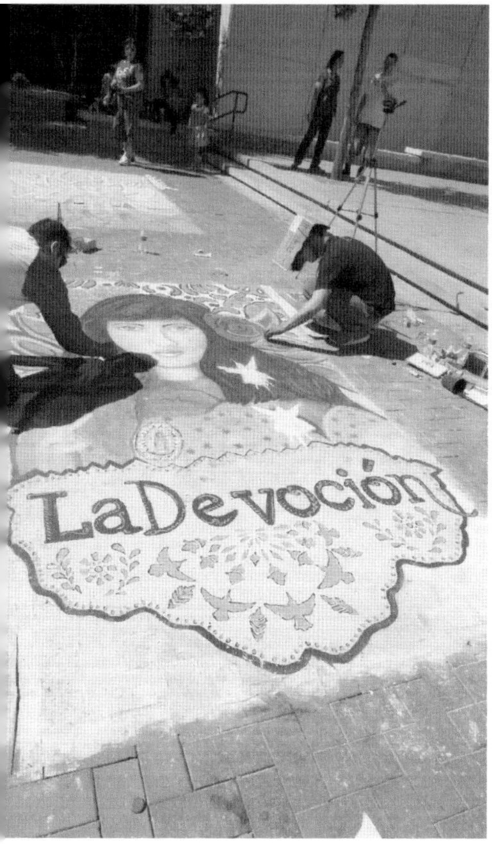

Chalk the Block

In 2008, a free outdoor event started downtown that would help introduce El Pasoans to the burgeoning artist community in the region. The festival, put together by volunteers like Jay and Chrissy Kleberg, has helped open more creative avenues for artists to share their passion with children and young adults in the community. Over 6,000 pieces of chalk were used in 2013, and more than 200 artists took part in the annual October event. Chalk the Block is a partnership between the city and the private sector, a partnership that continues to grow as the festival grows in popularity. (Both, courtesy of Chalk the Block.)

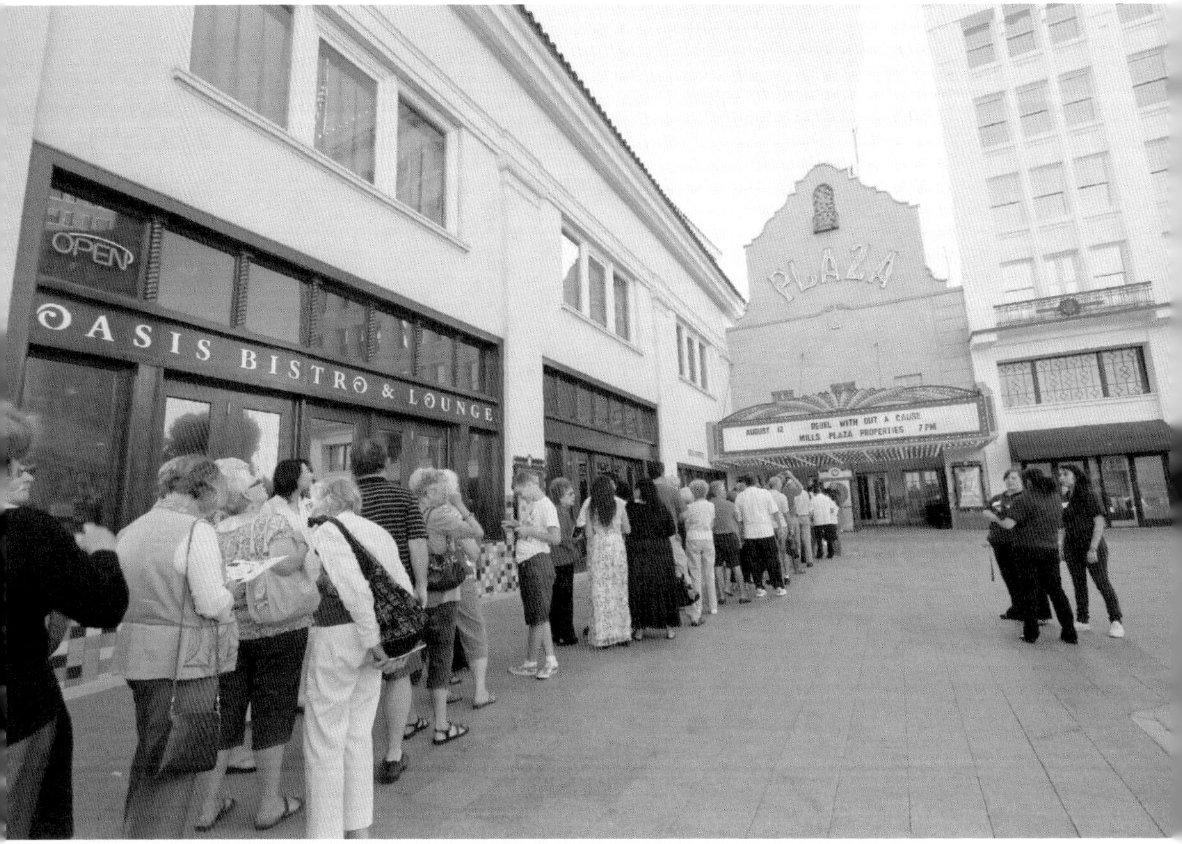

El Paso Community Foundation

In 1977, the El Paso Community Foundation began operations as a charitable endowment to serve the Paso del Norte region. The foundation began as a project of the El Paso Junior League and was born out of the ideas of Katherine Brennand and Richard Harlan "Rickie" Feuille. The first year saw foundation funds at $90,000. For 2015, the foundation has funds of over $120 million. The positive effects of the foundation can be found in projects like the restoration of the Plaza Theatre, Plaza Classic Film Festival, Wyler Aerial Tramway, and providing potable water to hundreds of people living in *colonias* (unincorporated settlements). Looking toward the future, the foundation is working with several initiatives such as sustainability and education partnerships that will have a positive lasting effect on the community. (Courtesy of the El Paso Community Foundation.)

Hunt Foundation

In 1987, Woody and Gayle Hunt created the Hunt Family Foundation with the vision that this organization would support not-for-profit organizations and projects that affect El Paso, Juarez, Las Cruces, and the surrounding areas. To date, the Hunt Family Foundation has given over $40 million to 507 organizations. The results of the foundation's work can be seen at organizations such as the YWCA, Kids Excel, El Paso Museum of Art, UTEP, and the El Paso Children's Hospital. (Courtesy of the Hunt Family Foundation.)

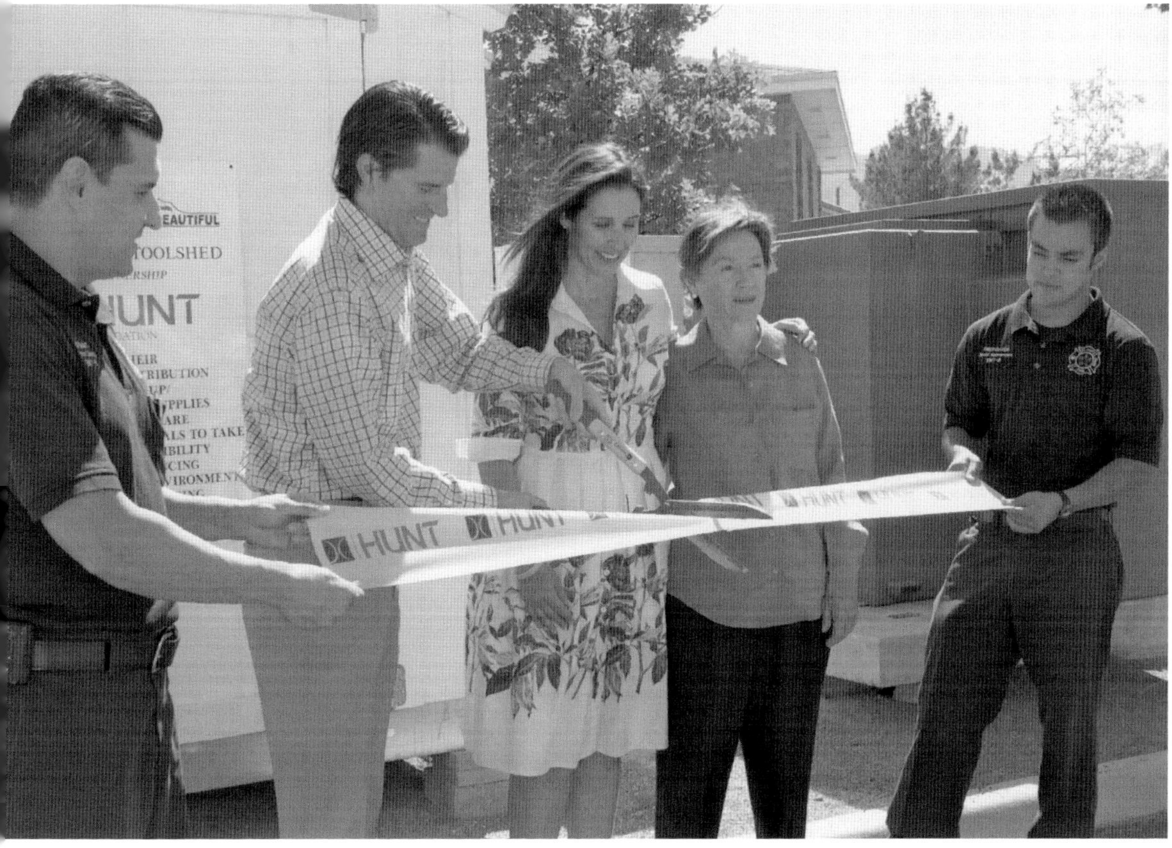

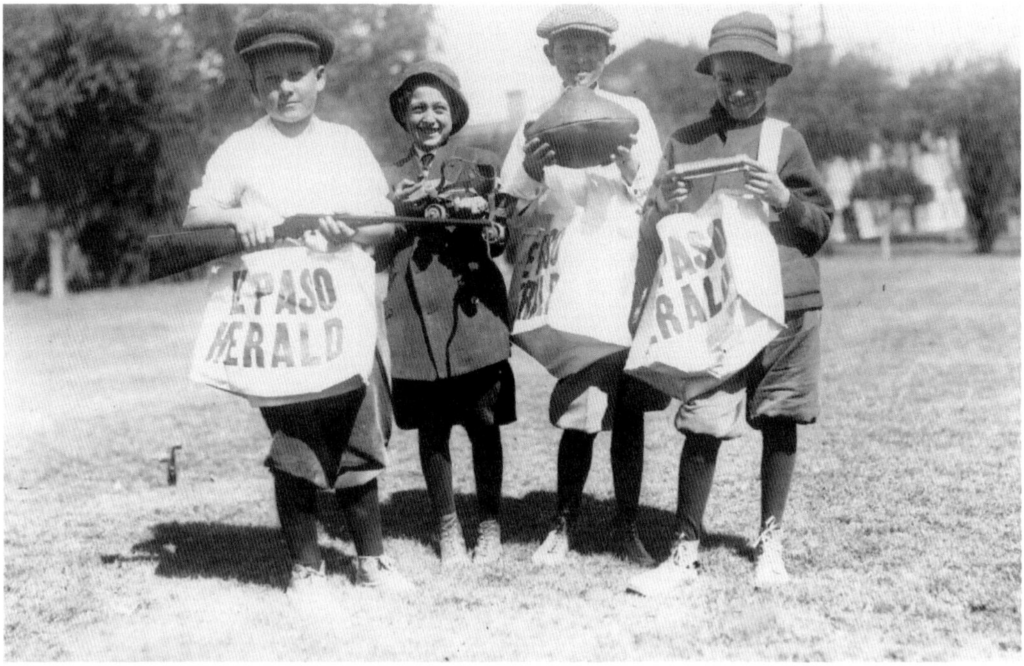

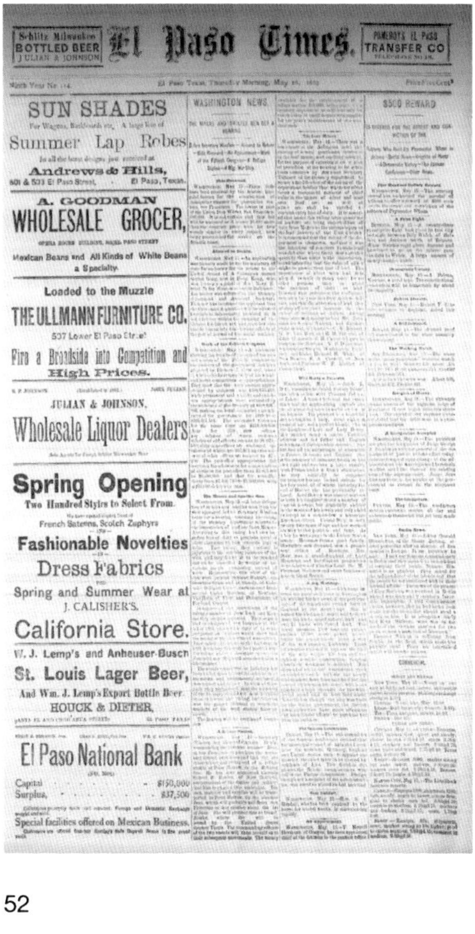

Schlitz Milwaukee
BOTTLED BEER
JULIAN & JOHNSON

El Paso Times.

POMEROY'S EL PASO
TRANSFER CO

SUN SHADES

Summer Lap Robes

Andrews & Hills,
601 & 503 El Paso Street, El Paso, Texas.

A. GOODMAN
WHOLESALE GROCER,

Mexican Beans and All Kinds of White Beans a Specialty.

Loaded to the Muzzle
THE ULLMANN FURNITURE CO.
507 Lower El Paso Street
Fire a Broadside into Competition and High Prices.

JULIAN & JOHNSON,
Wholesale Liquor Dealers

Spring Opening
Two Hundred Styles to Select From.
French Sateens, Scotch Zephyrs
Fashionable Novelties
Dress Fabrics
Spring and Summer Wear at
J. CALISHER'S.
California Store.

W. J. Lemp's and Anheuser-Busch
St. Louis Lager Beer,
And Wm. J. Lemp's Export Bottle Beer.
HOUCK & DIETER,

El Paso National Bank
Capital - - - - $150,000
Surplus, - - - - $37,500
Special facilities offered on Mexican Business.

WASHINGTON NEWS.

$500 REWARD

El Paso Newspapers

The newspaper has been a part of El Paso since the 1800s. At one time, the *El Paso Times and* the *El Paso Herald-Post* both shared the spotlight as the city's major papers. From the Mexican Revolution to the 1966 national championship and troops headed from Fort Bliss to fight the war on terror, the journalists in El Paso have covered the important stories of the day. Now, only the *El Paso Times* remains, but the legacy of the paper in El Paso will not be forgotten. (Above, courtesy of EPPL BHC; left, courtesy of the Abilene Library Consortium.)

CHAPTER FOUR

The Creatives

Inspiration can arise anywhere. It may be a rich colorful sky taking shape as the sun slowly sets behind the mountains. It could be the scene of war unfolding before one's eyes that makes such an impression that an artist like Tom Lea creates a painting that still serves as a reminder of the harsh realities of life during wartime.

The love of music took Jim Ward from playing high school gigs to touring across the world as he and his bandmates played shows from Asia to Europe. It is that inner well that people draw from that promotes the drive to achieve and express. Author Sergio Troncoso took hold of his passion and made his way from growing up with very little in Ysleta to attending several Ivy League institutions. He is now a professor and celebrated writer.

While many pushed their creativity into writing, music, and canvas, another individual pushed his ideas onto blueprints and would see those plans turn into buildings that would come to define El Paso. Henry Trost designed everything from houses to large commercial buildings and churches. His passion can still be shared today, as many of the buildings he designed are still standing and are being restored.

El Paso knows that the creative community is a key cog when it comes to having a healthy and well-balanced city. There are more public art projects under construction than in decades past. A new affordable artist community is being constructed with help from the El Paso Community Foundation and Art Space to provide artists a place to live, sell, and display their works.

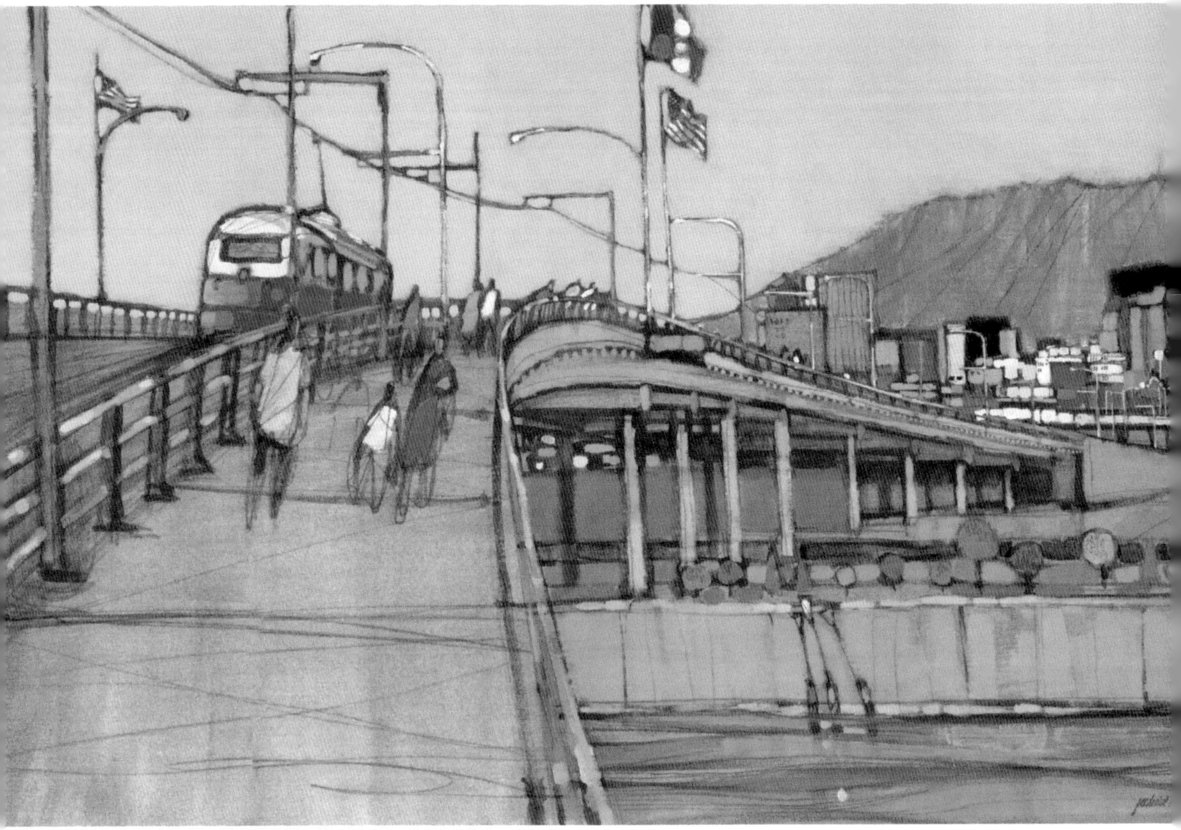

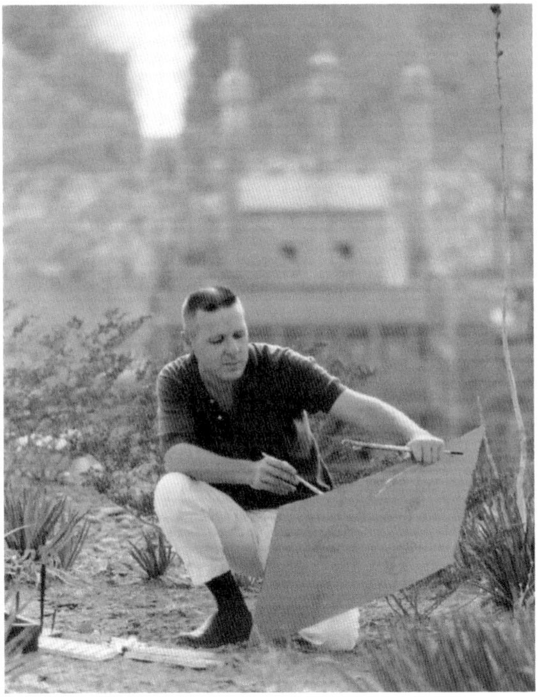

Frederick Carter

Frederick Carter (1925–2010) was born in Galveston, Texas, and attended Franklin School of Professional Arts in New York before making his way to El Paso, where he met his wife, Dottie. Some of his most iconic paintings have featured well-known El Paso locations such as Sunset Grocery, the International Bridge, and other street scenes in the area. Many people were drawn to his bright and vivid colors, and his talent was recognized when he was chosen as the Texas State Artist in 1995. Frederick Carter passed away in 2010, but his paintings will be shared for generations to come. Carter's *El Paso from the International Bridge*, painted in 1971, is pictured above. (Above, courtesy of Pancho and Donna Mangan; right, courtesy of the Frederick Carter family.)

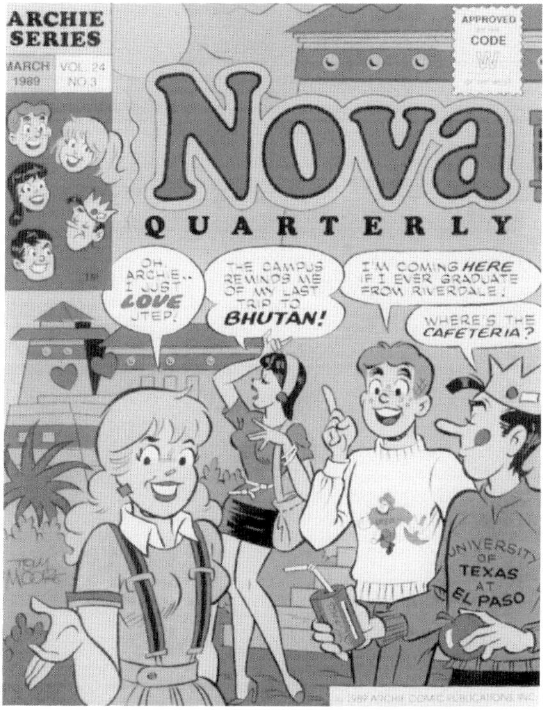

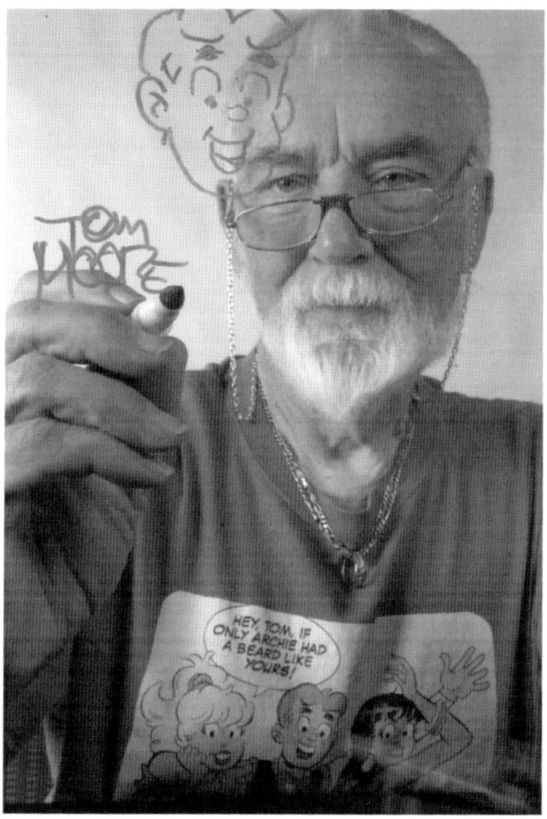

Tom Moore

To know more about *Archie* comics, look no further than Tom Moore. For close to 40 years, Moore was a cartoonist for the series. He attended Crockett Elementary and Austin High School, and his ink lines were influenced by cartoons like *Lil Abner* and *Little Orphan Annie*. Moore began drawing cartoons while in the Navy; he served at the tail end of World War II and in Korea. After he was out of the service, Moore was in New York City and happened to be at the right place at the right time and found a job writing and drawing for the *Archie* series. His wife, Ruth, also helped him throughout the years and provided the female point of view for Betty and Veronica. In the late 1980s, Moore took a leave of absence after a long and fruitful career. (Both, courtesy of Tom Moore.)

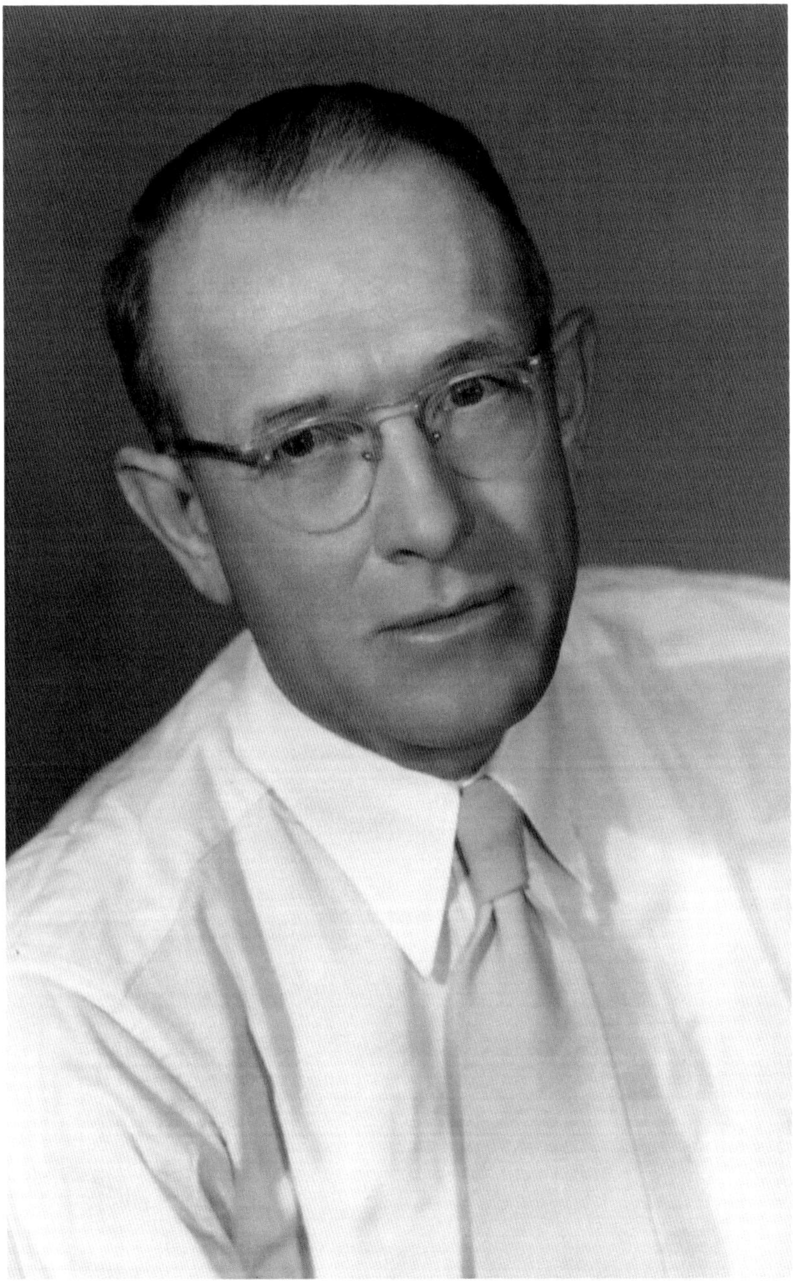

Charles Leland Sonnichsen

C.L. Sonnichsen (1901–1991) studied English literature while he was in school, but after moving to El Paso, he changed his focus. Once in the arid Southwest, his research and writing focused on the history and culture of the region. He wrote numerous books that covered topics from the Mesacalero Apaches to the history of the Pass of the North. Sonnichsen was a professor at the Texas College of Mines (UTEP) and served as president of the Texas Folklore Society. His writing educated generations of readers and students alike and will continue to do so into the future. (Courtesy of the El Paso County Historical Society.)

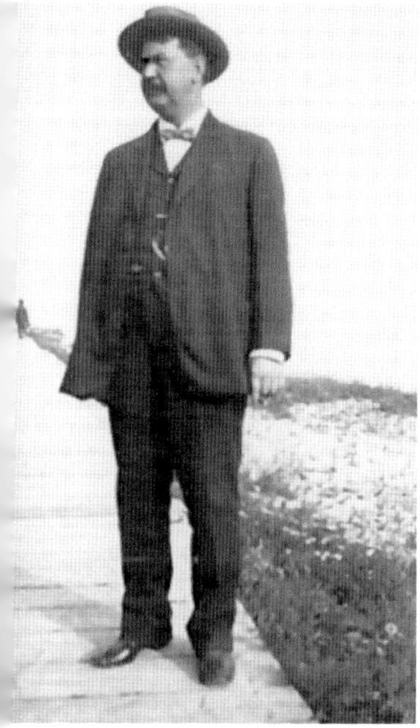

Henry Trost

Henry Trost and his brothers were a major influence on the architecture that can be seen today throughout El Paso and other areas of West Texas. Henry Trost was born in 1860 in Toledo, Ohio. After traveling around the country, he made his way to El Paso to start an architecture firm with his brothers. Trost & Trost would go on to design well-known landmarks throughout the city such as the Mills Building, Bassett Tower, El Paso High School, and Hotel Paseo Del Norte. Trost's knowledge of architectural styles was vast and many of those styles, from Victorian to Mission Revival, are found in structures throughout the city today. As El Paso has begun to see a downtown revival, a push has been made to make sure the architectural and design work of current Trost buildings remains protected and maintained. Henry Trost passed away in 1930, but it is to be hoped that the work of Trost & Trost will live on for generations to come. (Left, courtesy of Margaret Smith; below, courtesy of the El Paso County Historical Society.)

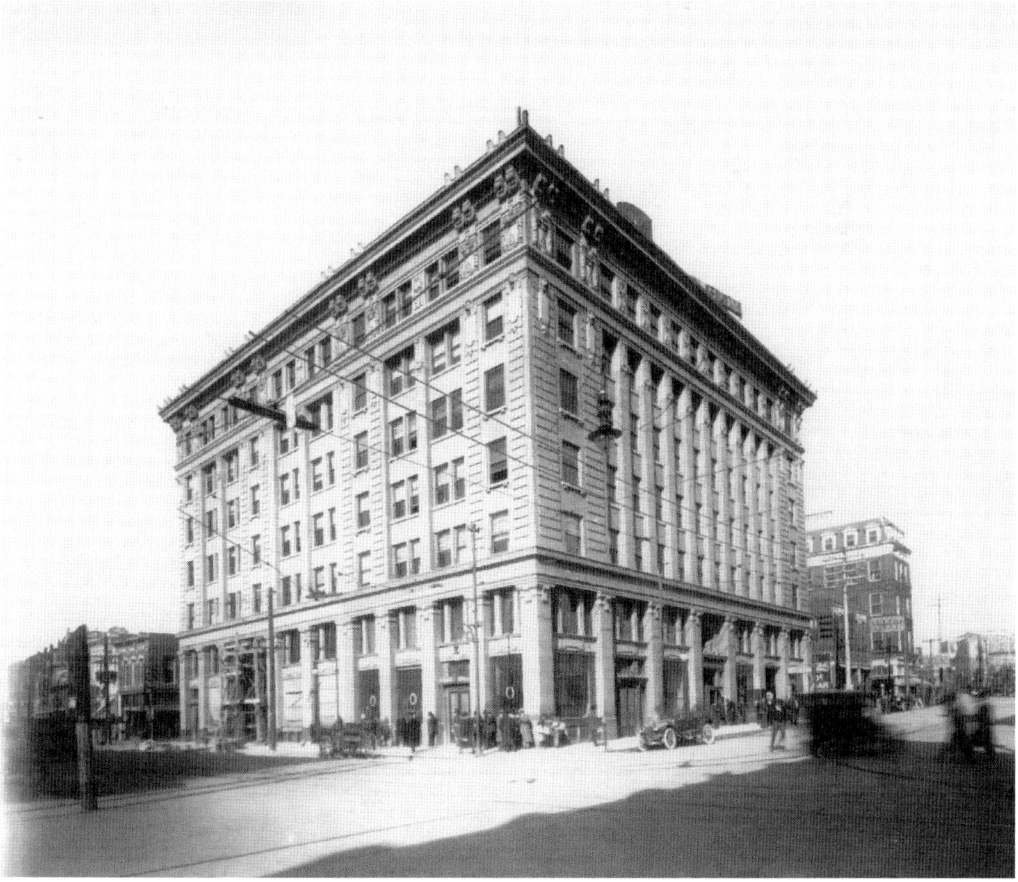

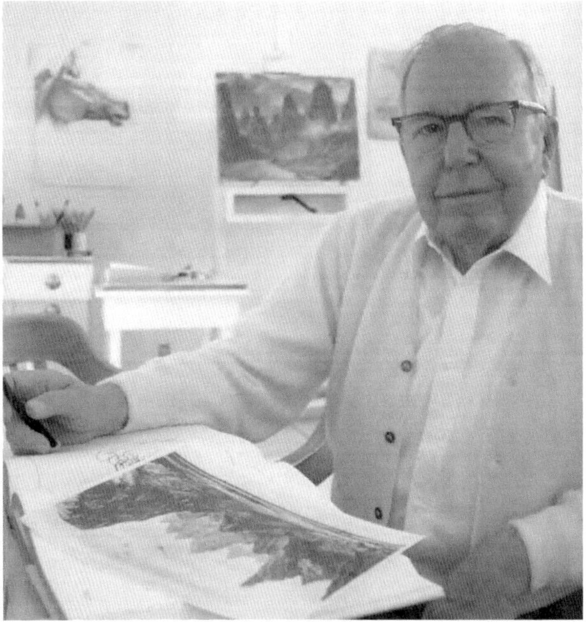

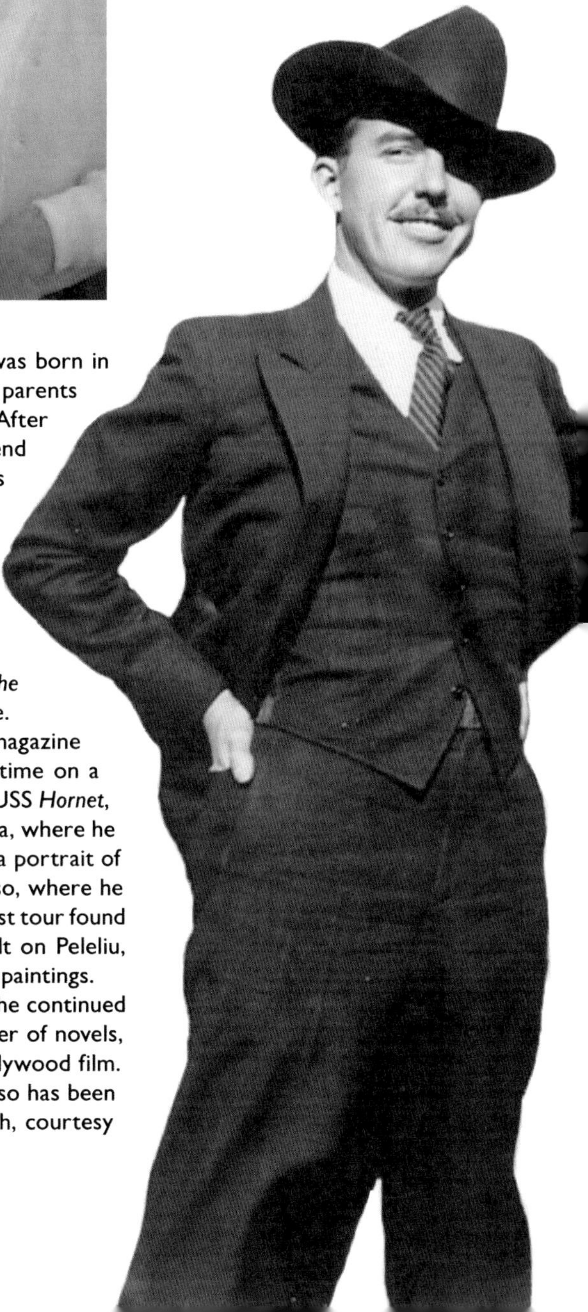

Tom Lea

One of the most influential artists in El Paso was born in 1907. Tom Lea grew up in a good home with parents who supported his desire to get into the arts. After graduating from El Paso High, he went on to attend the School of the Art Institute of Chicago. He was mentored by and apprenticed under muralist John Norton. During the Great Depression, Lea found work doing a number of murals through the treasury department. His first project was *The Nesters*, a mural for the Ben Franklin Post Office in Washington, DC. Lea created other murals, including the *Pass of the North* mural for the El Paso Federal Courthouse.

During World War II, Lea was invited by *Life* magazine to be an artist war correspondent. He spent time on a destroyer in the Atlantic, a few months on the USS *Hornet*, and traveled with bomber crews in North Africa, where he met Jimmy Doolittle and subsequently painted a portrait of him. After Pearl Harbor Lea returned to El Paso, where he turned in his first spread for *Life* magazine. His last tour found him embedded with Marines during the Assault on Peleliu, where the true face of war came through in his paintings.

Afterwards, Lea returned to El Paso, where he continued to paint and write as well. Lea penned a number of novels, and one, *The Brave Bulls*, was turned into a Hollywood film. Lea passed away in 2001, but his legacy in El Paso has been preserved through the Tom Lea Institute. (Both, courtesy of the Tom Lea Institute.)

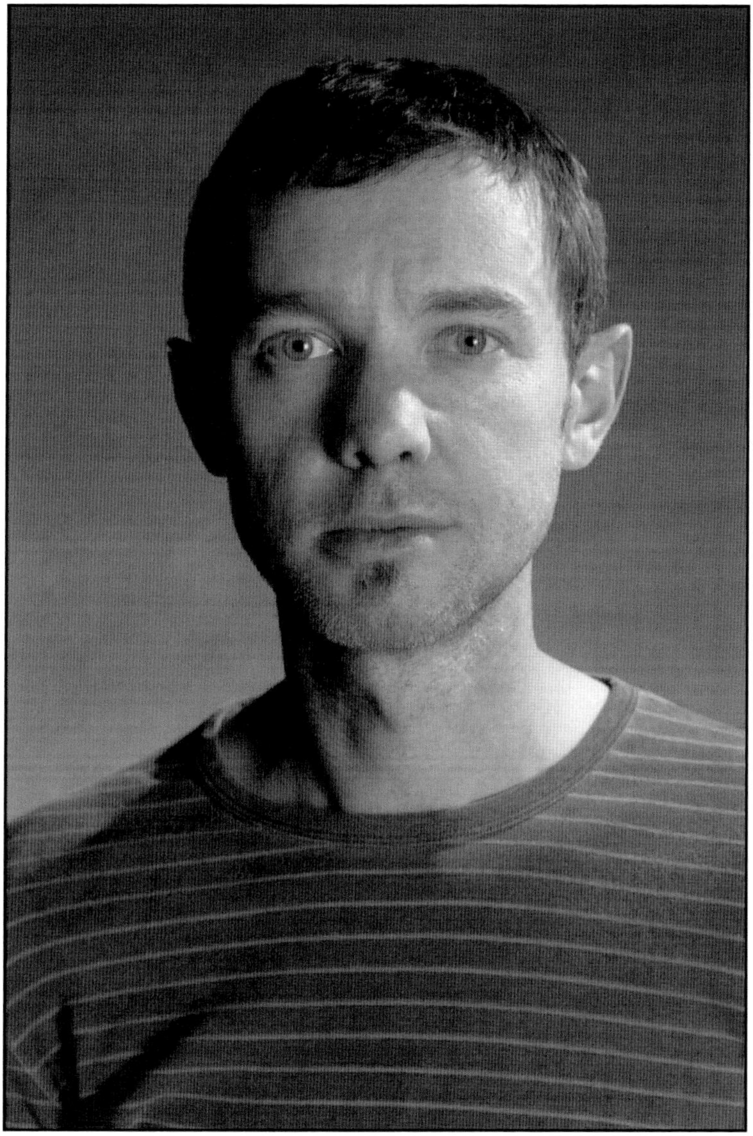

Jim Ward
Bright lights, screaming fans, and music venues across the globe is how Jim Ward (born in 1976) helped share a piece of the El Paso music scene with people across the world. Ward has fond memories of playing in Memorial Park as a child and playing some of his first shows while in school at El Paso High. First finding success with popular El Paso band At the Drive-In, Ward and fellow band members traveled across the world playing in venues from Holland to Japan.

Since then, they have formed more bands, including Sparta and Sleepercar, but the genre has stayed the same—rock. Behind every creative output is an influence, and for Jim, that is his wife, Kristine. They have been together for 17 years, and her inspiration has helped him in music and in their business ventures Tricky Falls/Bowie Feathers and Eloise. As for the future of the El Paso music scene, Ward believes El Paso "will be the next stop for the creatives that are being pushed out of cities like Austin/Phoenix/Albuquerque. I think El Paso is such a unique and fantastic place that will inspire those who come out here and stay." (Courtesy of Lindsey Best.)

Leon Metz

A number of great historians have lived in El Paso. One of the most notable and recent is Leon Metz. His name is synonymous with El Paso history. Born in 1930 in West Virginia, Metz made his way to El Paso via the US Air Force. He was the first archivist at UTEP and a very accomplished writer. He has authored over 19 books and helped document the lives of men like John Wesley Hardin and John Selman. Metz's expertise on the West has been valuable, and he has appeared on several historical programs and written many articles for the *El Paso Times*. Documenting the area's history is extremely important, and Leon Metz has accepted that responsibility since he arrived here in the 1950s. (Courtesy of EPPL BHC.)

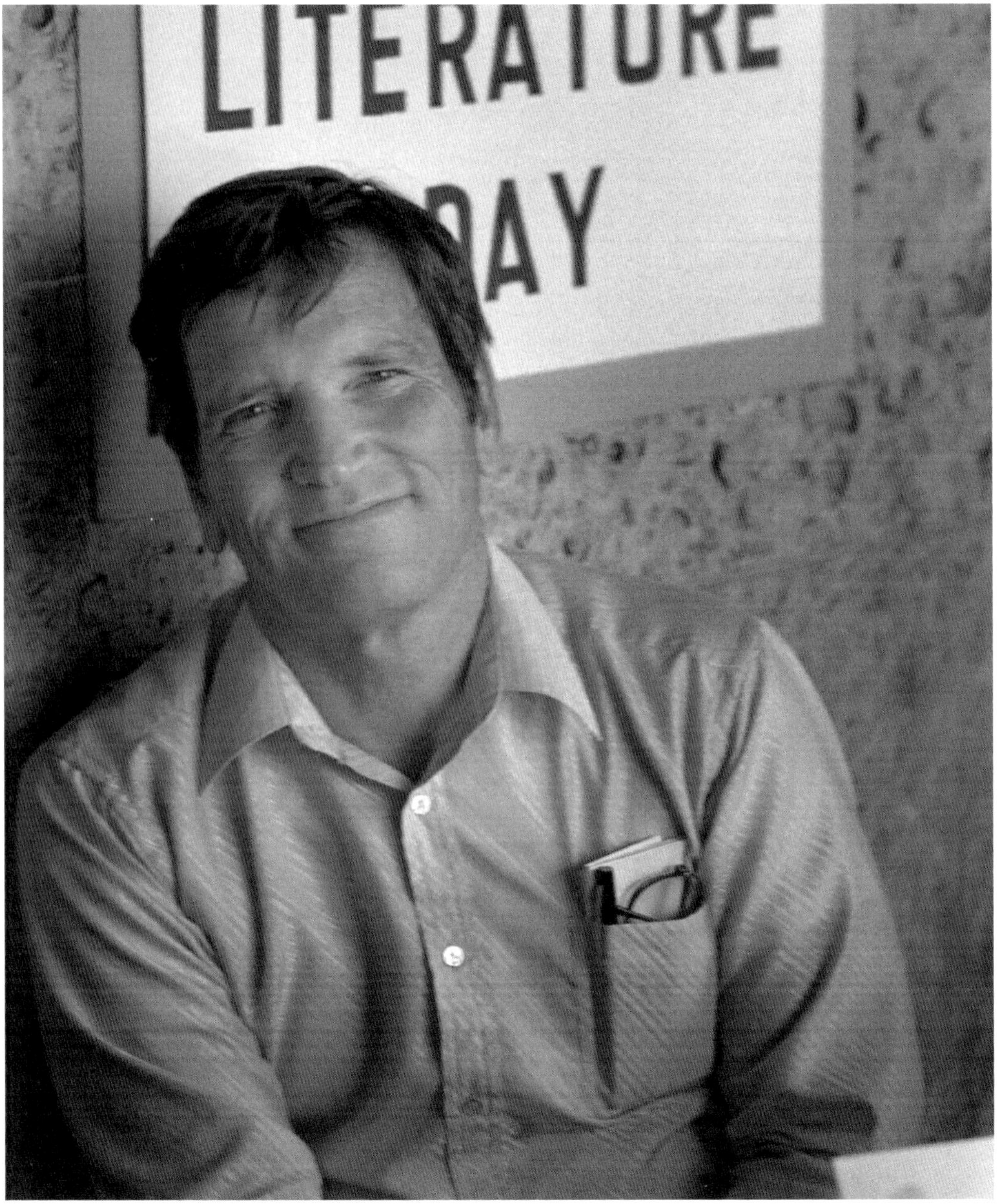

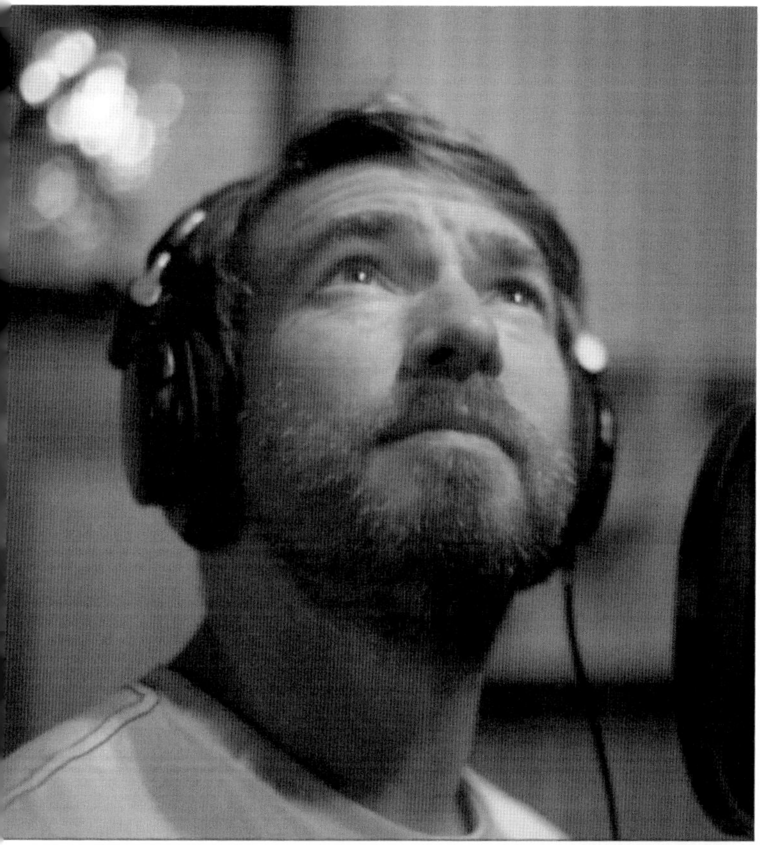

Sonic Ranch
Near Tornillo sits a 2,000-acre ranch that features pecan orchards and what has been called the world's largest residential studio-recording complex. Sonic Ranch was founded by Tony Rancich over two decades ago, but the ranch has been around for over 90 years. The solitude of the complex has provided a great retreat for bands looking to make their next record without all of the noise from the modern-day world. Bands such as the New Master Sounds, Ministry, the Yeah Yeah Yeahs, and more have all spent time making music within the peaceful confines of Sonic Ranch. (Photographs by Simon K. Allen.)

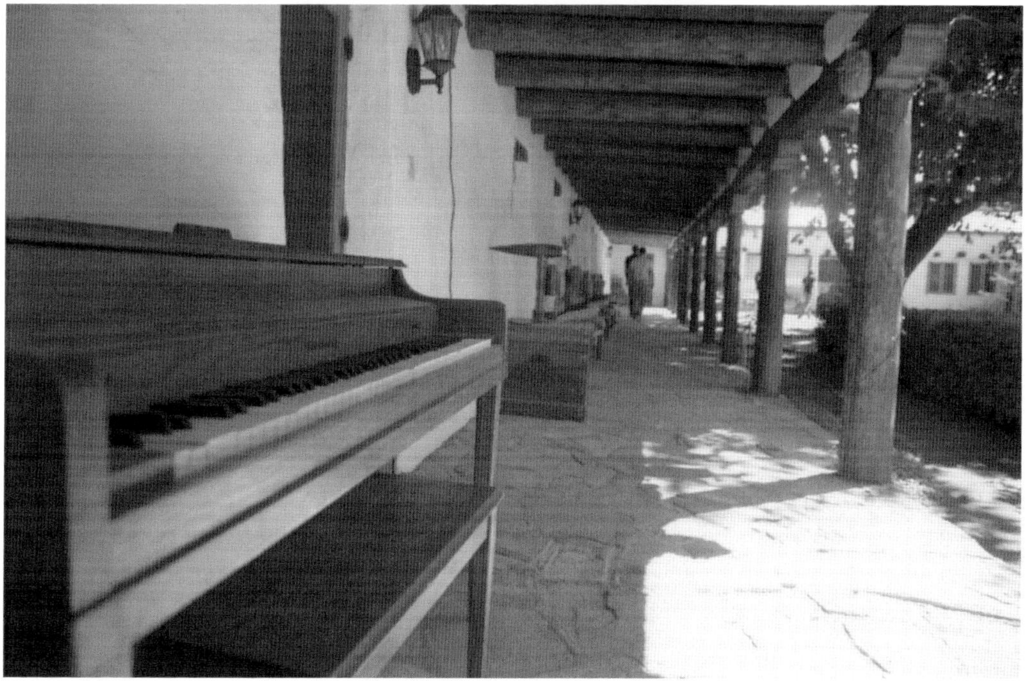

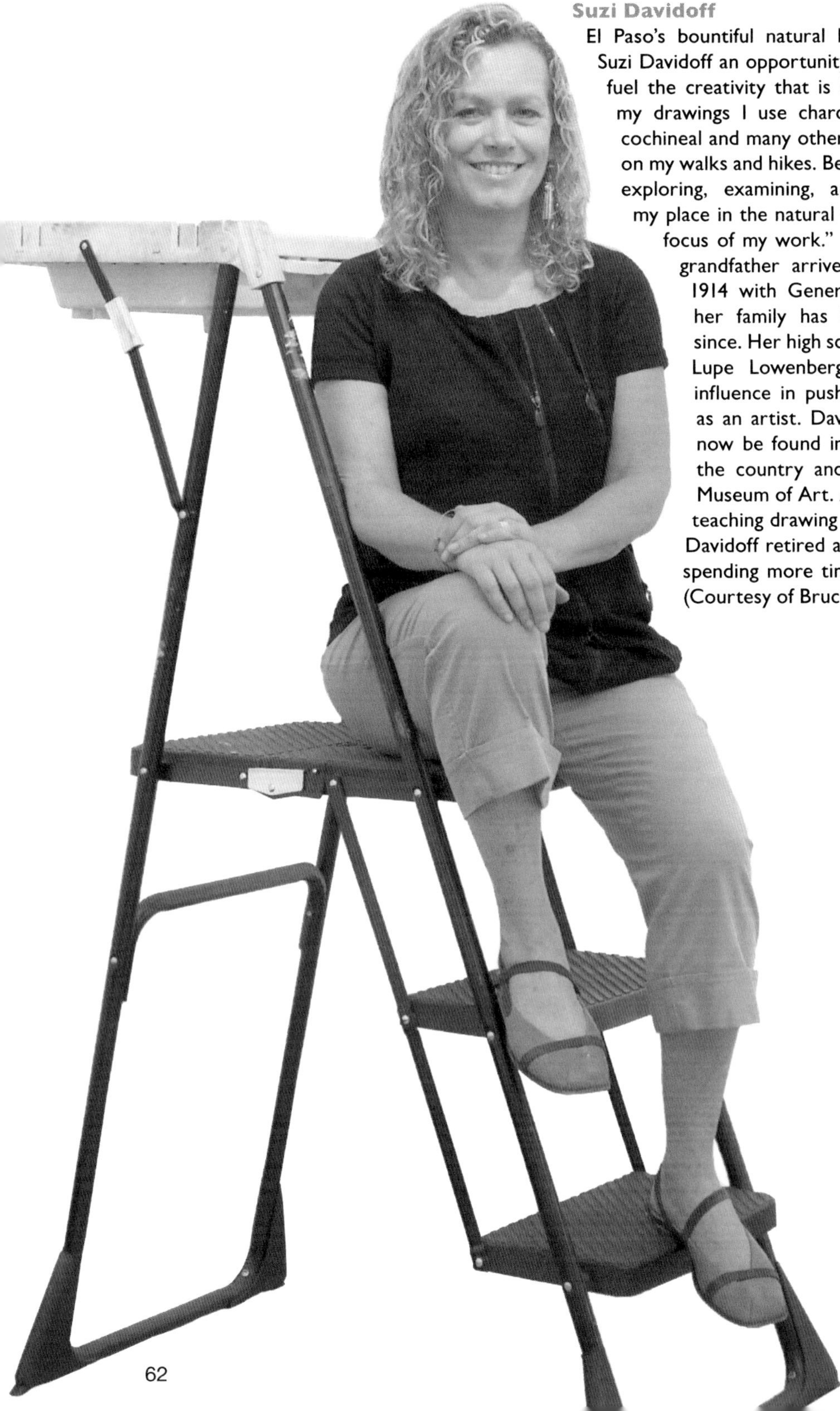

Suzi Davidoff

El Paso's bountiful natural landscape allows Suzi Davidoff an opportunity to explore and fuel the creativity that is her drawing. "In my drawings I use charcoal, earth, clay, cochineal and many other materials found on my walks and hikes. Being in nature and exploring, examining, and experiencing my place in the natural world is a major focus of my work." Davidoff's great-grandfather arrived in El Paso in 1914 with General Pershing, and her family has been here ever since. Her high school art teacher, Lupe Lowenberg, was a major influence in pushing her forward as an artist. Davidoff's work can now be found in galleries across the country and at the El Paso Museum of Art. After 25 years of teaching drawing and art at UTEP, Davidoff retired and now plans on spending more time in her studio. (Courtesy of Bruce Berman.)

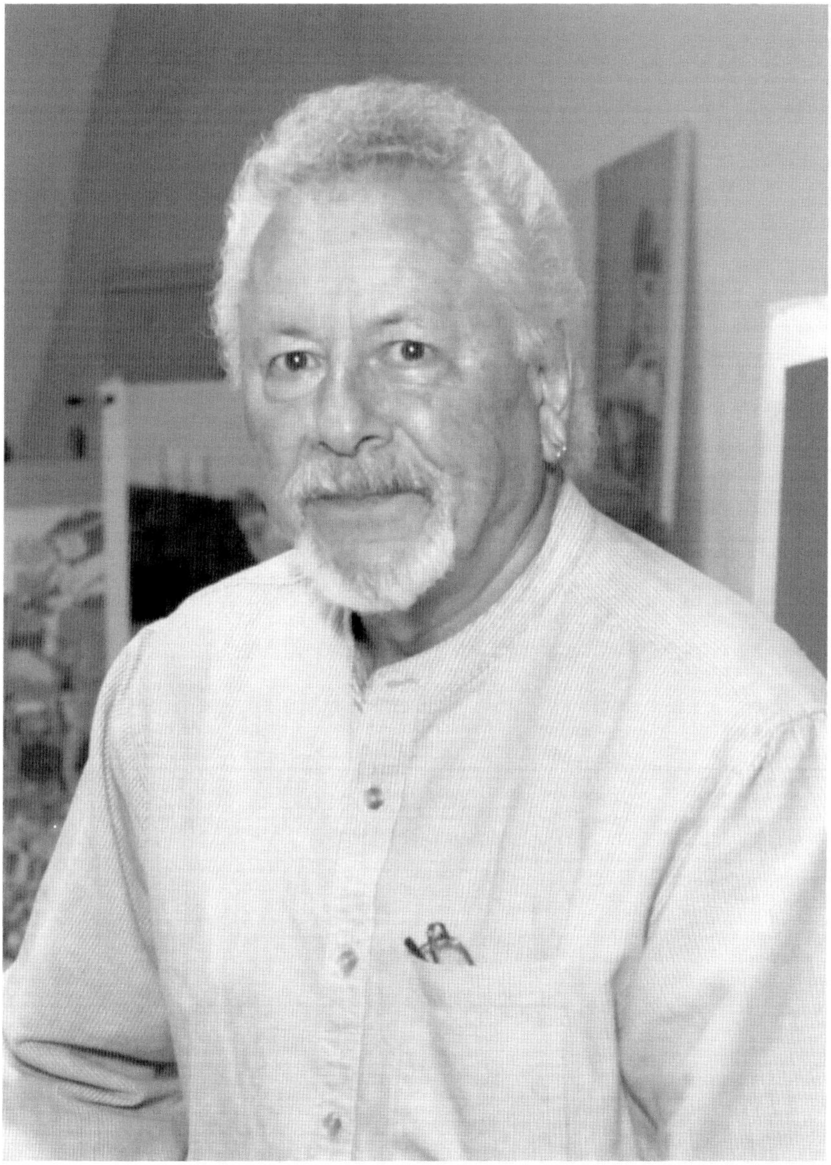

Gaspar Enriquez

In San Elizario, one can find Gaspar Enriquez at the studio within his restored 250-year-old adobe home working diligently on his latest project. Born in 1942 in the Segundo Barrio, Enriquez enjoyed El Paso as a child while "experiencing all of its flavors." His mother was a large influence in his life and a figure of strength who helped him overcome the temptations of an adolescent. He survived economic hardship and was able to get an education in the arts with a bachelor's degree from UTEP and a master's from New Mexico State University (NMSU). Mel Casas and Luis Jimenez influenced him in his craft, and many of the students he taught at Bowie High School became the inspiration for his portraits. His work is nationally acclaimed and has been sold to buyers all over, including the likes of Cheech Marin. The Chicano artist works mainly with acrylic on paper, canvas, and board. He has had an art exhibition at the El Paso Museum of Art and was commissioned to do murals for the El Paso Chihuahuas ballpark. (Courtesy of El Paso Inc.)

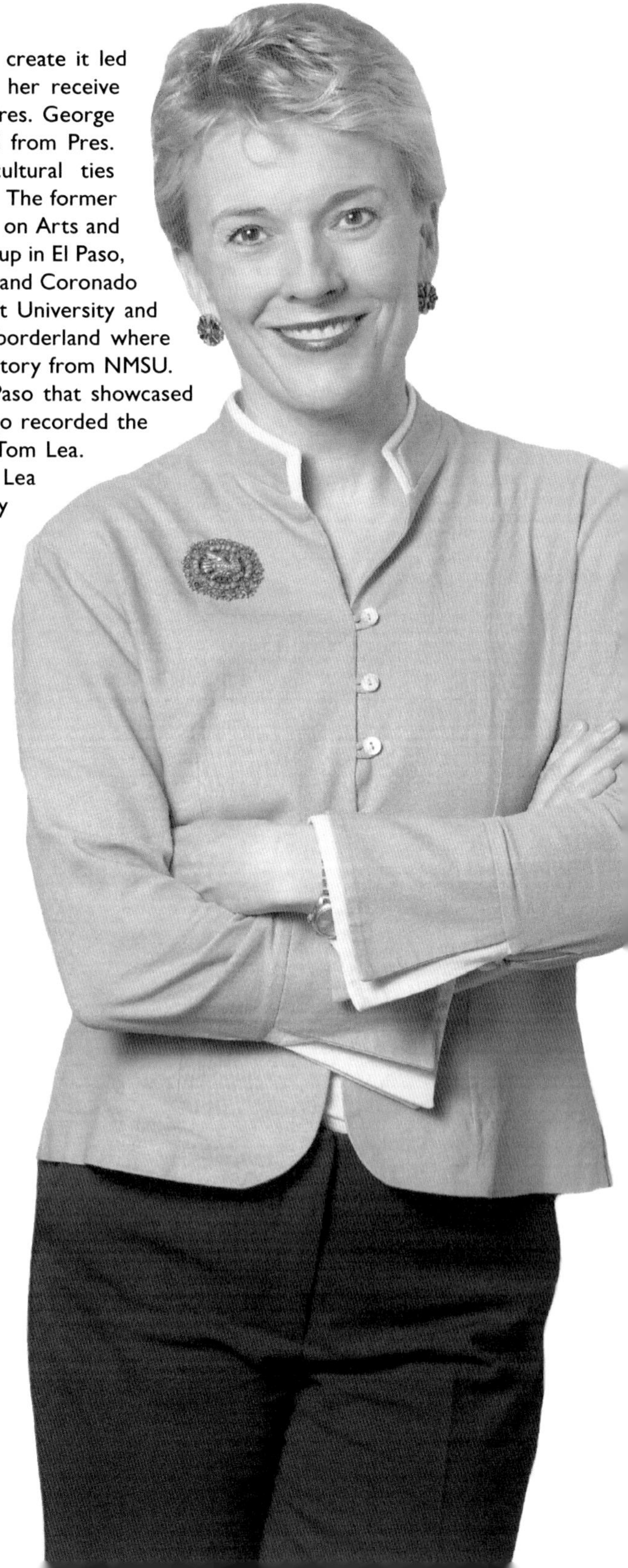

Adair Margo

A passion for art and the people who create it led Adair Margo on a path that has seen her receive the Presidential Citizens Medal from Pres. George W. Bush and the Aguila Azteca Medal from Pres. Felipe Calderón for strengthening cultural ties between the United States and Mexico. The former chairman of the President's Committee on Arts and Humanities was born in Japan but grew up in El Paso, where she attended Mesita Elementary and Coronado High School. After attending Vanderbilt University and studying abroad, she returned to the borderland where she earned a master's degree in art history from NMSU. For 25 years, she had a gallery in El Paso that showcased art from regional artists. In 1993, Margo recorded the oral history of local artist and writer Tom Lea. This eventually led her to open the Tom Lea Institute in 2009, in which Lea's legacy has been preserved and actively shared with people across the nation during Tom Lea Month every October. Margo has a vision for the future of arts in the area: "My hope for the arts in the borderland is that they will continue to flourish, and that a new generation of artists will look up and look out at the wonder of life around them." Adair and her husband, Dee, reside in El Paso and have two sons, William and Don. (Courtesy of the Tom Lea Institute.)

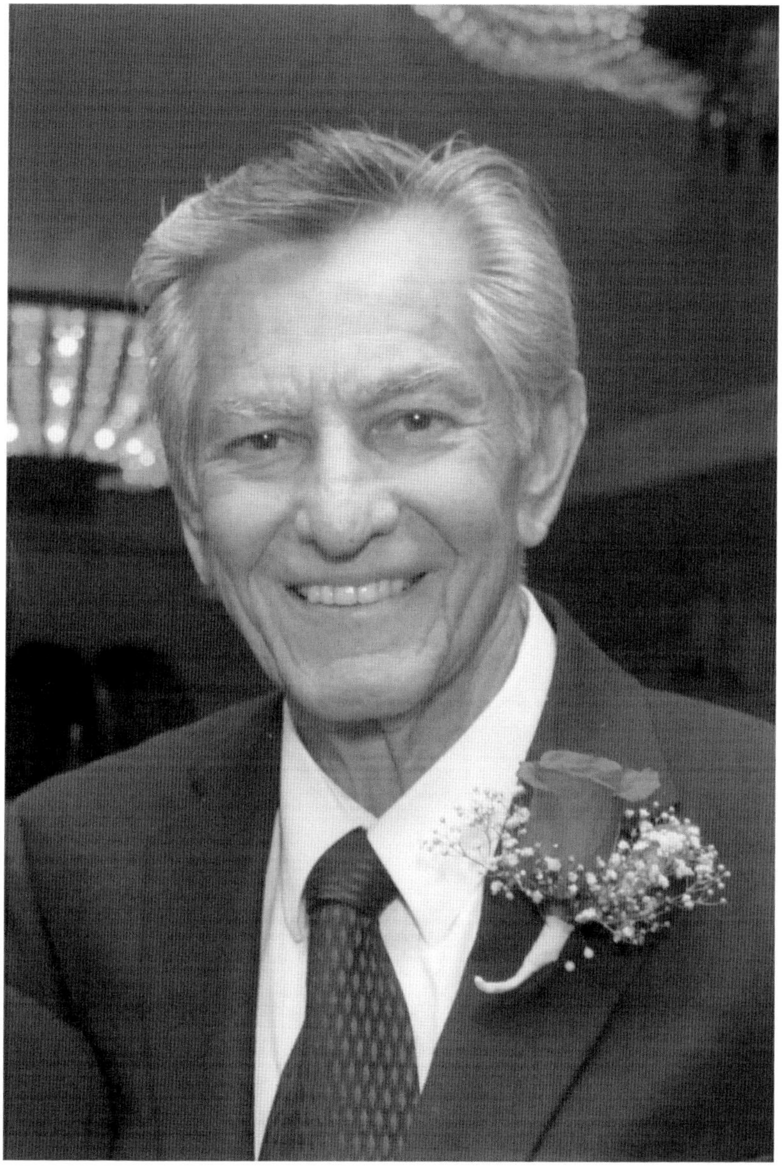

Nestor Valencia

Nestor Valencia is known as much for his work as a city planner as he is for his portraits that adorn the walls at the Plaza Theatre. Before entering a career with the city, Valencia attended college in 1963 at Texas Western, where he graduated with a bachelor's degree in art. He went on to get a master's in political science in 1969. The Air Force veteran held many roles throughout his 25-plus years at the city, working as an urban coordinator, regional planner, and director of planning. After his time at the city, Valencia joined the El Paso Community Foundation as the vice president for planning, and helped establish programs that focused on affordable housing, health, education, and culture. While at the foundation, Valencia helped push the restoration of the Plaza Theatre and Wyler Aerial Tramway. He has received the Conquistador Award from the city and also had the Mission Valley Transfer Station renamed after him. Valencia continues to paint portraits in his studio in Anthony, Texas, with his wife, Xochitl, and is actively involved in the community. (Courtesy of El Paso Inc.)

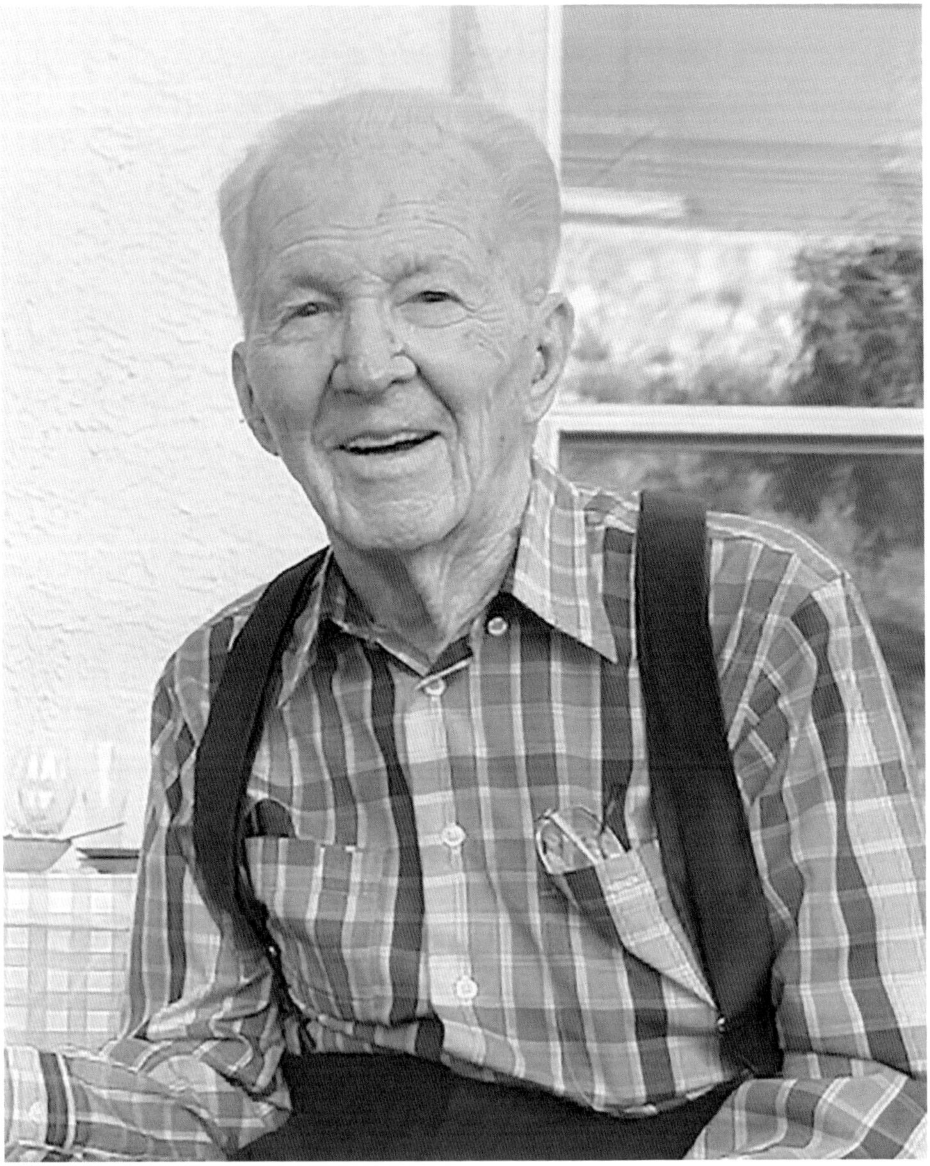

Sheldon Hall

The festival and reenactment of the first Thanksgiving that is held annually in San Elizario came to be because of the hard work and dedication of Sheldon Hall. Born in Ohio, Hall joined the US Army Air Corps and served as a pilot and test pilot. Several years after World War II, Hall made the move to El Paso, where he worked in construction before opening up his own company, which he sold in 1986. It was his work and dedication on the civic side where he really left a lasting impression on the community. As one of the founding members of the El Paso Mission Trail Association, he worked tirelessly to make sure that the El Paso area missions would not only be preserved but also promoted to bring awareness to the historical treasures that make up the Mission Trail. That dedication to El Paso's history and that of the Spaniards led to Hall's appointment as honorary consul to Spain, where he received the Encomienda de la Orden de Isabel Católica. The former bomber pilot continued to be a strong advocate for El Paso and its storied history up until his passing at the age of 95 in 2012. (Courtesy of El Paso Inc.)

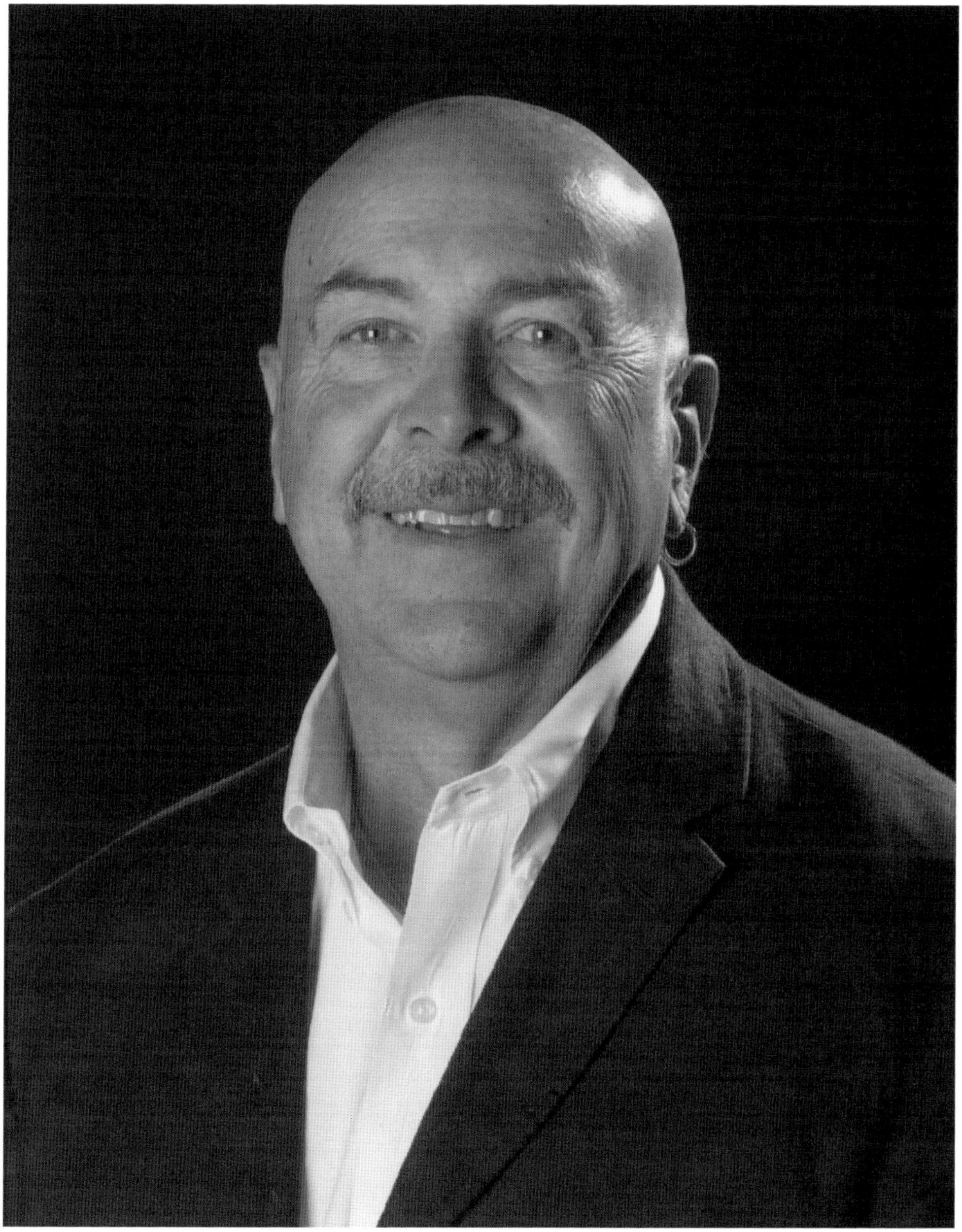

Bill Knight

As a senior at UT Arlington, Bill Knight took a journalism class out of curiosity. That class led him to change his major and set him on an award-winning path while covering iconic moments and people in sports. His newspaper columns and stories are an avenue to go deeper into the game than a box score or final result can provide. "I truly love sports, the sheer competition of all the games. And I love writing about it all. But, probably more than anything, I enjoy all the people I get to meet and actually get to know—the coaches and the athletes." While Knight's career as a journalist is his main focus, he has also published his first novel, *Into the Eyes of Life*, and has plans to write more fiction in the future. (Courtesy of Ruben Ramirez, *El Paso Times*.)

Benjamin Allire Saenz

Ben Saenz is an award-winning novelist and poet who has 20 works to his name. Before his writing career took off, Saenz attended St. Thomas Seminary, and went on to serve three years in the priesthood before leaving to pursue his true passion. After earning a master of fine arts degree at UTEP, Saenz received a fellowship at the University of Iowa and then a Wallace Stegner Fellowship in poetry from Stanford. His poetry and novels have helped capture the ups and downs of life in the Southwest and, more importantly, the border. His book *Everything Begins and Ends at the Kentucky Club* won the Pen/Faulkner Award for fiction in 2013. In addition to his life as a writer, Saenz also serves on the faculty at UTEP, where he has been since the 1990s. (Courtesy of EPPL BHC.)

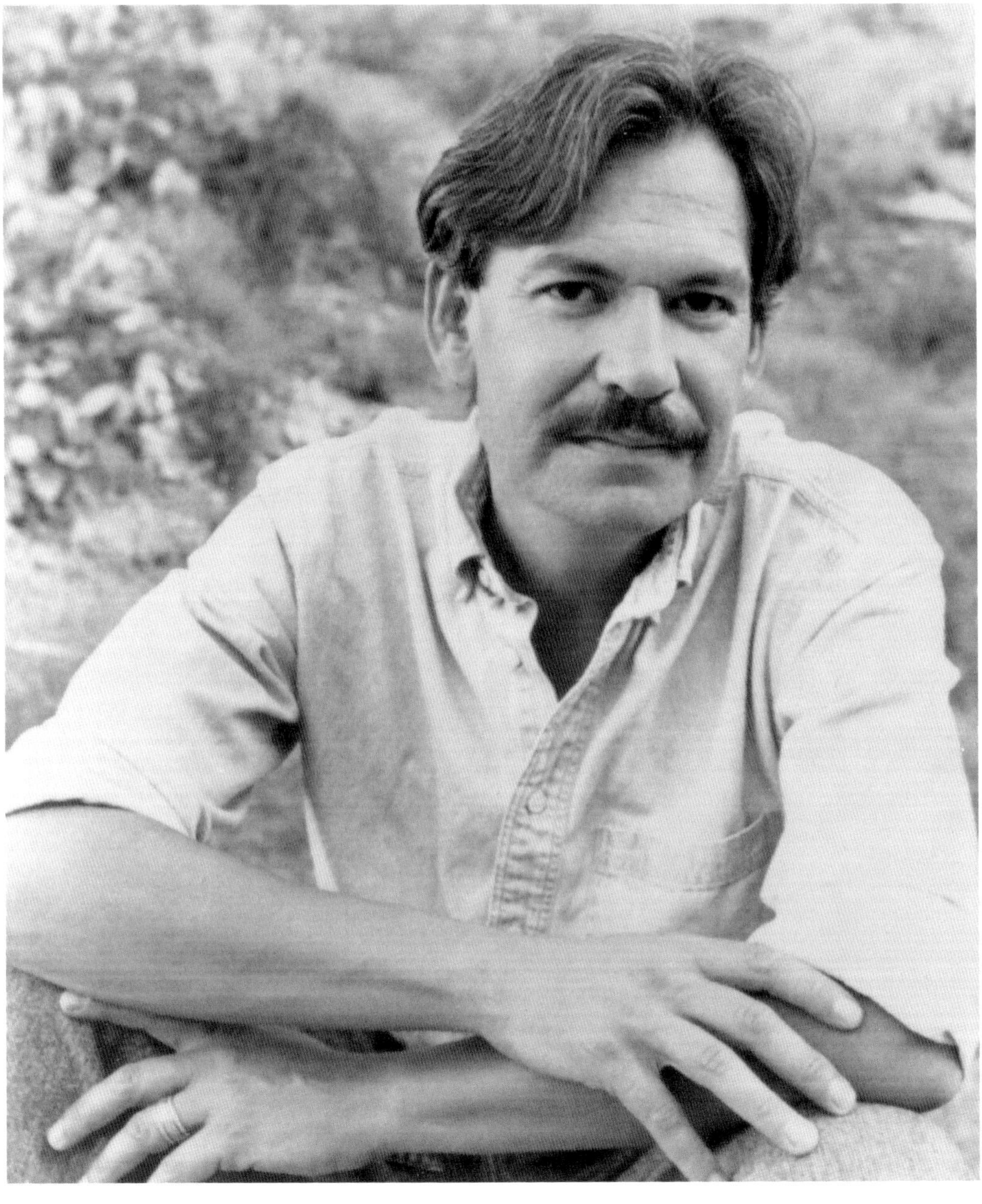

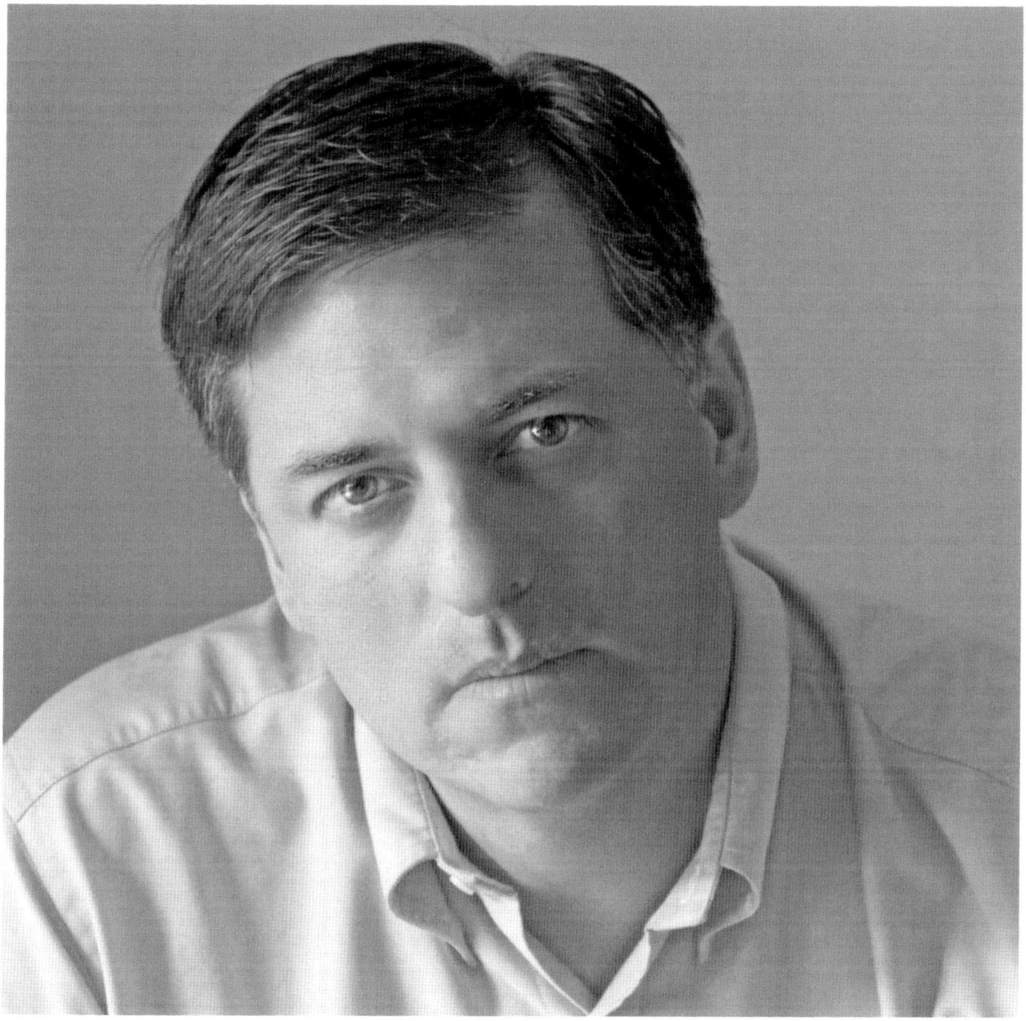

Sergio Troncoso

Growing up in one of El Paso's colonias was just a way of life for Sergio Troncoso. His family may have had to use an outhouse and kerosene lamps for a time, but it was these experiences that would help shape the future author. Born in 1961, early life in Ysleta was spent exploring canals and cotton fields that surrounded the family's adobe abode. The border was his home, but after encouragement from Irma Sanchez, his high school counselor at Ysleta, Troncoso applied to Harvard and was accepted. Transitioning from the border to Boston was not without its challenges. "I was the only Mexican-American in many of my classes, many said I had an accent, and I had only bell-bottom jeans and t-shirts when I arrived. I didn't know Boston got cold! But I received my first A- in Expository Writing freshman year, and that's when I knew I could survive."

After graduating from Harvard, Troncoso was awarded a Fulbright Scholarship to Mexico and then went on to study international relations and philosophy at Yale. He has published numerous books and is now a resident faculty member of the Yale Writer's Conference. Even though he resides in New York City with his wife, Laura, and their two sons, Aaron and Issac, he is sure to visit Licon's Dairy in San Elizario when he and his family come back to the borderland. (Courtesy of Sergio Troncoso.)

José Cisneros

José Cisneros was born in the city of Villa Ocampo, Mexico, in 1910. When the Mexican Revolution reached his town, his family was forced out of their home and embarked on a journey north. After facing a long and arduous trip with multiple stops along the way, Cisneros found himself in Juarez with his family. He was able to obtain a school passport and attended the Lydia Patterson Institute in El Paso. Several years later, Cisneros met Tom Lea and asked him to look at some drawings he had done on the back of a White House Department Store sign. Lea liked them so much that he wrote a letter to then-librarian Maud Sullivan telling her that Cisneros's work was "exceptional" and that maybe she should exhibit them. Cisneros really felt that was his first big break, and his career would only grow bigger over the decades. Many of his pieces of art focused on Spanish history and the Southwest, and can be found in museums across the nation. A few of the notable awards and honors he has received are the National Humanities Medal and a knighthood from King Juan Carlos I of Spain. For Cisneros, his life changed the moment his family was forced out of Villa Ocampo. He came to the United States with nothing, but left a legacy that will always be remembered. (Courtesy of the Tom Lea Institute.)

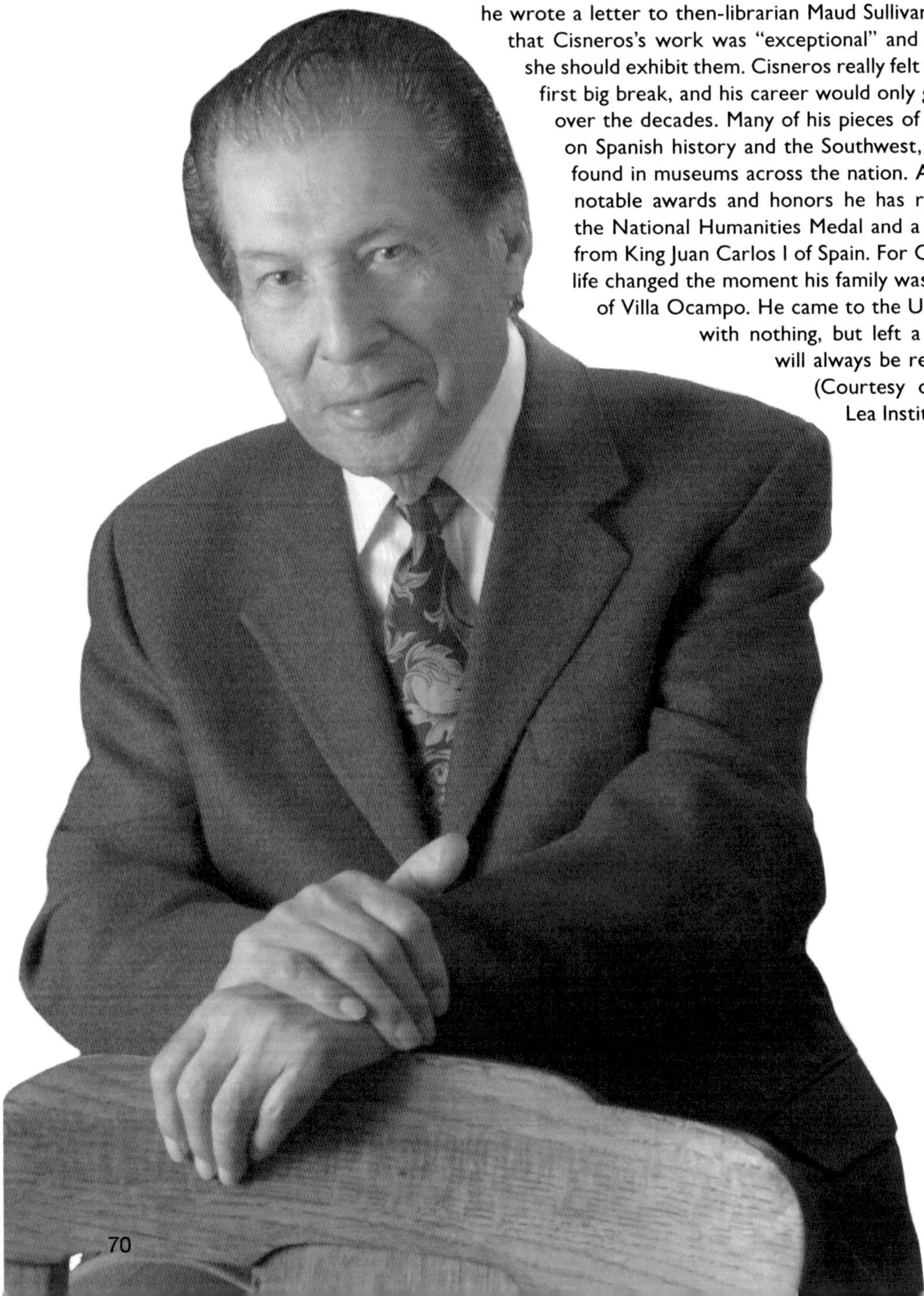

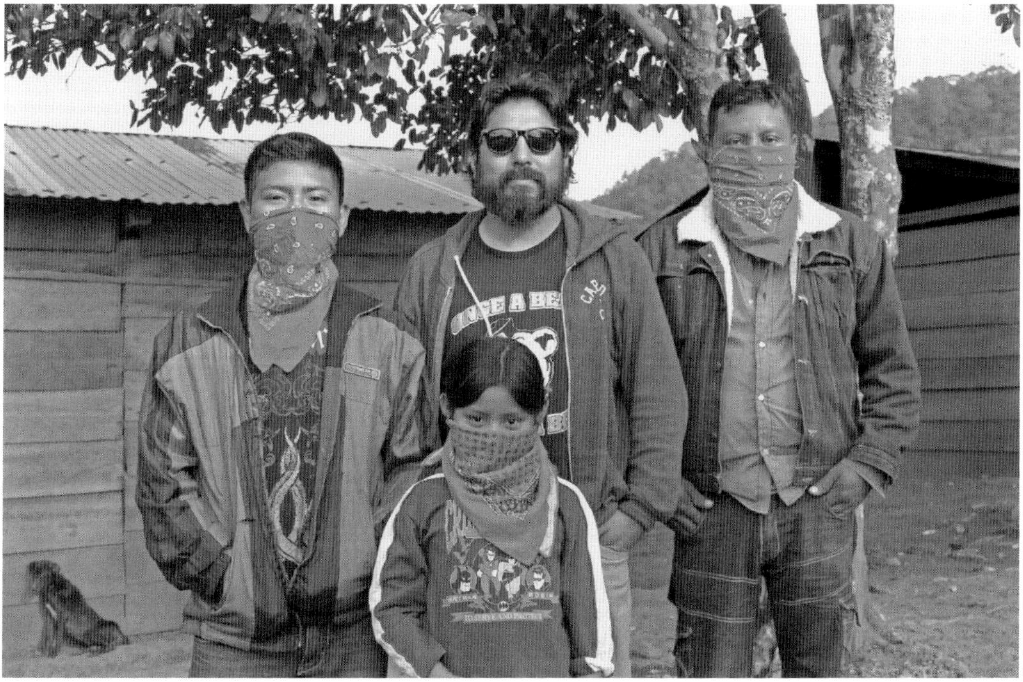

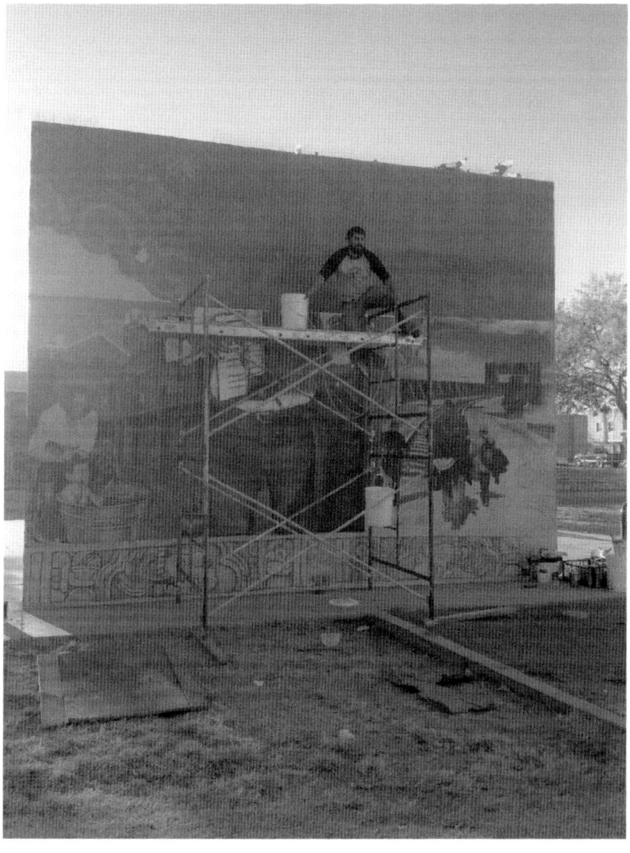

Jesus "Cimi" Alvarado

A young up-and-coming muralist from Segundo Barrio is slowly making a name for himself around the state. Cimi Alvarado's goal is to capture the story of his community and share it with others through his art. While attending Bowie High School, Cimi found a mentor in Gaspar Enriquez, who shaped him into the artist he is today. As his work gains notoriety, Alvarado has seen the requests for commission go up and has received more opportunities to showcase his work at different shows. (Both, courtesy of Jesus "Cimi" Alvarado.)

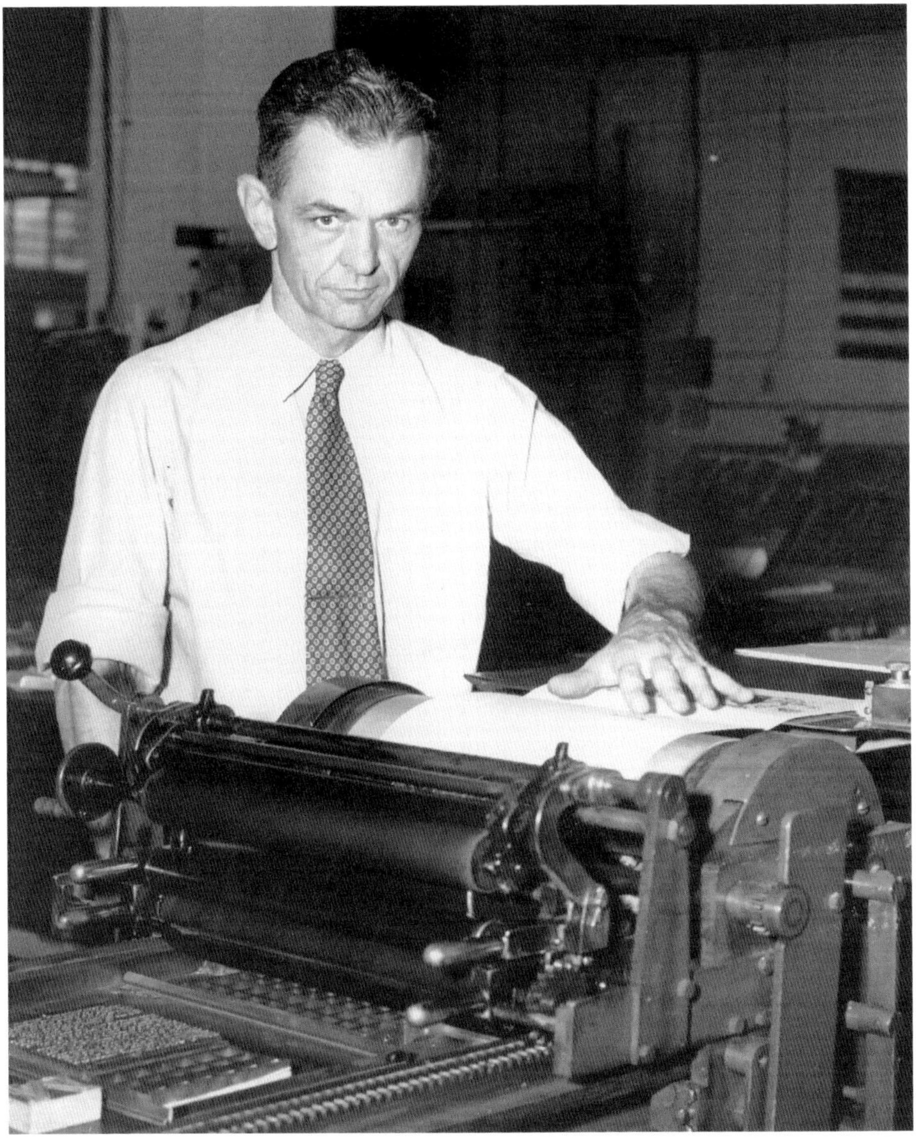

Carl Hertzog

One of the finest book designers in the state of Texas called El Paso home when he moved to the city after answering an advertisement for a printing job at W.S. McMath Company. Hertzog received his first printing press from his stepfather when he was just 10 years old. That press was the catalyst for one of the finest print designers years later. Hertzog met Tom Lea in 1937 and went on to print and design several of Lea's books, such as *Peleliu Landing*.

After working for several companies, Hertzog branched out and started his own printing company with partner Dale Resler. His skill in fine printing was second to none. He did printing for a multitude of publishers across the country, including Little, Brown, and Company and Alfred Knopf. When Hertzog was not creating fine print pieces and commercial work, he was involved with the Texas Folklore Society and the Rotarians. Carl Hertzog was detail oriented with every book, and that attention to detail is why he will forever be remembered as one of the finest printers the industry has ever seen. Hertzog passed way in 1984. (Courtesy of the EPPL BHC.)

CHAPTER FIVE

Educators, Coaches, and Athletes

The formative years are when many people come in contact with individuals who have a profound influence on the trajectory of their lives. The encouraging words of a coach to an athlete at a young age can be the same words that propel that same athlete into the professional leagues. An educator's passion can help inspire a student to expand their horizons and shoot for goals believed impossible.

For Diana Natalicio, life has led her to becoming an influential leader in the world of higher education throughout the borderland and beyond. Jorge Avendano turned his love of music into a passion for educating El Paso's own aspiring musicians. Many times he would buy instruments for his students who were not able to afford them. There were El Paso sports teams that fought discrimination to reach the pinnacles of their leagues, like the 1949 state champion Bowie Bears and the 1966 Texas Western NCAA championship team. The countless hours and sleepless nights that go into structuring the week's lesson plans or preparing the team for the upcoming game can go unnoticed, but it is that dedication that has made the people on the following pages legends in the El Paso area.

Speak with many of them, and they will say that when doing what one loves, the time and effort that is required is a minor speed bump for the joy and feelings of accomplishment that come with achieving their goals.

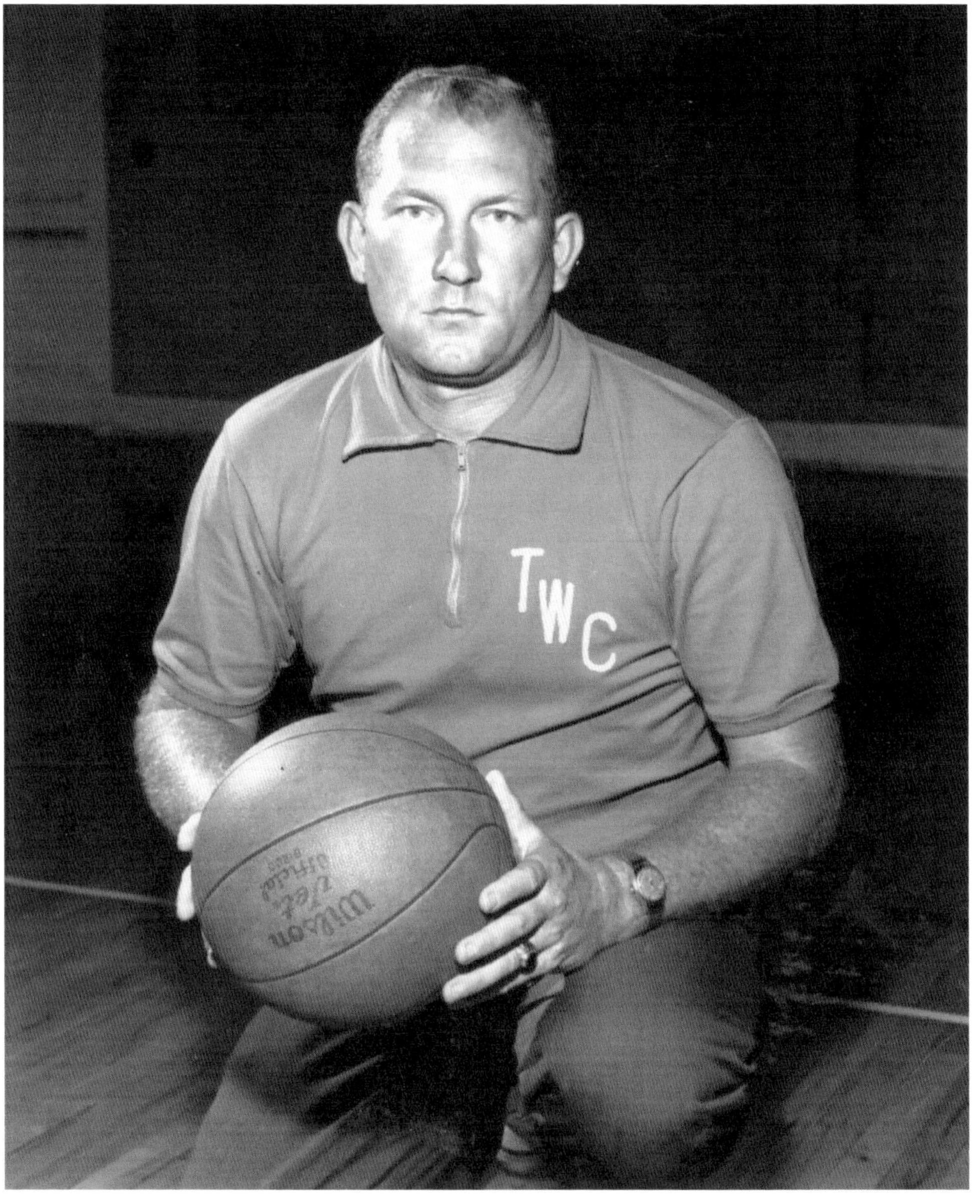

Don Haskins

From a small town in Oklahoma, Don Haskins grew up to become one of the most successful and revered coaches in El Paso and across college athletics. After playing college basketball at Oklahoma A&M, Haskins, known as The Bear, went into coaching and eventually made his way to El Paso for the Texas Western job in 1961. That first season was the start of a long run of success that saw numerous players go to the NBA, like Tim Hardaway and Antonio Davis. The moment in his career that has forever been etched into history was when his squad beat Adolph Rupp and the Kentucky Wildcats in the 1966 national championship. The team's story was made into the movie *Glory Road* in 2006. Over his career, the Miners made the NCAA tournament 14 times and won just as many conference championships. He was inducted into the Naismith Basketball Hall of Fame in 1997 and is the gold standard when it comes to UTEP basketball. Haskins passed away in 2008. (Courtesy of UTEP Special Collections.)

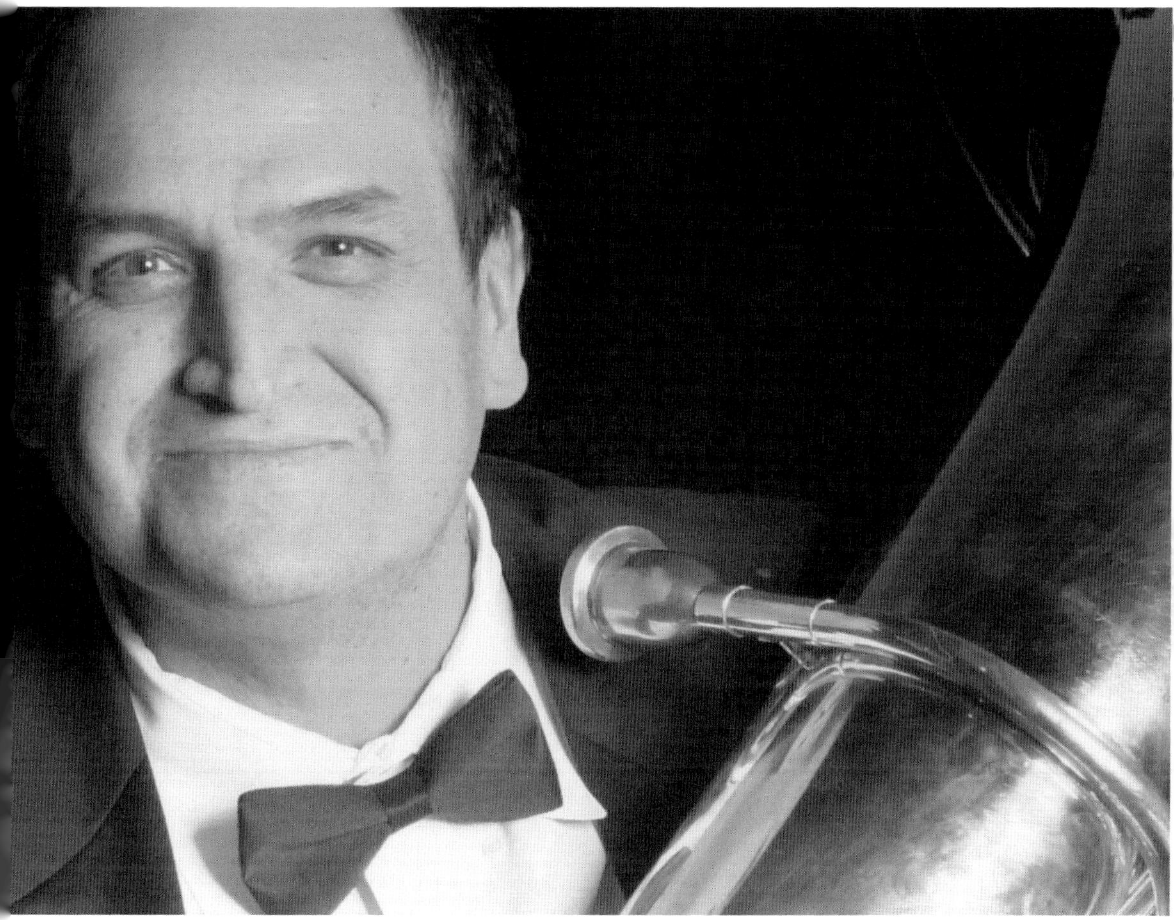

Jorge Avendaño

One of El Paso's most dedicated music educators was born in Mexico City in 1962. Jorge Avendaño moved out to El Paso in 1982 and attended UTEP, graduating with a degree in music and English. The El Paso Symphony tuba player knew from age 12 that he loved music. As an educator, he not only taught El Paso children how to play music but showed them how having discipline in life can lead to success. He took great pride in watching his students succeed.

His 20-year career as a music teacher saw him at multiple elementary schools and finally at Hornedo Middle School. Avendaño was known for his generosity and would give instruments to students whose families could not afford them. His passing in 2006 was hard for the El Paso music community. Thankfully, his influence on students was so strong that many have gone on to become music educators themselves, and they continue to teach the lessons that "Mr. A" taught them. (Courtesy of Enrique Avendaño.)

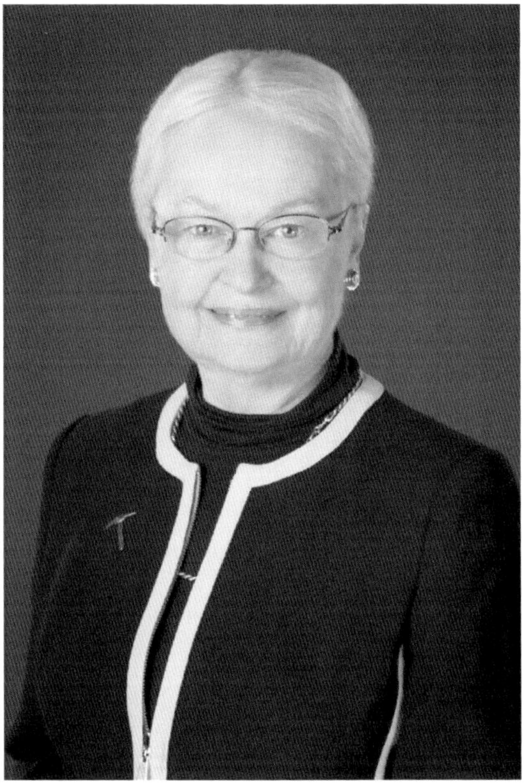

Diana Natalicio

The values of hard work were instilled at a very young age for UTEP president Diana Natalicio as she watched her father work tirelessly to run his small dairy business. "One of the things that characterized our family was that everybody seemed to like what they did and worked hard at it." Born in St. Louis, Missouri, early life in school provided a great base, but her time in high school was not as fruitful. "They set low expectations for us. They really didn't think we would go to college. We were not affluent enough in their view. There were career tracks and the girls typically went into home economics and secretarial work."

After high school, Natalicio went to work as a switchboard operator for about month before she realized that she had to do something else. She ended up attending St. Louis University and worked part time as a secretary. "I struggled a lot the first year. There were days when I thought going to school was a mistake but I made sure to put one foot forward and work hard."

After being awarded a Fulbright Scholarship to Brazil, the world was opened to her. Her time there led to an opportunity with the University of Texas, where she earned a doctorate in linguistics. With a new degree in hand, she made her way to El Paso and became a professor at UTEP. In 1988, Natalicio was named the president of UTEP. During her presidency, UTEP enrollment increased to over 23,000 students, annual research dollars are nearing $100 million, more doctoral programs are being offered, and the campus has seen new buildings constructed, campus beautification projects, and many renovations. "People are really willing to do what it takes to be successful. I admire their resiliency."

Retirement is not on the table right now. "As long as I get up in the morning and feel like we are going to have an impact today, I feel that's what I want to be doing. This is so rewarding, it's great work. I think we are making a difference." Looking forward, Natalicio continues to have big aspirations for the university. With more students graduating, there are still not enough opportunities to keep all graduates here in the region, but she is hopeful that job opportunities will begin to change as the region comes together and holds onto its talent. (Courtesy of UTEP, Office of the President.)

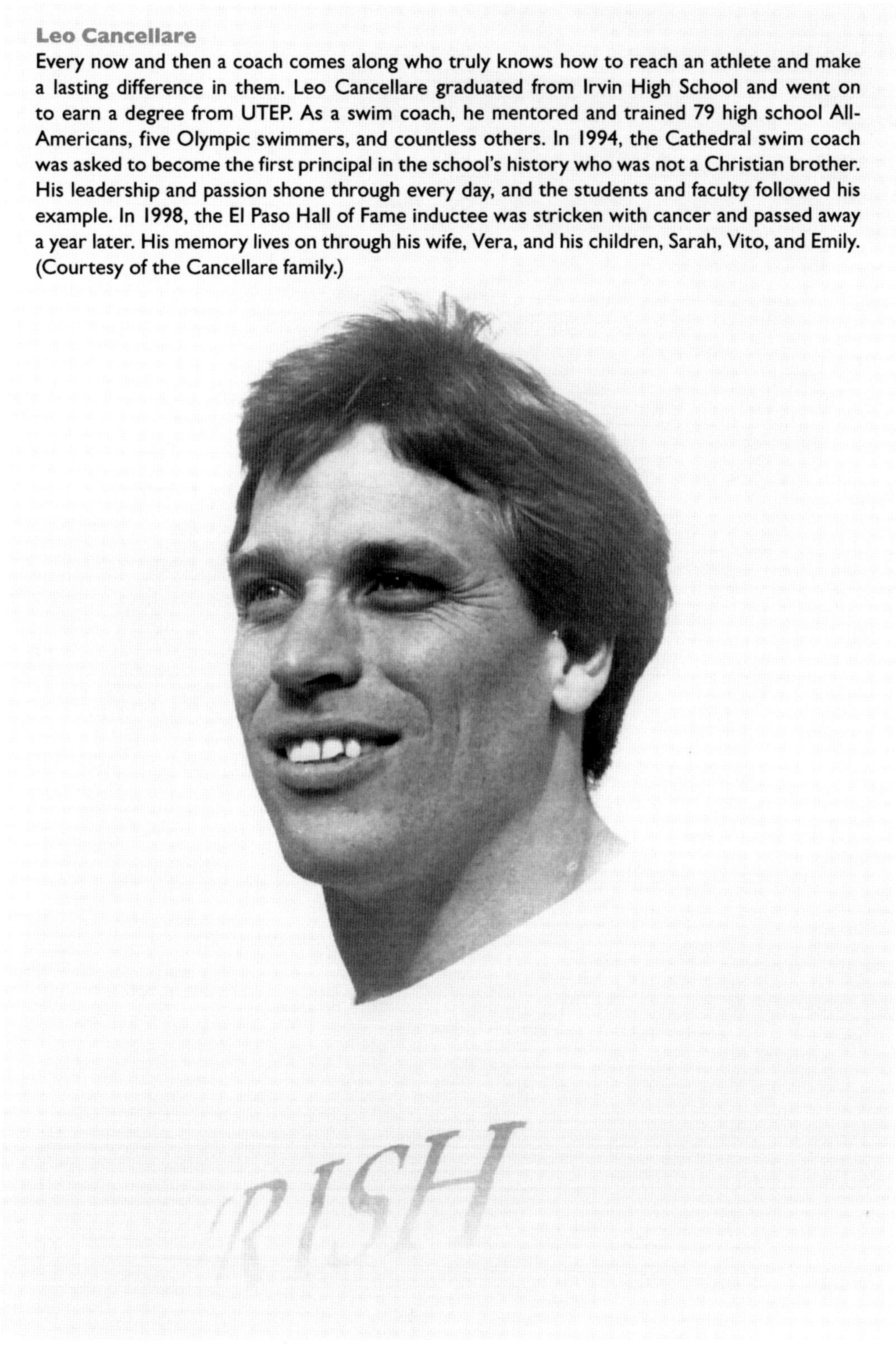

Leo Cancellare

Every now and then a coach comes along who truly knows how to reach an athlete and make a lasting difference in them. Leo Cancellare graduated from Irvin High School and went on to earn a degree from UTEP. As a swim coach, he mentored and trained 79 high school All-Americans, five Olympic swimmers, and countless others. In 1994, the Cathedral swim coach was asked to become the first principal in the school's history who was not a Christian brother. His leadership and passion shone through every day, and the students and faculty followed his example. In 1998, the El Paso Hall of Fame inductee was stricken with cancer and passed away a year later. His memory lives on through his wife, Vera, and his children, Sarah, Vito, and Emily. (Courtesy of the Cancellare family.)

Lee Trevino

One of golf's most well-liked personalities ventured out to El Paso in 1966, where he worked for $30 a week at Horizon Golf Club. He gave lessons, ran the pro shop, and occasionally played a round against the members for a wager. Originally from Dallas, Trevino began to develop a serious interest in golf while serving in the Marines. A tireless worker of his craft, Trevino placed fifth in the US Open in 1967 and wound up winning it the following year. He continued to win multiple majors and other PGA tournaments, becoming one of the most liked and successful golfers in the sport. When he was not on the tour, he could be found playing and practicing at El Paso Country Club. Trevino now resides in Dallas, where he continues to play golf daily. (Courtesy of the EPPL BHC.)

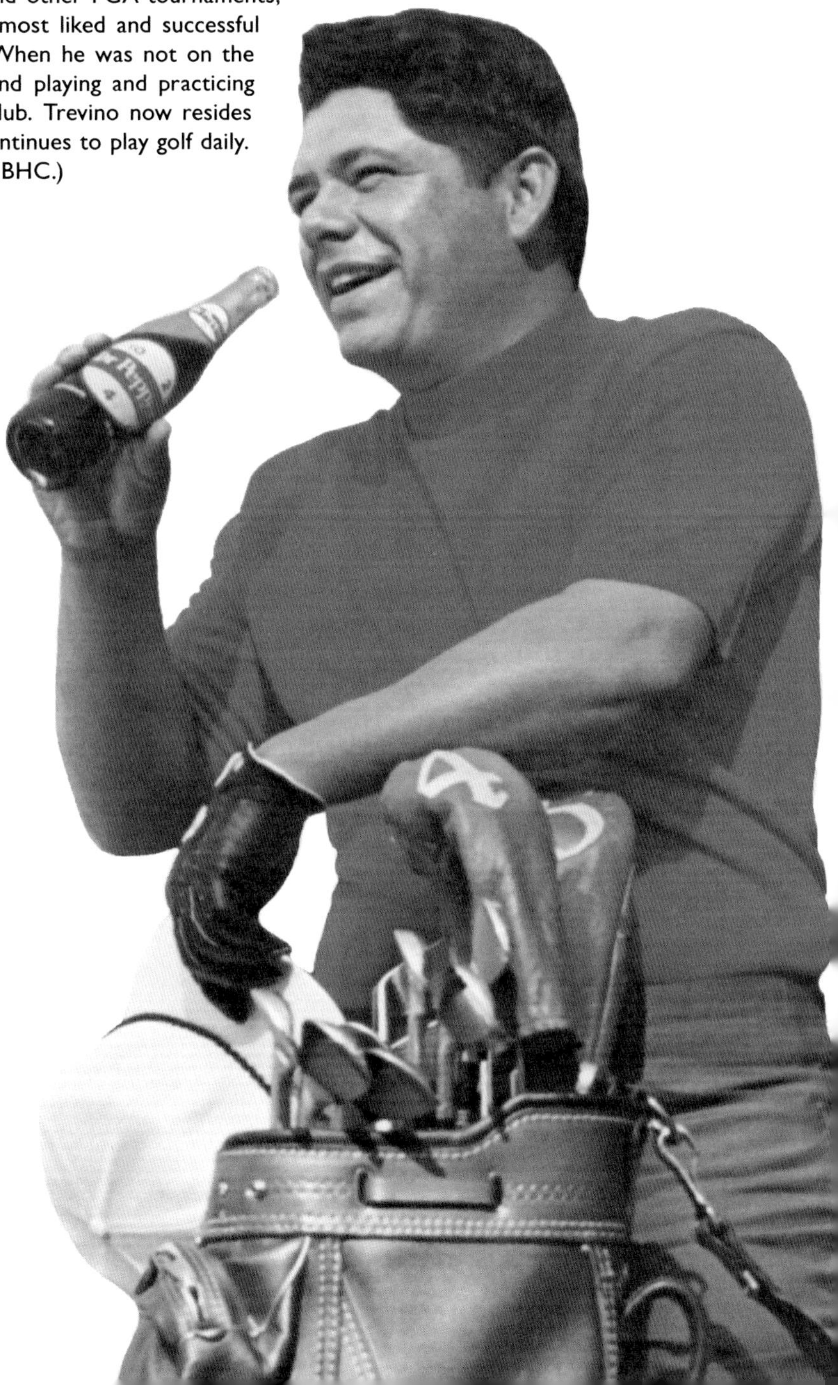

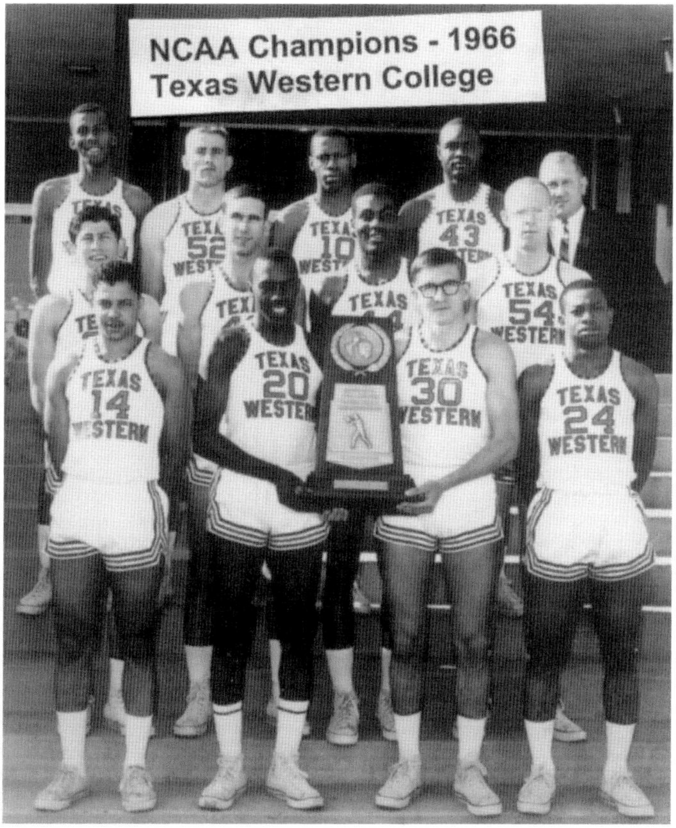

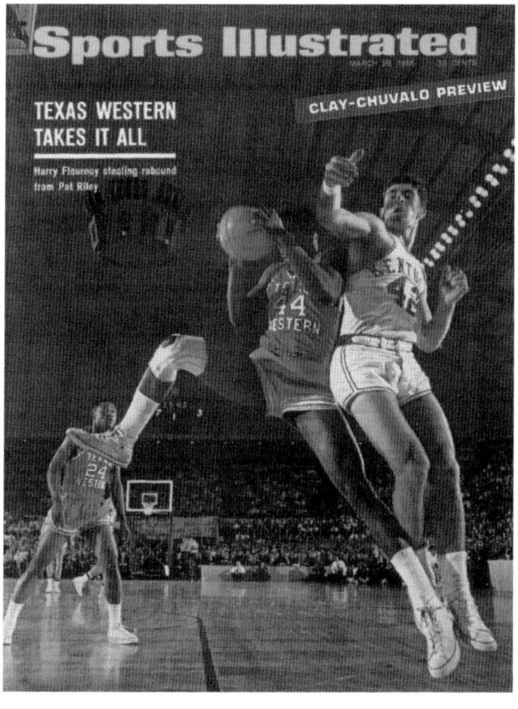

1966 NCAA Champions
In 1966, Don Haskins led Texas Western to a victory over Adolph Rupp and the Kentucky Wildcats for the NCAA basketball championship. Players Willie Cager, Bobby Joe Hill, and David Lattin graced the court. The game was a significant turning point and one of the most important games in sports history, as Texas Western had an all-black starting five against Kentucky's all-white starting five. The 1966 team was inducted into the Naismith Basketball Hall of Fame in 2007, and Disney produced a movie about them in 2006. (Both, courtesy of the El Paso County Historical Society.)

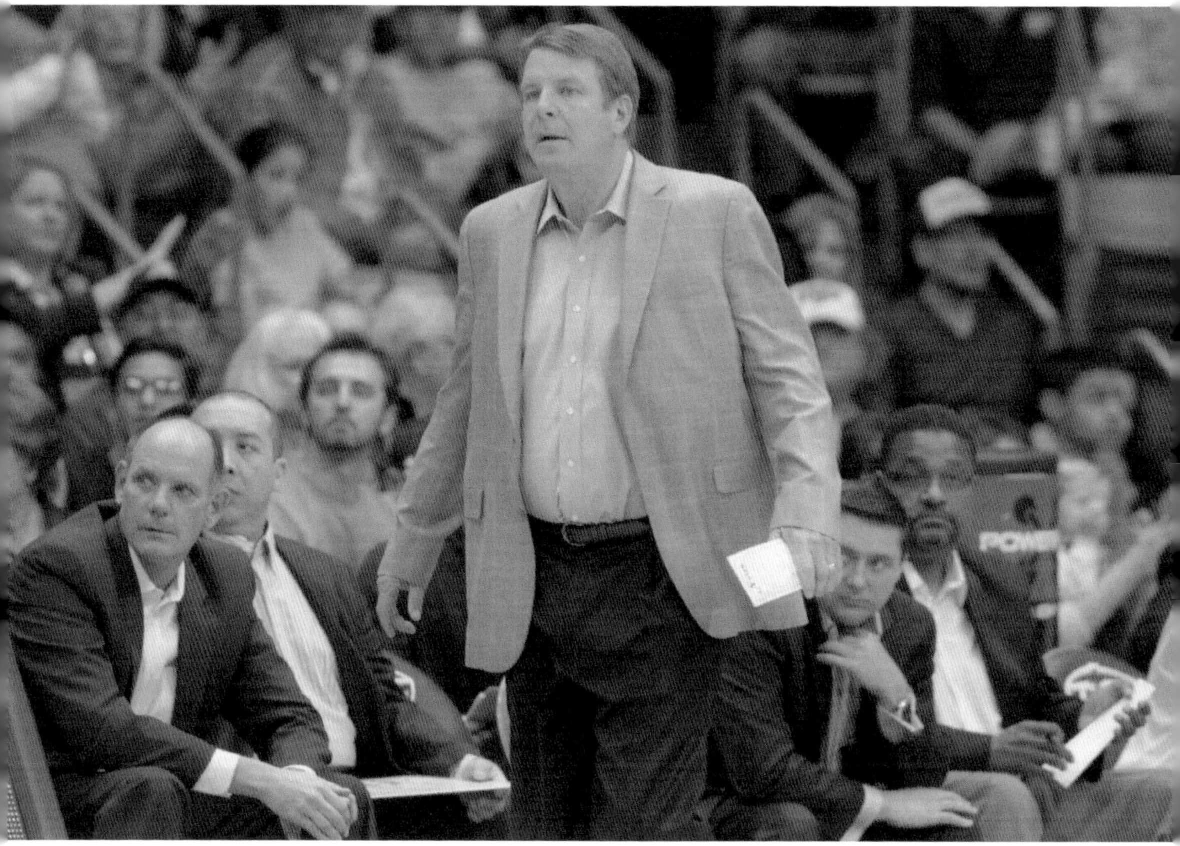

Tim Floyd

In Miner country, expectations and emotions are sky high during basketball season. In 2010, UTEP was able to bring a branch from the Haskins coaching tree back to the Sun City when it hired Tim Floyd. Floyd got his full-time start in coaching as an assistant under Don Haskins from 1978 to 1986. Floyd took his knowledge to head coaching jobs at Iowa State and USC, to name a few. He also was a head coach in the NBA, where he led the Chicago Bulls and New Orleans Hornets. Now back in the Sun City where it all started, Floyd has already led the Miners to multiple post-season tournament berths. (Courtesy of UTEP Athletics.)

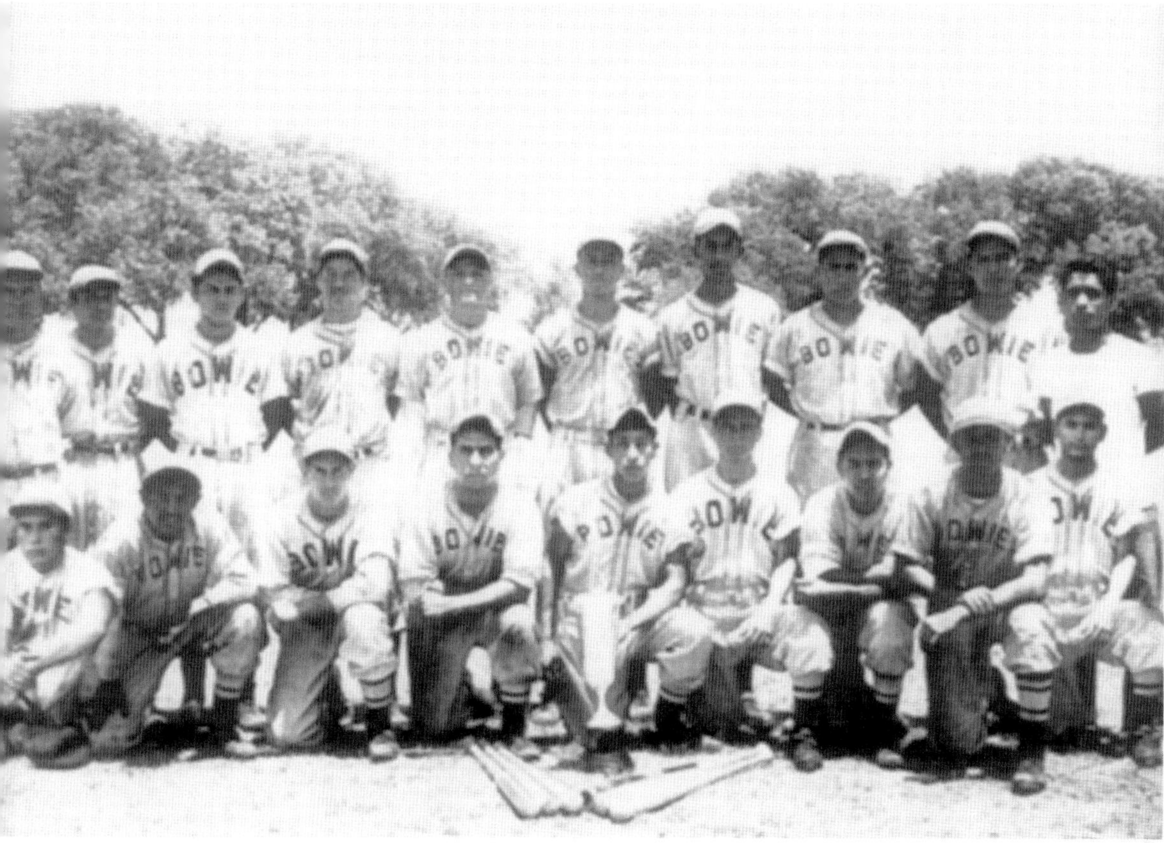

1949 Bowie Bears

In 1949, the first state champion in high school baseball was crowned in Texas. It just so happened that the team to win it all hailed from El Paso. This part of the Lone Star State can be forgotten when it comes to high school sports, but this group of underprivileged kids from Segundo Barrio made sure everyone understood that El Paso, and Bowie High School, knew its way around a baseball field. Under the direction of Coach William "Nemo" Herrera, the Bowie Bears made their way through the high school playoffs, battling opposing teams and constant discrimination. The team's spirit and skill overcame all of the obstacles in their way and they beat Stephen F. Austin High School 3-2 and came back home with the championship trophy. (Courtesy of Bowie High School.)

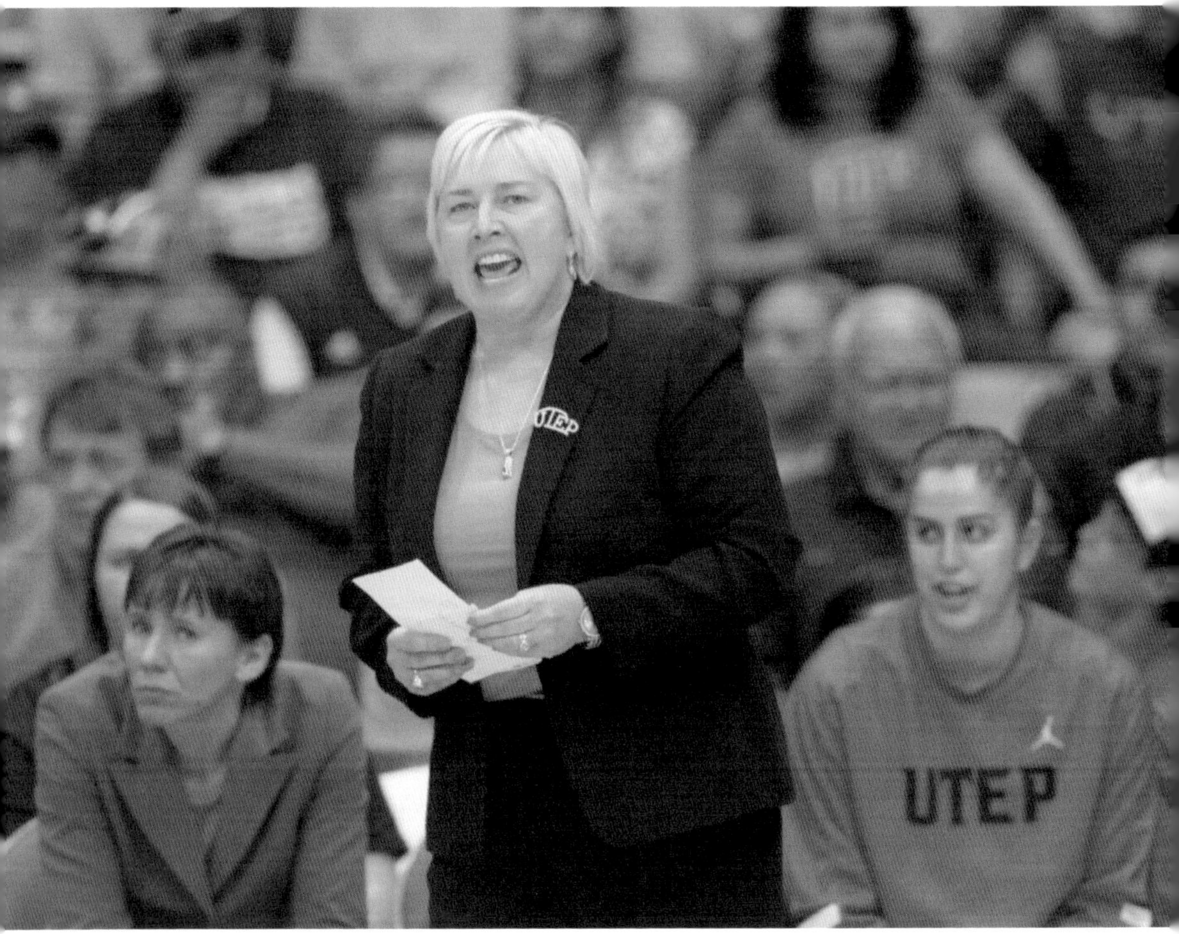

Keitha Adams

There was women's basketball before Keitha Adams came to be the head coach at UTEP, but the Lady Miners had experienced nowhere near the success they achieved under Adams. After her arrival in 2001, the Lady Miners won three league titles, went to the NCAAs multiple times, and were runners-up in the 2014 Women's National Invitational Tournament. Adams's leadership and mentoring continue off the court, where she stresses academics to her players and helps prepare them for life after college. Under Adams, UTEP has been able to build a nationally recognized winning tradition in the women's basketball program, where the peak has yet to be surmounted. (Courtesy of UTEP Athletic Department.)

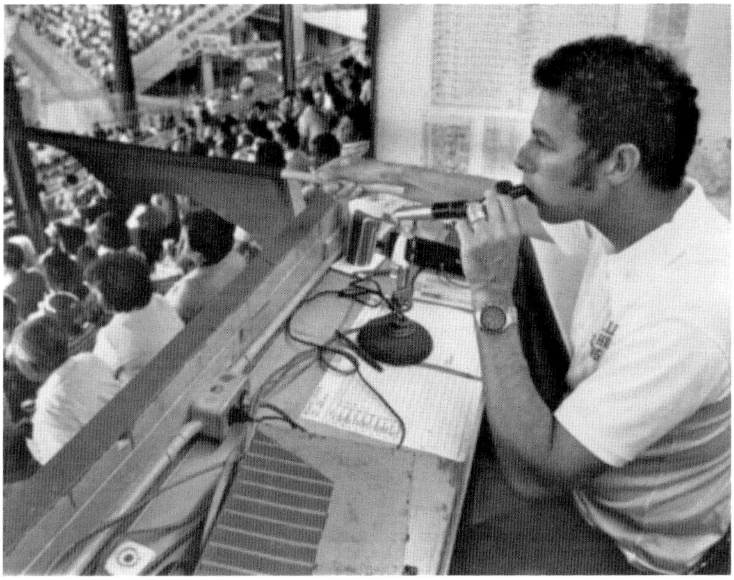

Paul Strelzin

If one is to travel over 2,000 miles from Brooklyn to El Paso, it is best to make the most of the journey. Paul Strelzin called El Paso his home and fully embraced the culture. His wife, Darlyne Valle, an elementary school teacher, guided him into education, where he had a 30-year career as a teacher, vice principal, and principal. Known as "Strelz" since childhood, that would become his moniker around town. Jim Paul recruited him to be the announcer for the Diablos, El Paso's then Double-A affiliate. His deep voice pumped up crowds as yelled, "We Wanna Hit, We Wanna Hit!"

Strelzin also worked the Miner basketball games and was well known for getting under the skin of opposing teams. A coach once commented that Strelzin and UTEP had no class. The next time the teams met, Strelzin walked out in a tuxedo with tails, cane, and hat.

His enthusiasm behind the microphone got him suspended a couple of times, but he was a fan favorite and one of the best to ever fill the seat. While his antics were well known, his love for education and the students in his schools were just as important. (Both, courtesy of Laura Strelzin and family.)

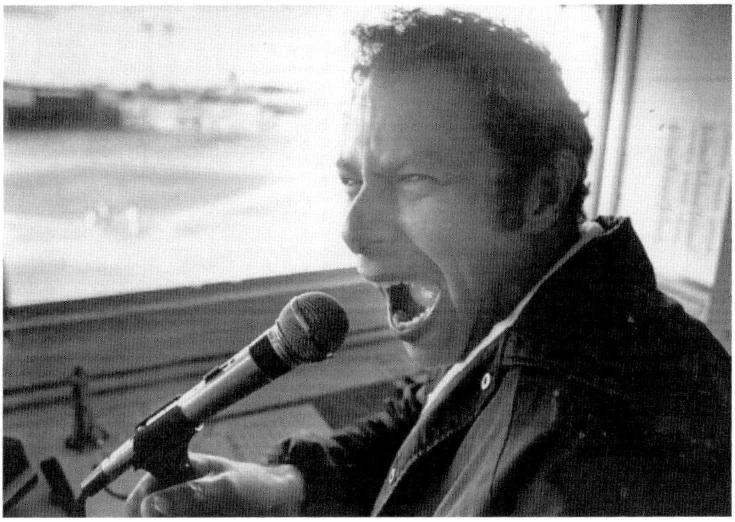

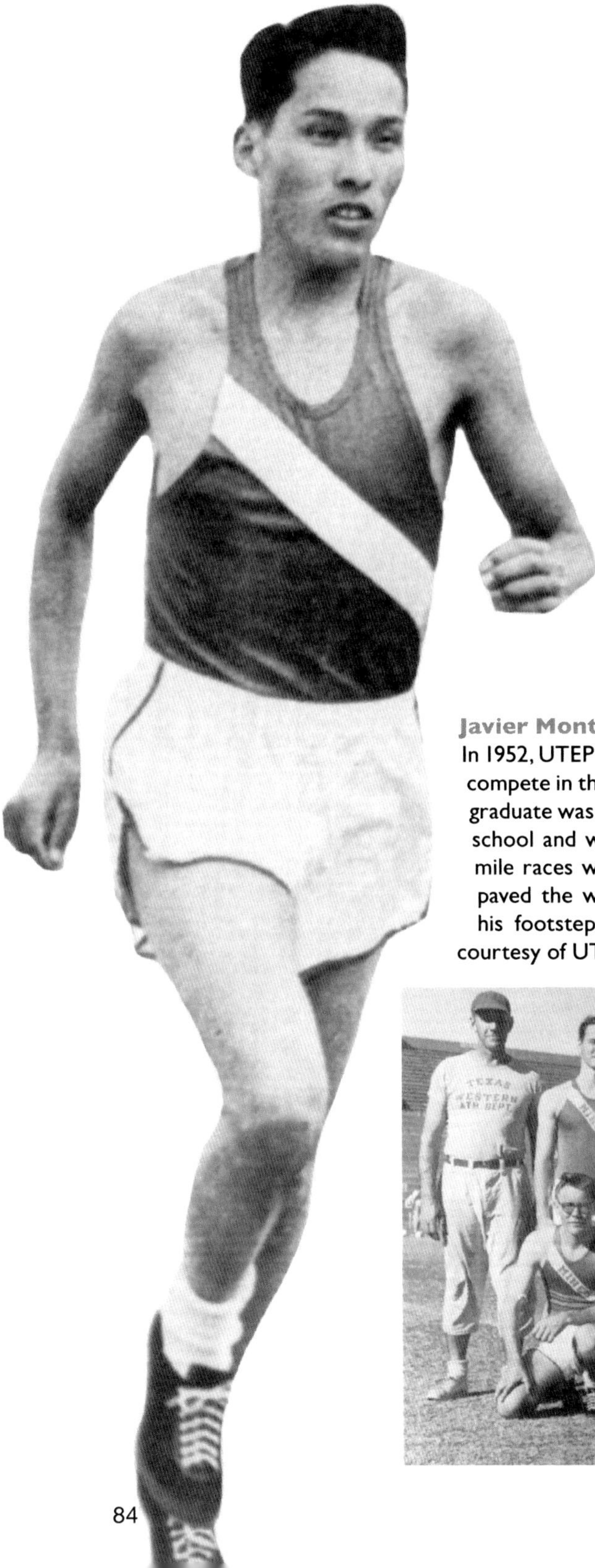

Javier Montez

In 1952, UTEP's first Olympian made his way to Helsinki, Finland, to compete in the games, representing the United States. The Bowie graduate was awarded a scholarship for track and field out of high school and went on to compete and win at the one- and two-mile races while in college. Javier Monte's run in the Olympics paved the way for many UTEP athletes who have followed in his footsteps, representing their respective countries. (Both, courtesy of UTEP Special Collections.)

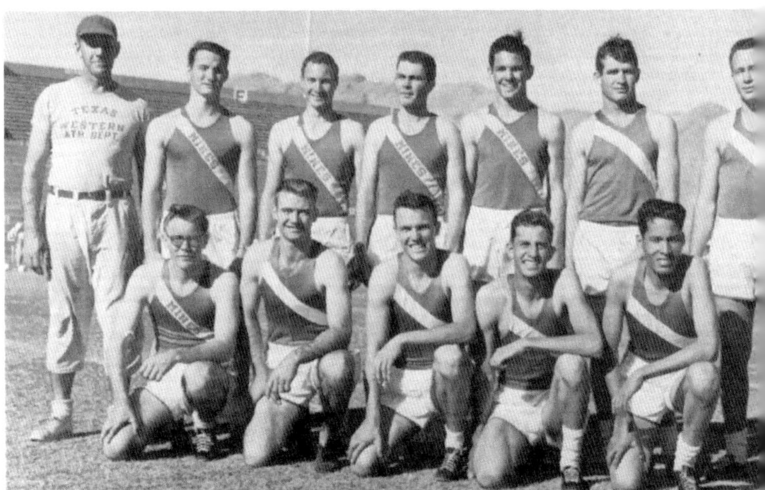

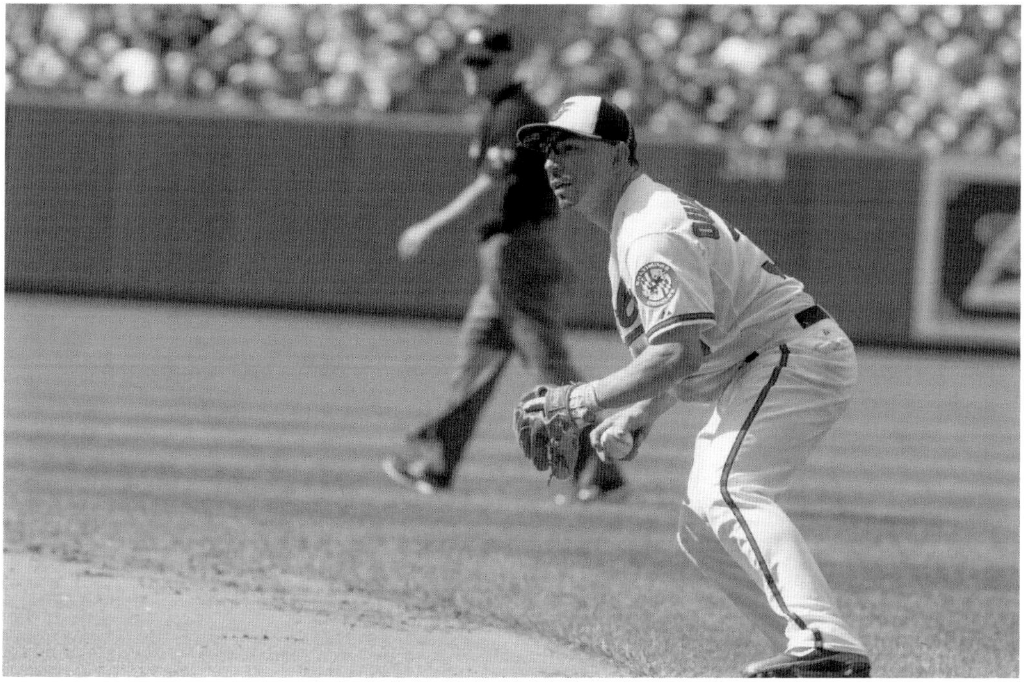

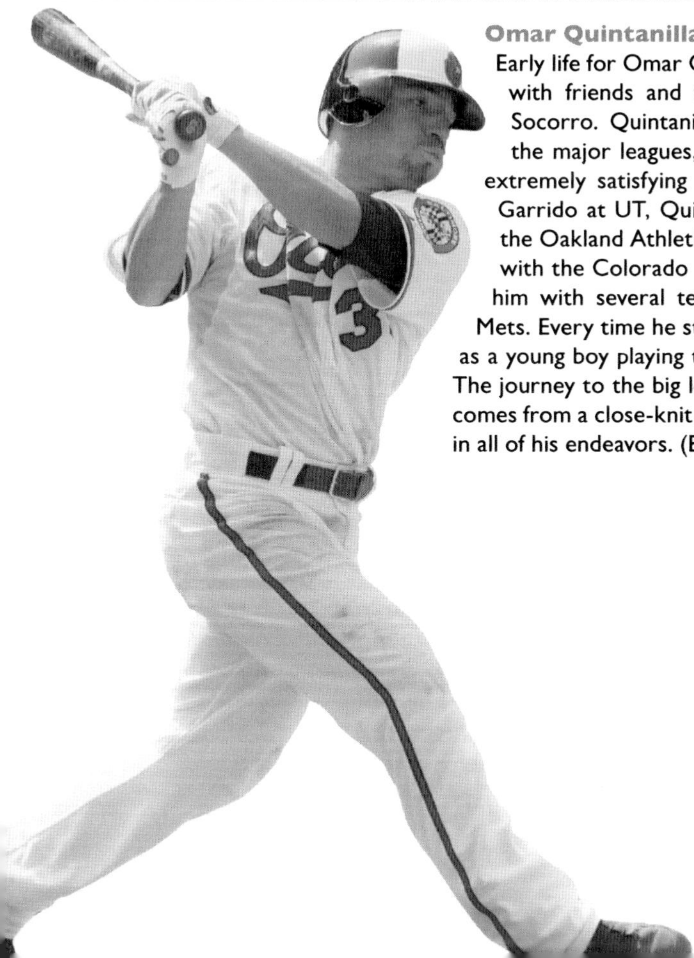

Omar Quintanilla

Early life for Omar Quintanilla was spent playing baseball with friends and family near his childhood home in Socorro. Quintanilla always had dreams of playing in the major leagues, and to see it come to fruition was extremely satisfying for him. After playing under Augie Garrido at UT, Quintanilla was drafted 33rd overall by the Oakland Athletics. His first major-league start came with the Colorado Rockies. His playing career has seen him with several teams, most recently the New York Mets. Every time he steps on the field, that passion he had as a young boy playing the game for the first time reignites. The journey to the big leagues was not easy, but Quintanilla comes from a close-knit family that continues to support him in all of his endeavors. (Both, courtesy of Keith Allison.)

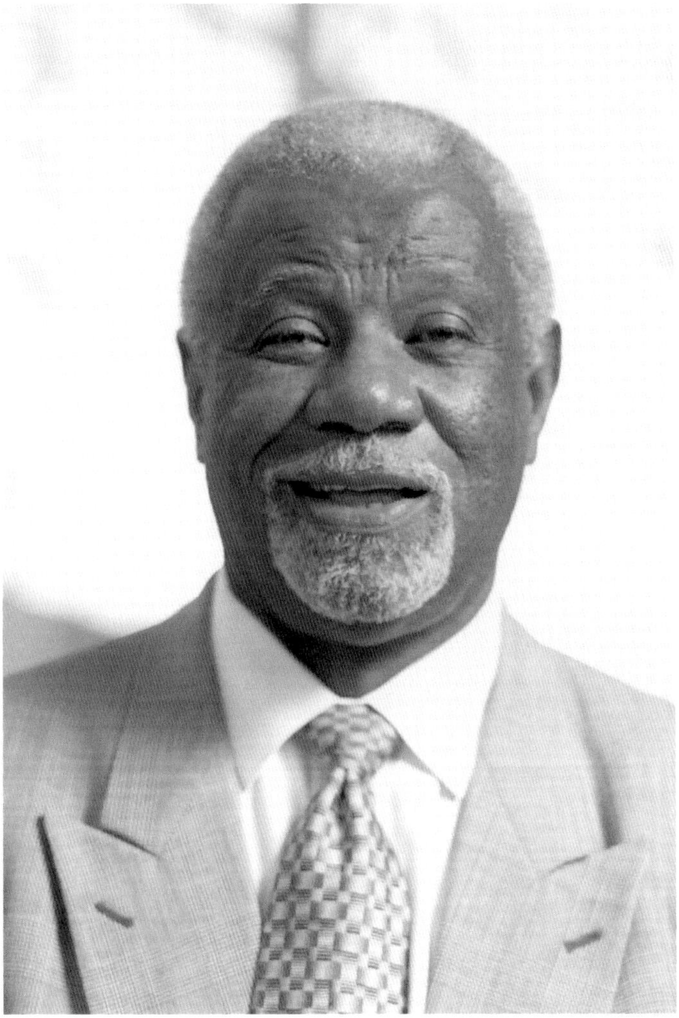

Nolan Richardson

One of the best athletes to ever come out of El Paso is Nolan Richardson. Growing up, he was most influenced by his grandmother Rose "Ole Mama" Richardson. The Bowie High School alum's athletic prowess led him to Texas Western, where he played basketball under Don Haskins. Richardson was one of the first to meet Haskins when he got to Texas Western and helped him and his family move in to the athletic dorms. His time under Coach Haskins helped influence Richardson in developing his "40 Minutes of Hell" playing style.

A dream came true when Richardson got the coaching job at Bowie High School, and he led the team to the 1974 district championship. After leaving high school for the college ranks, Richardson went on to win the 1980 national junior college championship at Western Texas with a 39-0 record, the 1981 National Invitational Tournament at Tulsa, and the 1994 national championship at the University of Arkansas. He is the only college coach to win all three titles in the history of the game and has been inducted into numerous halls of fame, with the latest being the Naismith Memorial Basketball Hall of Fame in 2014.

The hall-of-fame coach had a way of connecting with his players. His advice to them was to come to practice with a positive attitude because his definition of attitude was how one feels about working. This is what unlocked the door to success. (Courtesy of Madalyn Richardson and family.)

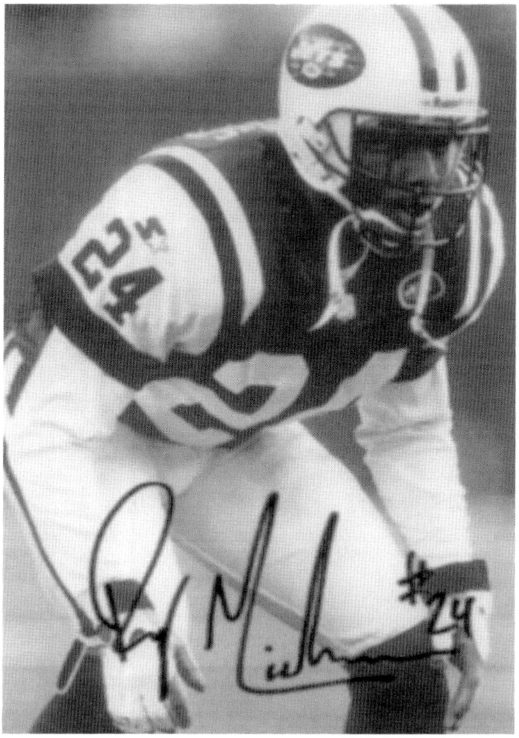

Ray Mickens

Playing in the NFL is a dream for many young boys. Growing up in Northeast El Paso, Ray Mickens started football at the age of seven with the Northeast Raiders. After attending Andress High School, he played for Texas A&M and became one of the best defensive backs in the country and was an All-American. After college, Mickens was drafted by the New York Jets, and played 10 seasons before retiring in 2006. Post-NFL, Mickens lives in Dallas but is still active in the El Paso area, where his foundation supports educational initiatives through programming that benefits children throughout the city. (Courtesy of Ray Mickens.)

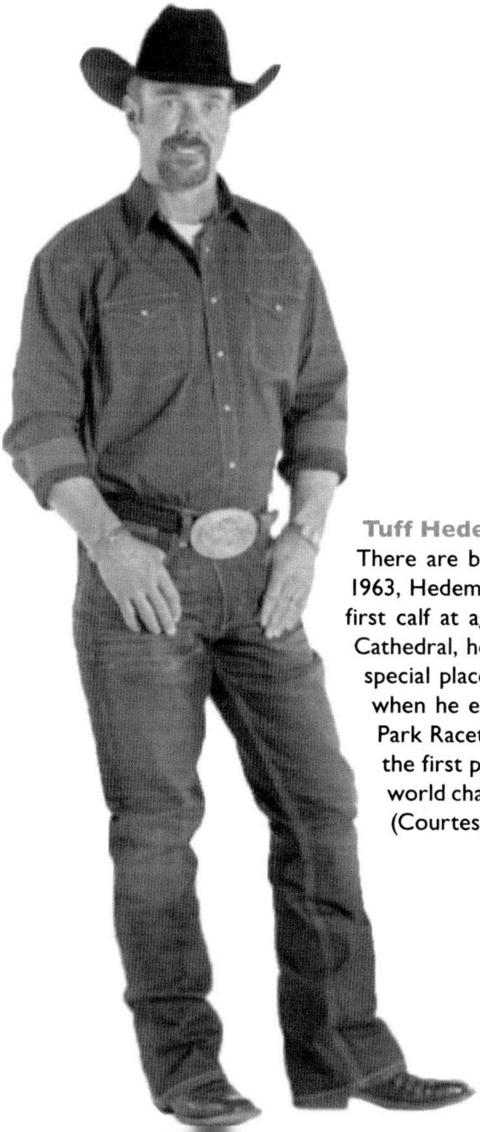

Tuff Hedeman

There are bull riders, and then there is Tuff Hedeman. Born in 1963, Hedeman was riding his first horse at two years old and his first calf at age four. By the time he was getting ready to go to Cathedral, he had already ridden his first big bull. El Paso holds a special place in his heart, and one of his fondest memories was when he exercised race horses as the sun rose at the Sunland Park Racetrack. Tuff Hedeman is a legend in bull riding and was the first person to win $1 million riding bulls. He is a four-time world champion and an inductee of the Pro Rodeo Hall of Fame. (Courtesy of Tuff Hedeman.)

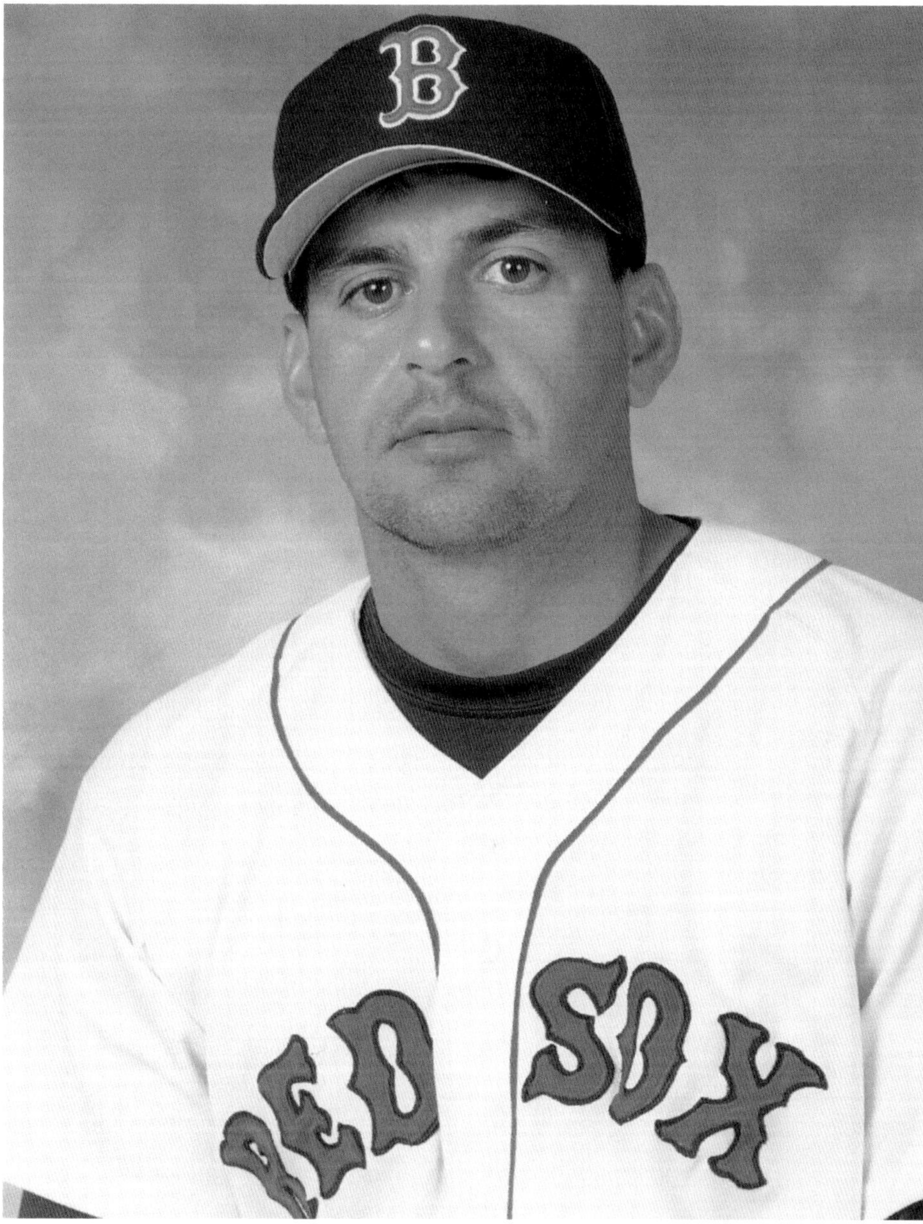

Frank Castillo

The tradition of baseball is strong in El Paso, and many have the dream of playing in the major leagues. In 1987, Frank Castillo was drafted out of Eastwood High School in the sixth round by the Chicago Cubs, and moved his way up the minor-league system and had his first major-league start in 1991. The right-handed pitcher went on to play 14 seasons and win a World Series ring in 2004 with the Boston Red Sox.

His best season occurred in 1995 when he posted a 3.21 ERA and came within one pitch of throwing a no-hitter during a game at Wrigley Field. After retirement, Castillo moved to Arizona with his family. In 2013, Castillo drowned on vacation while boating. He is survived by his two daughters, Cadin and Camden. (Courtesy of the EPPL BHC.)

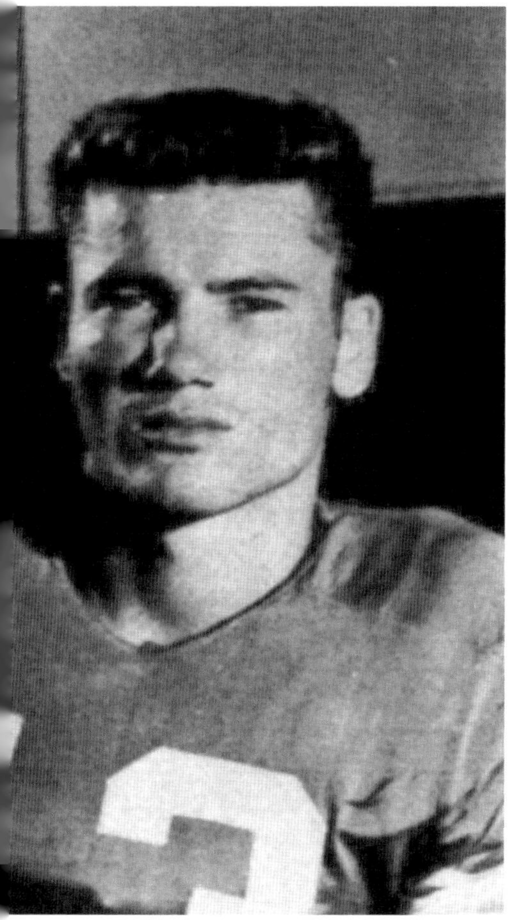

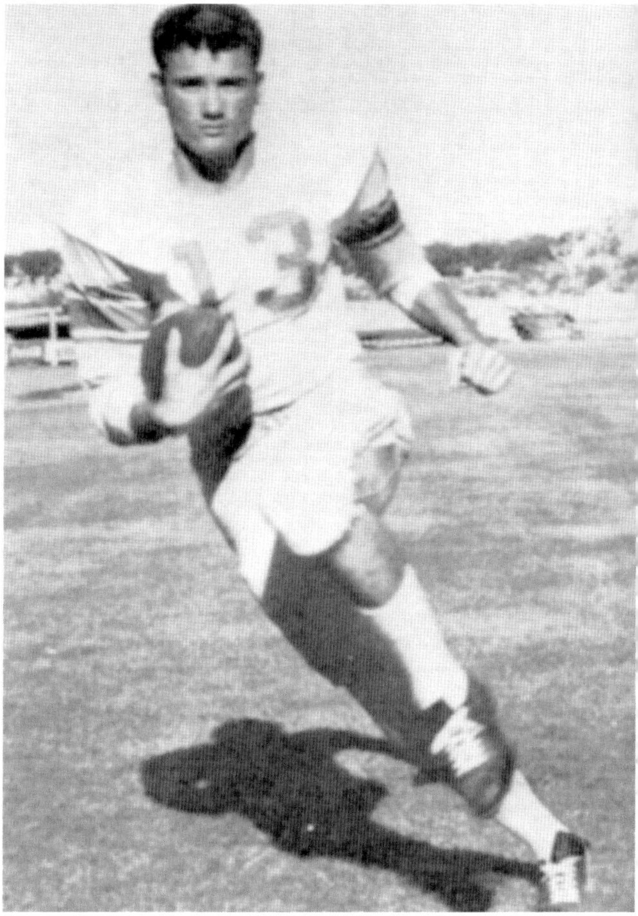

Don Maynard

Joe Namath had a favorite wide receiver, and it happened to be a player out of Texas Western. That receiver was Don Maynard, who won Super Bowl III against the Baltimore Colts and was inducted into the Pro Football Hall of Fame in 1987. Born in Crosbyton, Texas, Maynard found himself at Texas Western playing under coach Mike Brumbelow.

After being drafted by the New York Giants in 1958, Maynard played his rookie season next to NFL greats like Frank Gifford and coaches Tom Landry and Vince Lombardi. Maynard then landed with the New York Titans (now New York Jets). There, he became one of the most iconic players for the Jets. He finished his career with 633 receptions and 11,834 yards. (Courtesy of UTEP Special Collections and UTEP Athletics.)

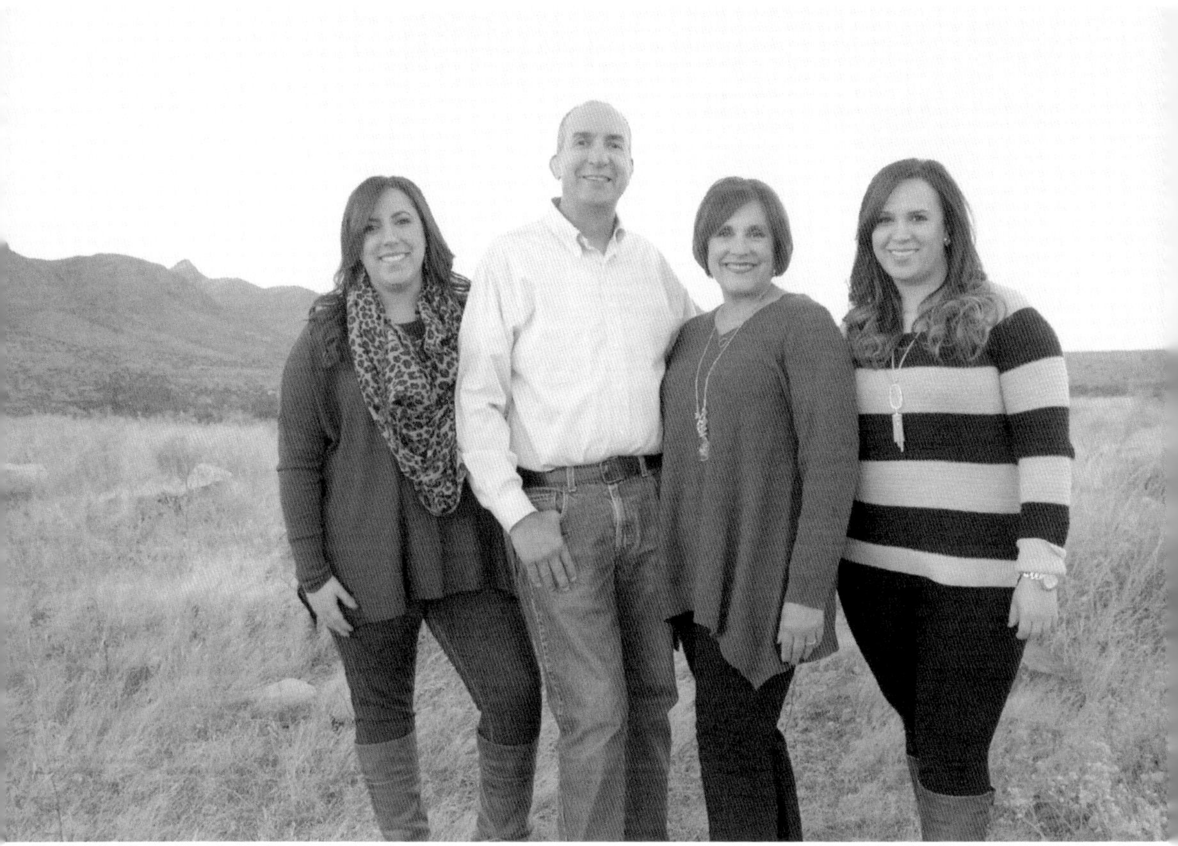

Ben Avalos

Relentless training, a can-do spirit, and great support helped transform Ben Avalos from a lanky freshman wrestler at Irvin High School to a city and state champion by his senior year. After high school, Avalos entered the Air Force. While in the service, he participated in the Interservice Freestyle and Greco-Roman Wrestling Championships. After his time in the military, Avalos earned an undergraduate and graduate degree from UTEP. With a focus in physical education and health, he entered into teaching and coaching. He coached the Eastwood High wrestling team to six city and regional championships with top-10 finishes at state competitions every year. Avalos's teaching career spanned 28 years; during that time, he helped implement PE Day for Ysleta ISD, which helped promote the importance of physical education. The hall-of-fame coach continues to teach at UTEP, helping influence future educators. (Courtesy of Ben Avalos.)

CHAPTER SIX

Professionals and Public Servants

Public servants are on the front lines of both positive press and strong criticism. One day they are celebrating a neighborhood improvement project while the next they are defending a tax increase. El Paso has seen some exceptional leaders through the years, and while all have faced struggles, they have done their best to represent their constituents and help improve the borderland region. Congressional leaders like R.E Thomason, Silvestre Reyes, and Beto O'Rourke have each gone to Washington to represent El Paso's interests and stand up for what they believe is right. Sandra Day O'Connor, former US Supreme Court justice, spent her childhood going to school in El Paso. She later made a profound difference in Washington, DC, where she served as the first woman on the US Supreme Court and was a key swing vote in many cases. While some El Pasoans have made a name for themselves in public service, others have accomplished notoriety in other ways.

Danny Olivas took El Paso to space when he became an astronaut and performed multiple spacewalks. While Fort Bliss may be hard to spot from space, it has been an integral part of El Paso for a long time, and recently, an El Pasoan was tapped to lead the military installation. Gen. Dana Pittard made his way back to El Paso in 2010 and ran the post for several years, overseeing a multibillion-dollar transformation. Whether it is on Fort Bliss or down in the valley, El Pasoans have their radios dialed in to Steve Kaplowitz starting at 4:00 p.m. as he delivers sports talk all across the Sun City. This variety of personalities helped shape the political aspect of El Paso and added to the identity of a city looking for inspiration from its own citizens.

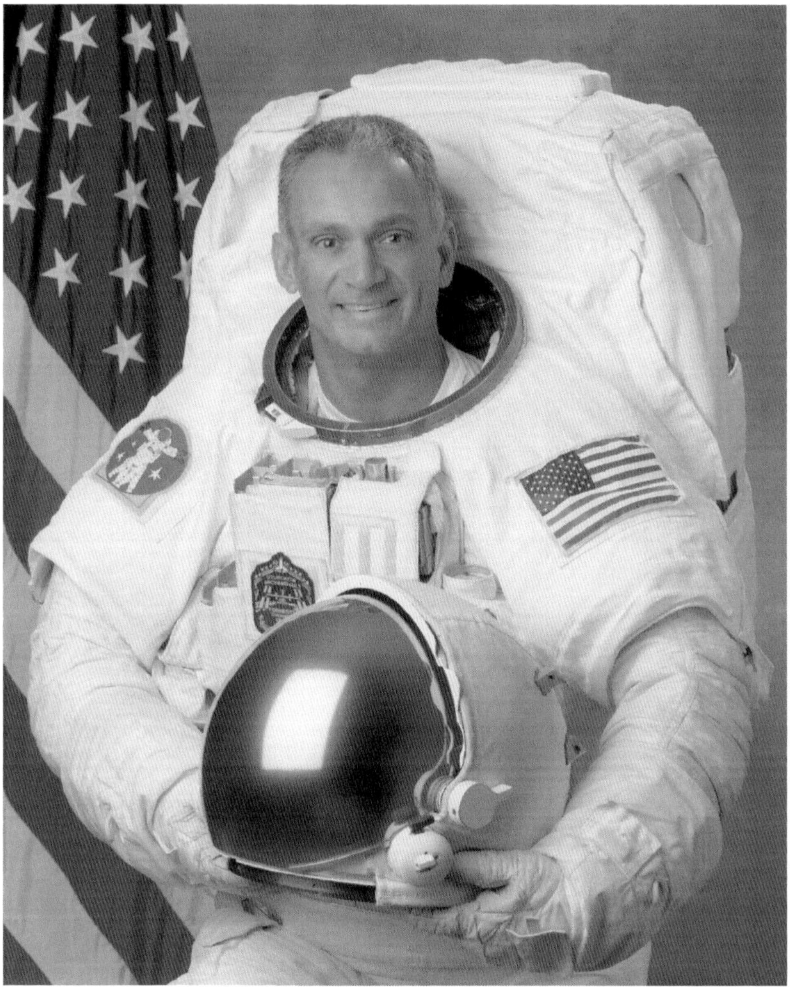

John "Danny" Olivas (ABOVE AND OPPOSITE PAGE)
The next time there is a clear evening, take a look up at the night sky. The vastness of space and the twinkling of stars can overwhelm the senses. Danny Olivas spent time looking up at the stars when he was young and looking down at Earth later in life while performing multiple spacewalks for NASA. A trip at age seven to the Johnson Space Center in Houston was the spark that began his motivation to become an astronaut.

Before traveling in the space shuttle, Olivas was busy learning the value of hard work and dedication. Early in his life, his jobs included unloading boxcars, working at fast-food restaurants, refueling airplanes, and working as a bank teller. After graduating from Burgess High School, he attended UTEP, where he met his wife, Marie Schwarzkopf, and graduated with a degree in mechanical engineering. Olivas earned a master's degree from the University of Houston and a doctorate from Rice University.

Retiring as a mission specialist with NASA in 2010 after 12 years of service, he created Olivas & Associates, an engineering consulting firm. In 2013, the University of Texas El Paso announced Olivas as the new director of space initiatives; he is helping build a center that aims to assist the commercial space flight sector.

Currently living in Los Angeles, Olivas maintains strong bonds with friends, colleagues, and family in the El Paso area. He and his wife have five children, Isabella, James, Anthony, Joseph, and Gabrielle. (Courtesy of John "Danny" Olivas.)

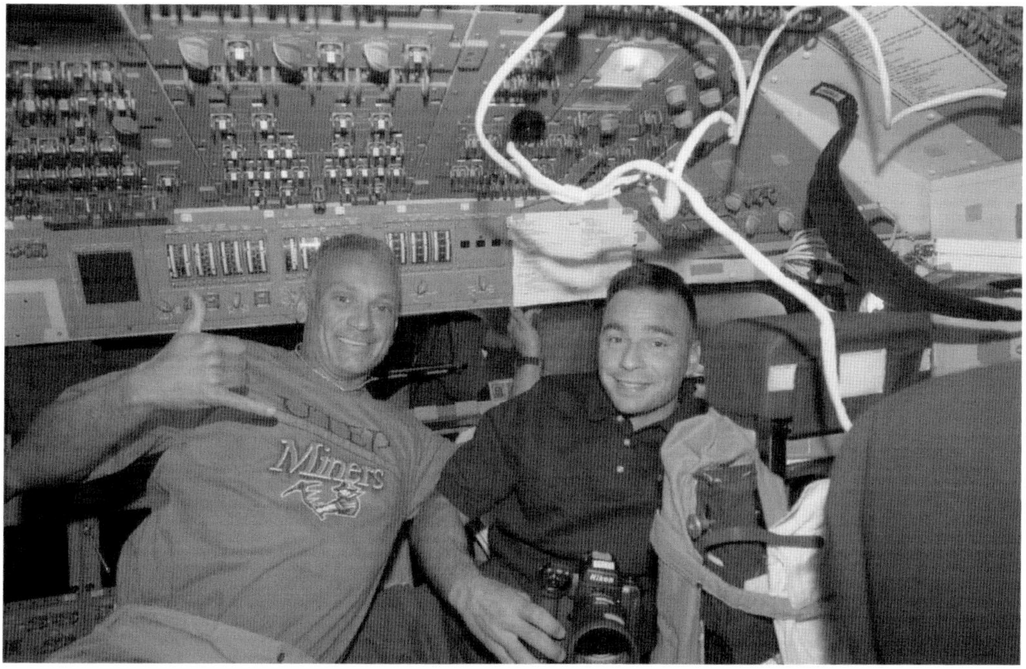
Miners

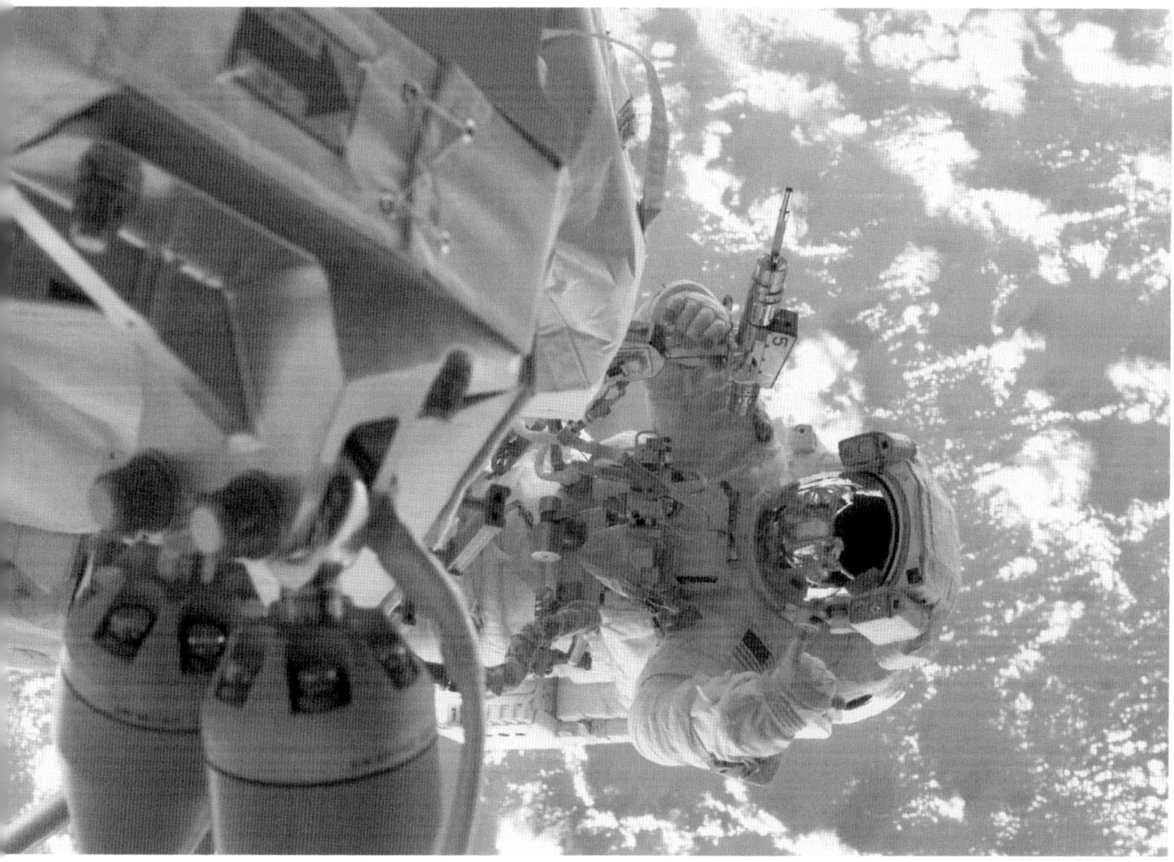

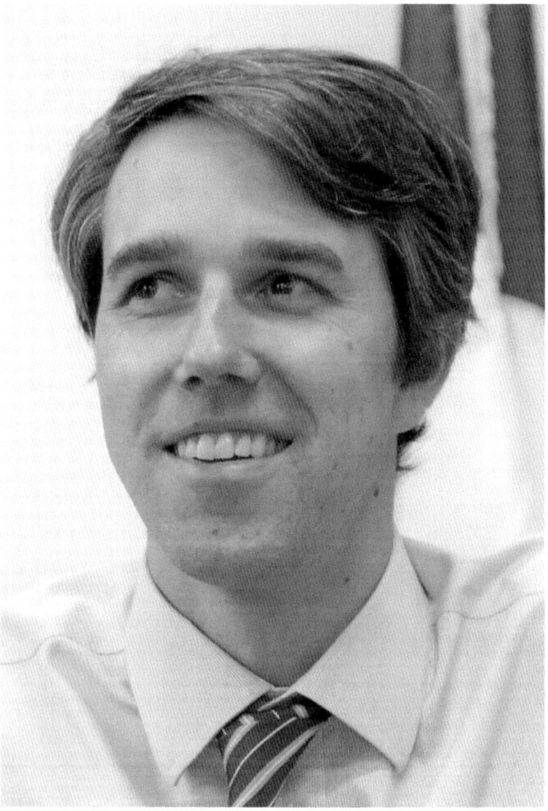

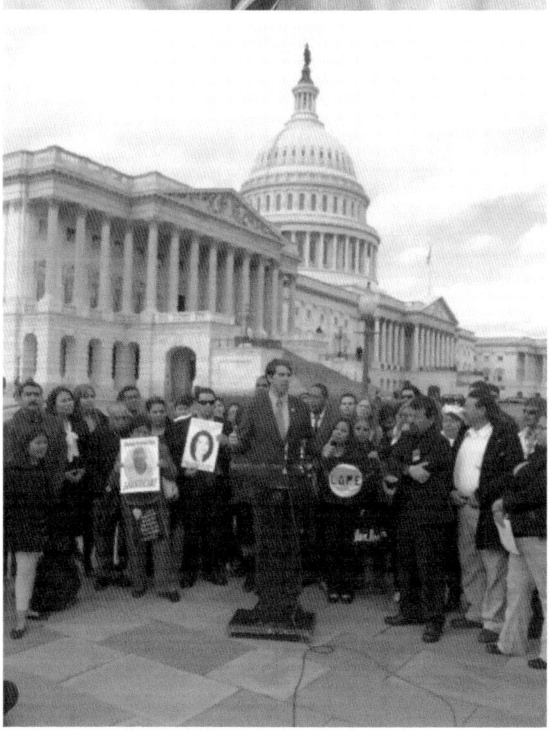

Beto O'Rourke

One of El Paso's most influential young leaders is Beto O'Rourke. Born into a family that has always understood the weight of civil service made O'Rourke consider other paths. Growing up, Congress was not exactly what he dreamt about at night. Instead, music was going to be his ticket. He attended Columbia University and graduated in 1995, working in New York City for a few years. The allure of being close to family pulled him back to El Paso, where he opened Stanton Street Technology. His first foray into civic life came through involvement in the Hispanic Chamber of Commerce. Shortly thereafter, he ran for city council in 2005, and his message to constituents was one of hope and what El Paso could be in the future. During his time on city council, downtown revitalization began, and improved transit options were built throughout the city.

After O'Rourke finished his time on city council, he ran for the 16th Congressional District. After winning the congressional seat, he made his way to Washington, DC, where he continues to champion border issues and be a voice for the citizens of El Paso and the region. For O'Rourke, El Paso's future is bright. "This is the most exciting time to live here. I really think we are on the rise again. We are at the very beginning of a very big expansion of our potential." (Courtesy of Beto O'Rourke.)

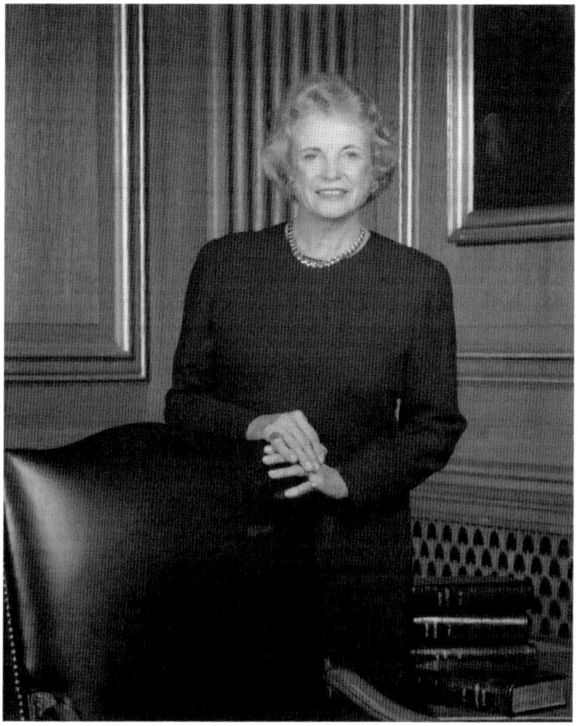

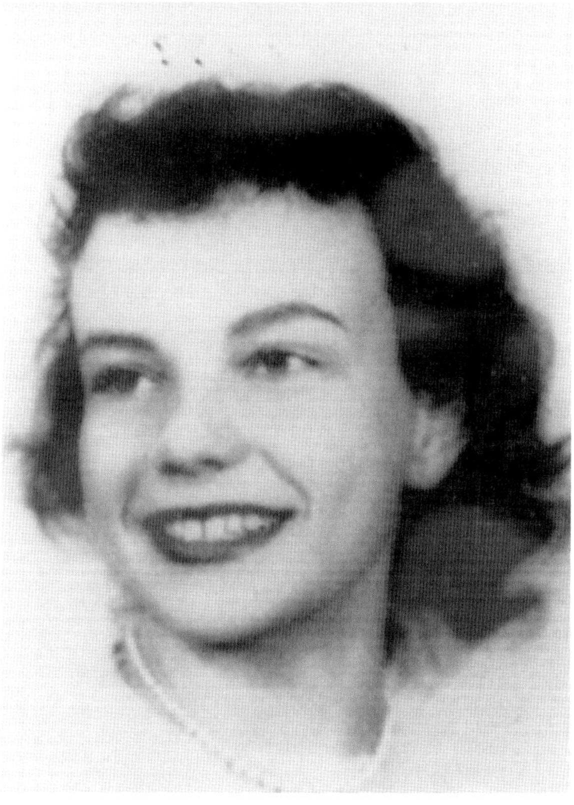

Sandra Day O'Connor
Who knew a small-town girl who grew up on a ranch called the Lazy B would be nominated by Ronald Reagan to be the first woman US Supreme Court justice? O'Connor spent her summers on the Lazy B but lived with her grandmother in El Paso to attend the Radford School during the year. Born in 1930 in El Paso, O'Connor was very close to her family. Although they had different personalities, O'Connor looked at her mother and father as strong, positive influences in her life. After attending Stanford University, she was motivated by Prof. John Rathburn to attend law school. Despite her qualifications, O'Connor had trouble landing a job as a female attorney.

In 1958, she moved to Arizona, where she served as the assistant attorney general, a state senator, and an appeals court judge before her appointment as associate justice of the US Supreme Court. As a justice, who was typically in line with other conservative court members, she was a key swing vote. After retiring from the court in 2006, O'Connor has written several books, started a company called iCivics, and is an active public speaker. (Top, courtesy of Collection of the Supreme Court of the United States; bottom, courtesy of the El Paso County Historical Society.)

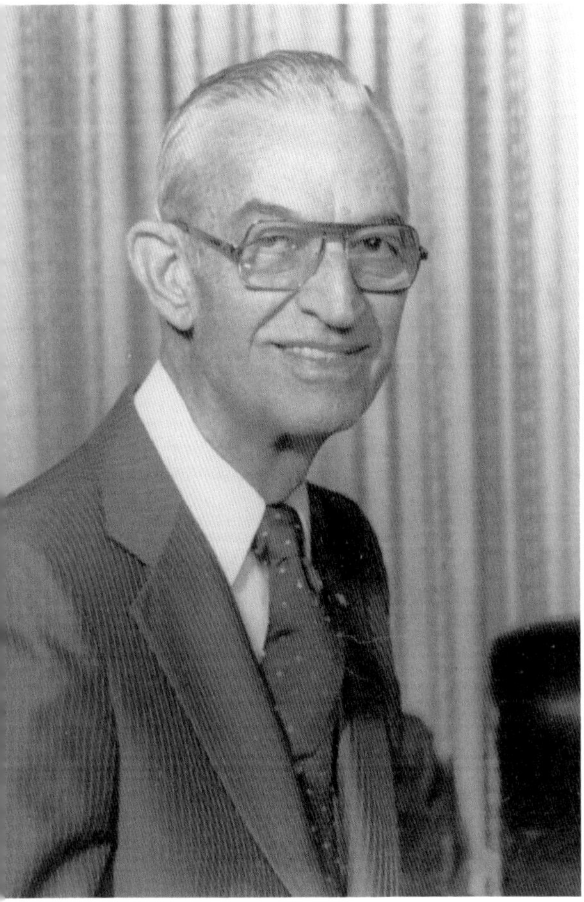

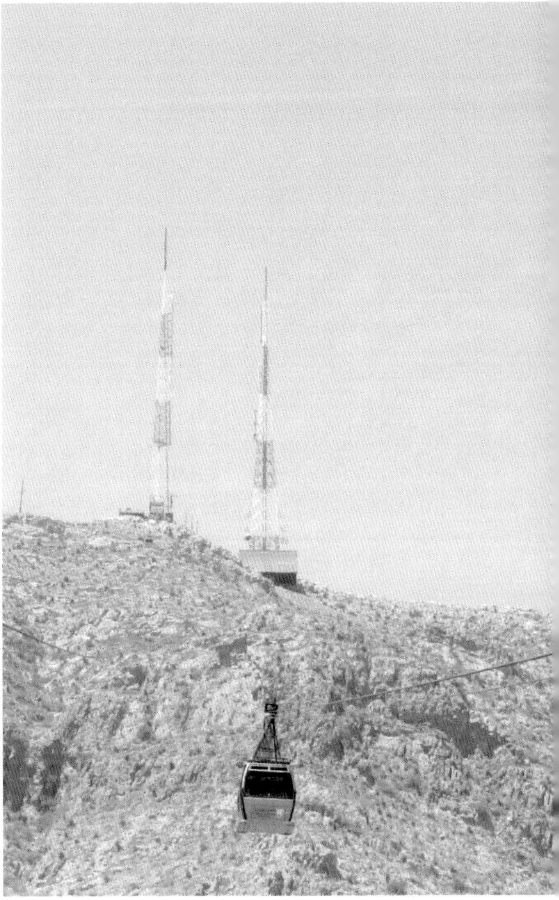

Karl O. Wyler

Karl Wyler was one of the main pioneers in early television and radio broadcasting in El Paso. Wyler became a fixture in radio during the 1930s, when he worked at KTSM. He eventually became a stockholder and president of the station. In 1953, KTSM's television signal went live. The station later put its transmission tower on Ranger Peak and built what is now called the Wyler Aerial Tramway to ferry workers and equipment up to the site. When Wyler passed away in 1990, he left a majority of the stock in both the radio and television station to the El Paso Community Foundation. He also donated the tramway that now bears his name to Texas Parks and Wildlife so that the public could enjoy the views from the mountain. (Both, courtesy of the El Paso County Historical Society.)

Raymond Telles

Raymond Telles was one of El Paso's most successful politicians. Born in 1915, he attended Cathedral High and then the Texas College of Mines (UTEP). He served with distinction in both World War II and the Korean War and achieved the rank of colonel. In 1948, Telles made his first foray into politics when he won the county clerk seat. That election and subsequent re-elections led Telles to the 1957 El Paso mayoral race. His win made him the first Mexican American to hold the mayoral seat of a major US city. After two terms as mayor, Pres. John F. Kennedy broke barriers when he appointed Telles as the ambassador to Costa Rica. He served seven years as ambassador and was appointed to the Equal Employment Commission by Presidents Nixon and Ford. Telles, who passed in 2013, paved the way for other Mexican Americans striving to serve in public office. (Courtesy of EPPL BHC.)

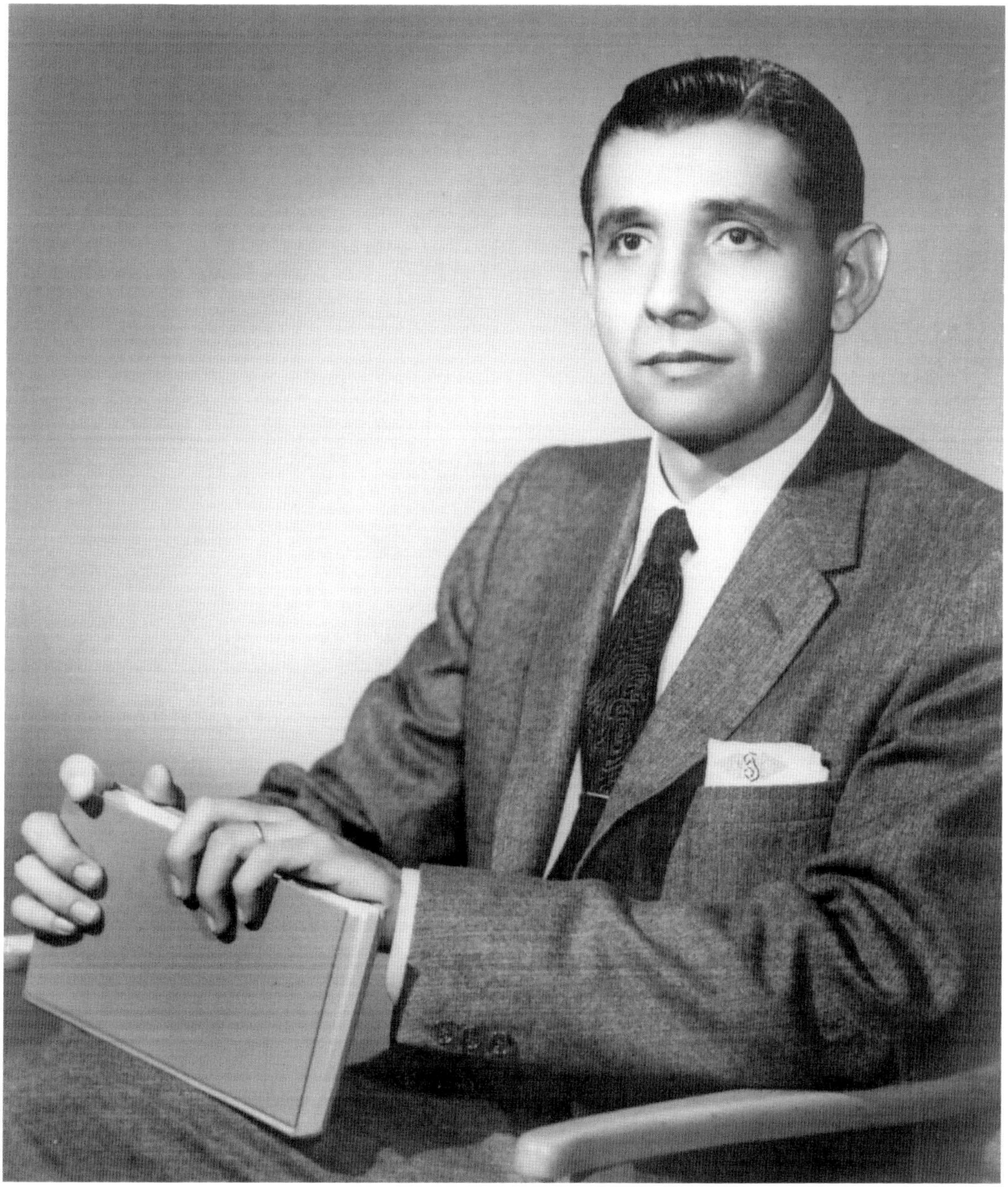

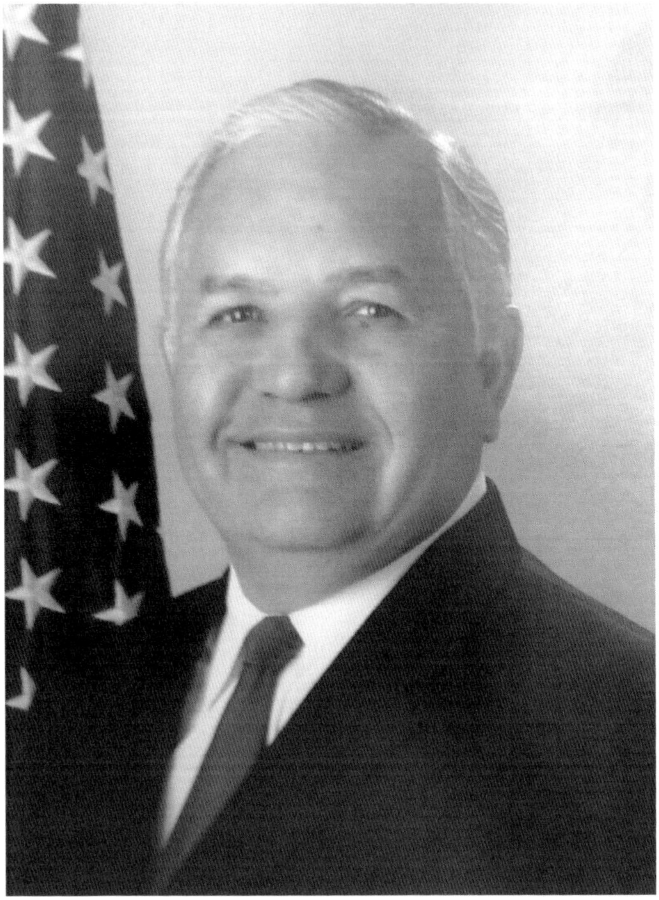

Silvestre Reyes

As the oldest of 10 children, Silvestre Reyes has carried responsibility since he was a young child growing up on the family farm in Canutillo, Texas. The values of hard work and responsibility he learned as a child would be the building blocks that would lead to an illustrious and storied career. His parents valued education and made sure all of their children valued it as well. "I remember the day my Dad invested in getting us the *World Book Encyclopedia*, which opened a window to the world and further fueled our love of reading and learning." In 1966, Reyes was drafted and entered the Army. As a helicopter crew chief and gunner on a UH-1 Huey, Reyes spent a 13-month combat tour in Vietnam.

Once his military career ended, Reyes worked a job with the border patrol and eventually became the chief. Along the way, he implemented drug and canine programs, reinstated horse patrols, and implemented the high-speed boat interdiction program on the Gulf Coast. As a chief in the border patrol and back in El Paso, Reyes implemented Operation Hold the Line, which proved to be a successful strategy in entry deterrence rather than entry apprehension. After getting pushback from Washington regarding the program, Reyes's brother Chuy convinced him to run for Congress.

Reyes announced his candidacy for Congress at the end of 1995, and much was accomplished during his 16 years in the legislature. Some of the more notable achievements were helping protect Fort Bliss from base closure, getting the largest inland desalination plant in the world built in El Paso, and helping convince the Pentagon to invest over $6 billion in Fort Bliss. During his time in office, he was appointed chairman of the House Intelligence Committee in 2006, the first Latino to ever hold the position. Now retired, Reyes and his wife, Caroline, reside in El Paso and enjoy time with their children and grandchildren. (Courtesy of Silvestre Reyes.)

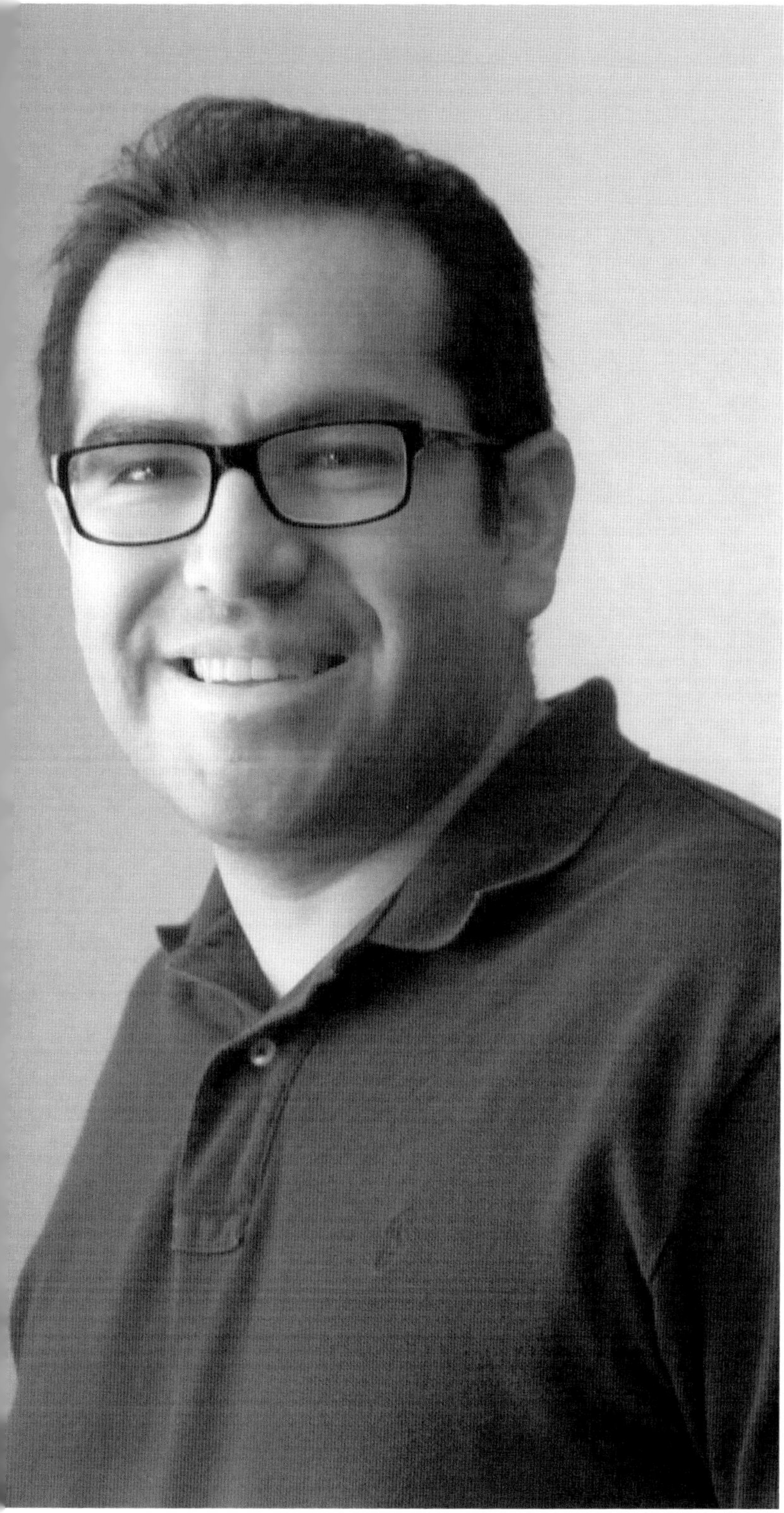

Steve Ortega
Public service can be a thankless job at times, but seeing projects that benefit the community come to fruition is where those in the position find fulfillment. For Steve Ortega, born in 1973 in El Paso, his term as a city councilman saw projects like the downtown arts market and the Pasodale Neighborhood street reconstruction and sidewalk beautification completed. His term in office coincided with a time when El Paso began entering into a new era of progress. "Change is always hard, especially in a community that has not had much, but the experience was very rewarding." (Courtesy of El Paso Inc.)

Jonathan Rogers

Jonathan Rogers served four terms as mayor of El Paso, from 1981 to 1989. The mortgage banker and philanthropist brought a sharp business mind to the city and made only three small tax increases during his time in office. His leadership and financial skills helped the city stabilize after being in financial disarray. While in office, he did not allow neckties to be worn between Memorial Day and Labor Day and was known for cutting ties off when challenged. Rogers's love for El Paso was strong, and he donated millions of dollars to schools such as UTEP and Texas Tech Medical School. The West Star Bank founder passed away in 2006, but his life and leadership will be remembered for ages. (Courtesy of EPPL BHC.)

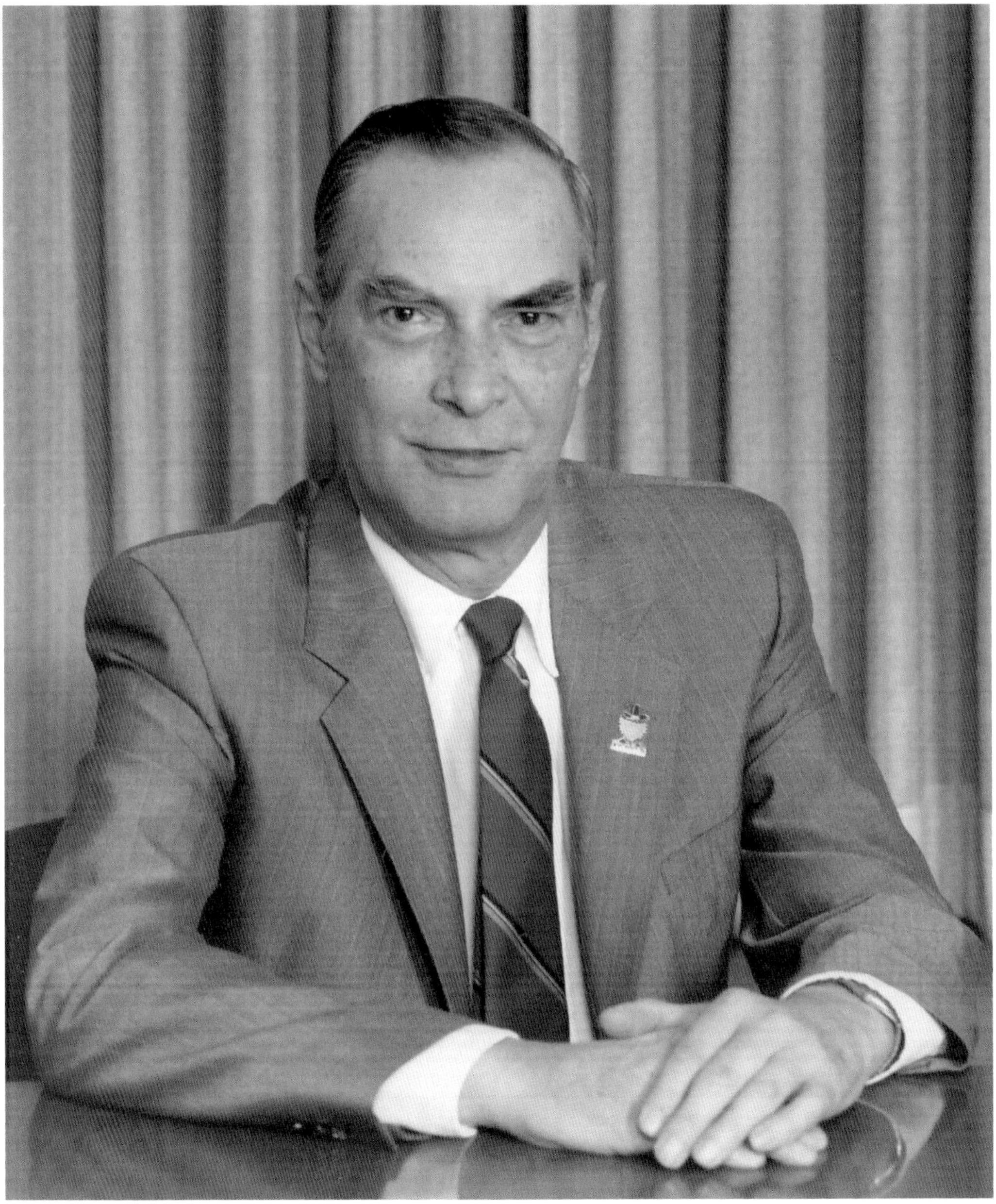

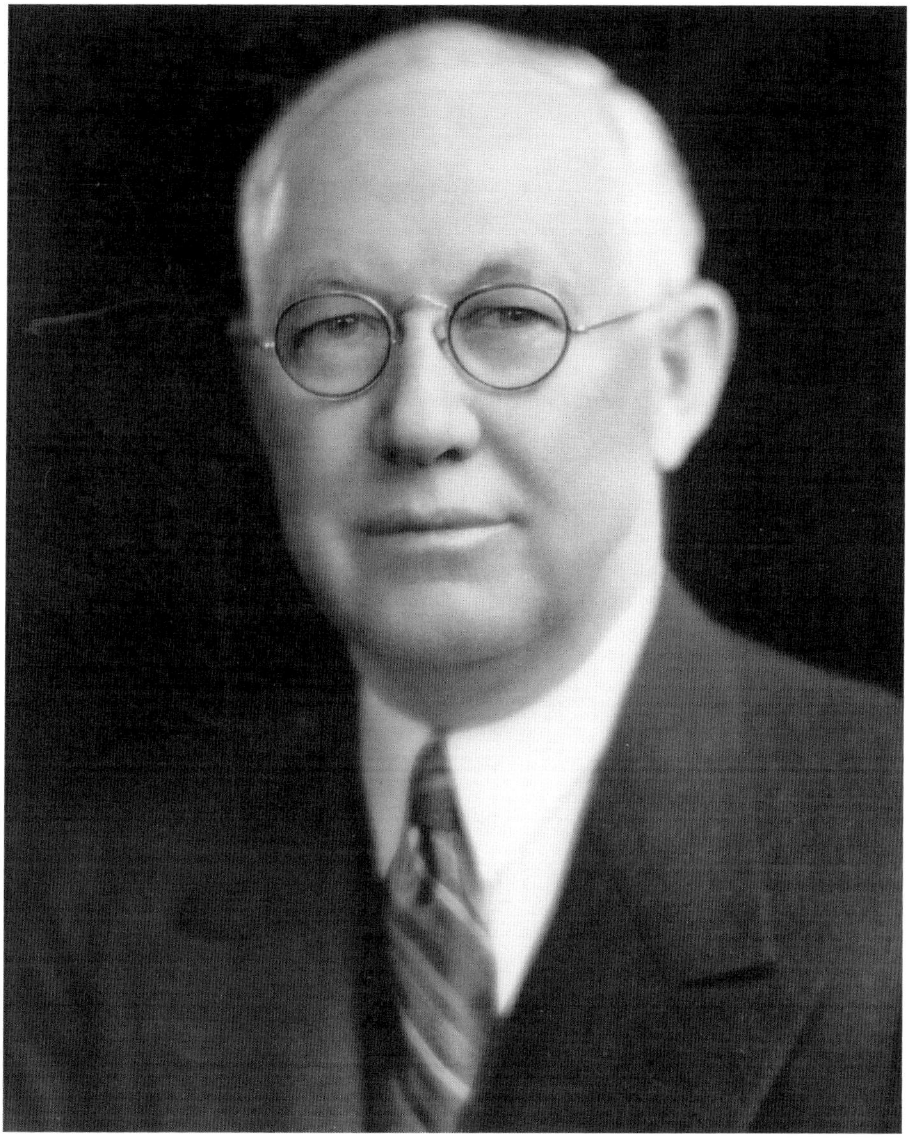

Robert Ewing Thomason
Born in Tennessee, Thomason's family moved to Texas when he was a small child. After college, he attended the University of Texas Law School and became an attorney. After moving to El Paso in 1912, he opened a law firm. He made a move into public office when he ran for a seat in the state legislature. He served two terms and became the speaker of the house. Thomason made a bid for governor but came up short in the election. In 1927, he won the election for mayor of El Paso. One of his significant accomplishments while mayor was opening the city's first municipal airport and introducing the city's first traffic-light system.

When his second term ended, Thomason made a bid for Congress. He held that seat for 13 terms and helped establish Big Bend National Park, and was a ranking member on the House Armed Services Committee through World War II. After serving in Congress, Thomason was appointed as a federal judge and served 16 years. R.E. Thomason's life was dedicated to public service in El Paso, and the area benefited greatly from his leadership. Thomason passed away in 1973. (Courtesy of EPPL BHC.)

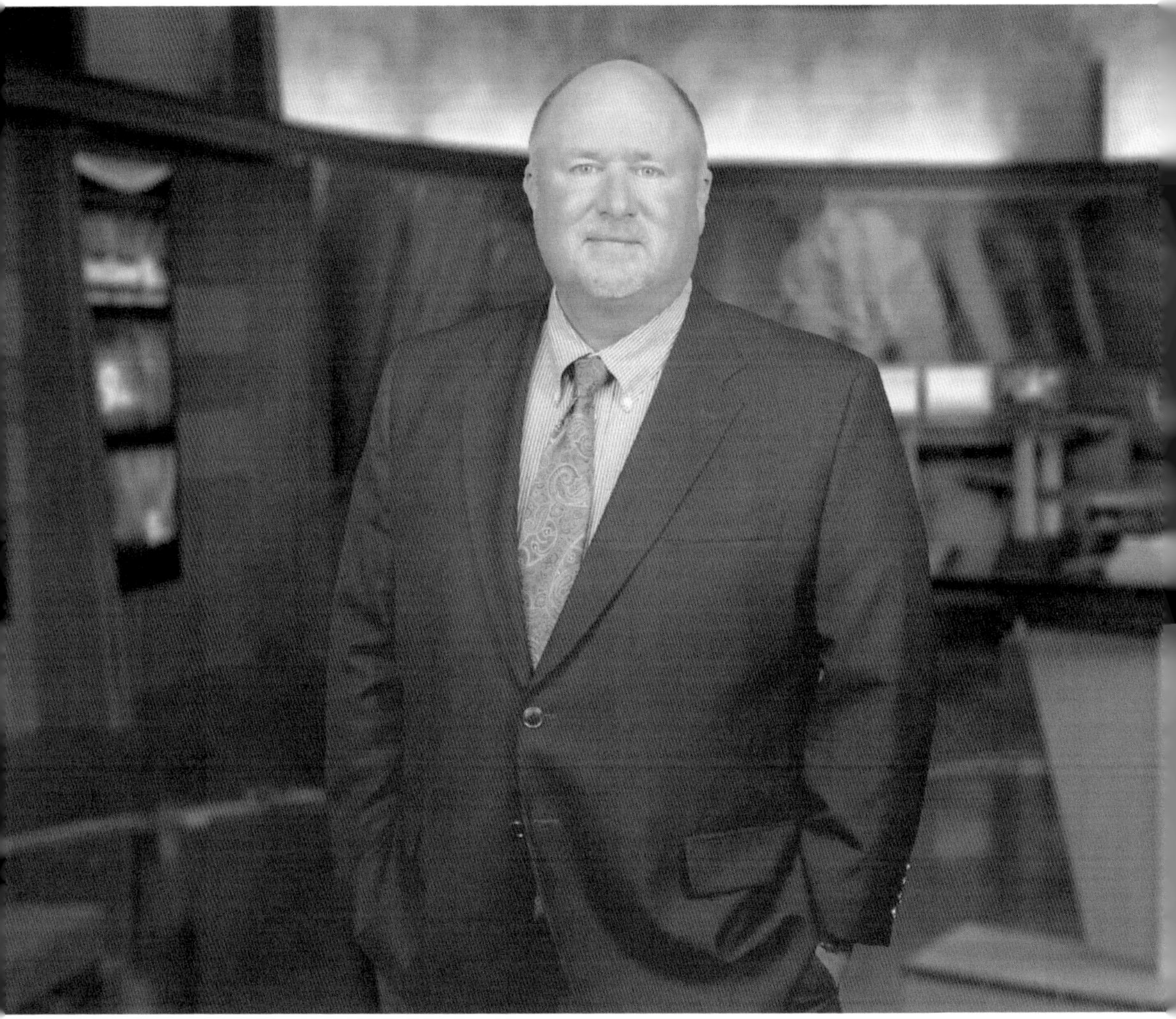

Fred Albers

As an aspiring sportscaster right out of the premier journalism school at the University of Missouri, Fred Albers knew that he would have a lot of moves in his future. The first five years as a sportscaster saw him in towns like Tupelo, Mississippi, and Montgomery, Alabama. Each move was necessary to move up in his career, but each stop had its moments. One memory that will never go away was from his time in Montgomery. "Every week I would drive to Tuscaloosa and talk with Bear Bryant. I didn't realize how lucky I was at the time to talk to Coach Bryant and get to know him a little bit." Eventually, Albers made his way to El Paso in 1980, where he worked for 12 years at Channel 7 before moving to Channel 9.

While here, the KTSM sportscaster was able to pick up national assignments doing live golf coverage for ESPN. Now, he works 25 weeks at Channel 9 and spends 25 weeks covering PGA Tour events for PGA Tour Radio. He has done play-by-play for tournaments such as the Masters and the US Open, and while his work takes him out of El Paso for part of the year, his heart is always here in the Sun City. He has been inducted into the El Paso Athletic Hall of Fame and Golf Hall of Fame. (Courtesy of KTSM.)

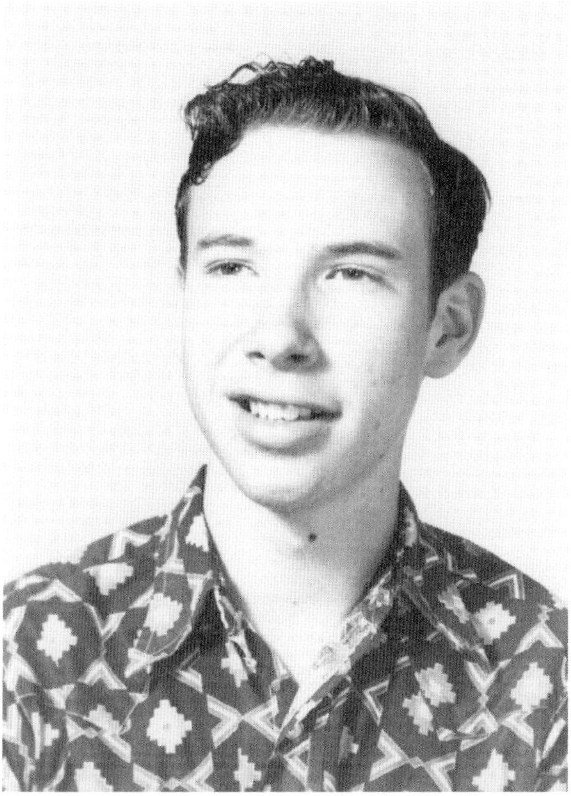

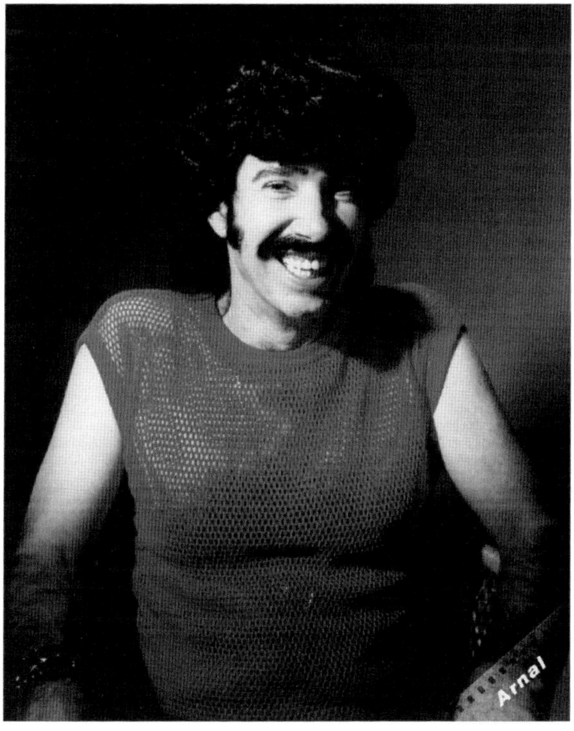

Steve Crosno

The radio was where Steve Crosno belonged. His voice would come over the airwaves on KELP and keep listeners entertained for hours. Crosno got into radio when he was 16, and in the 1960s and 1970s, he hosted the Crosno Hop. His ability to connect to his audience made him a ratings king. Crosno had a pretty simple solution for ratings, as he discussed in an interview some years back. "Getting and keeping ratings is so deceptively simple. Find out what they want and give it to them. The audience knows what they want." The disc jockey with the eccentric personality and wigs to go along with it faced highs and lows in his career but always found success through hard work that endeared him to generations of El Pasoans. (Both, courtesy of Manny Rivera.)

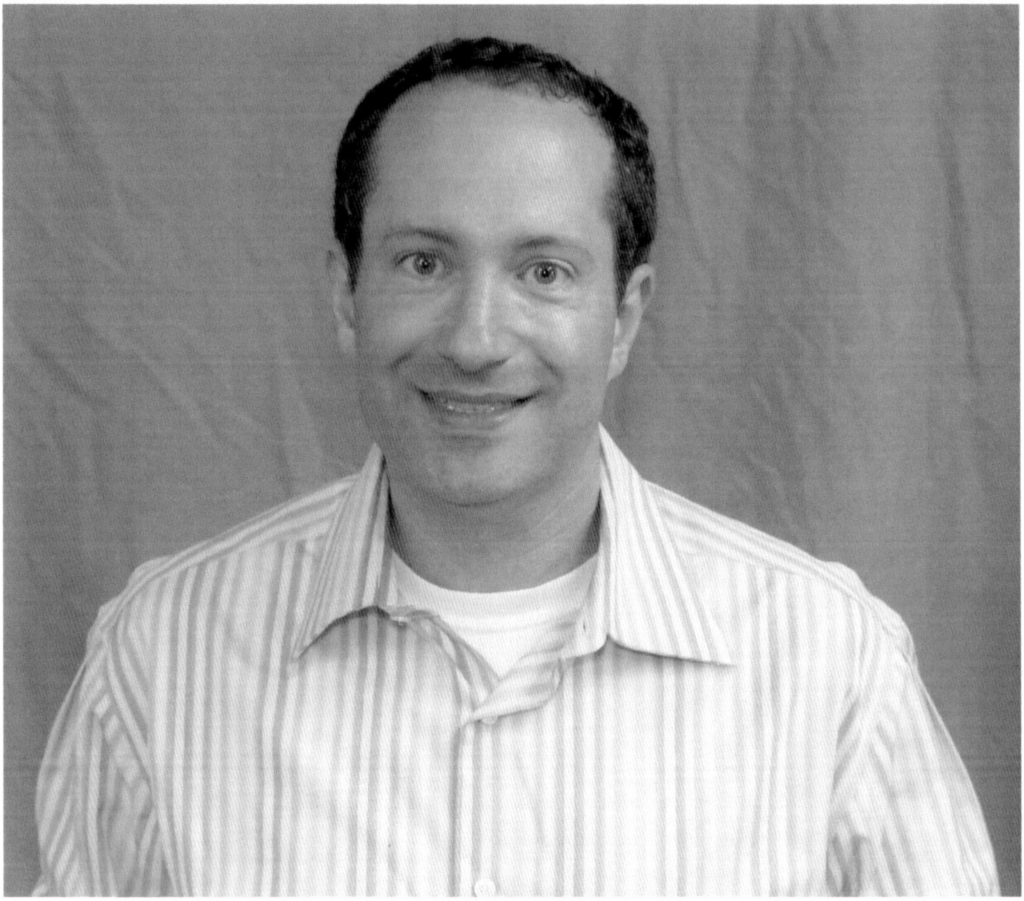

Steve Kaplowitz

As a child, Steve Kaplowitz felt that the world was truly for the taking. Brooklyn-born Kaplowitz saw himself playing under the bright lights in right field for the New York Mets. At the age of five, he and his family moved to El Paso to get away from the hustle and bustle of Long Island.

His junior year at Coronado, he went into journalism and wrote for the school paper after an injury ended his baseball-playing days. When he got to the University of Texas, he became a broadcast journalism student and wound up hosting a sports show on the school's student radio channel. This job opened doors for the 20-year-old, and he found himself covering games for teams like the Spurs and encountering media types such as Marv Albert and Bob Coozie. The job had its perks. "We had free parking, they fed us. We sat right there at mid court and you look behind and you see people who are probably millionaires paying $500 a ticket and here I am 20 years old sitting here for free. So that's when I decided that this would be the life."

His career in sports radio was almost a fleeting thought. After failing to secure a job after graduation, Kaplowitz was ready to throw in the towel and head back to school to get an accounting degree. Fortunately, a call came in, and he was brought on as an intern for Buzz Adams's morning show. Two decades later, Kaplowitz finds himself on the airwaves of El Paso hosting a very successful sports radio program. "The show is for the community. A sports radio show should be about your listeners. It's important for them to have that opportunity to comment on big stories when they break." An inductee of the El Paso Athletic Hall of Fame, Kaplowitz plans on continuing El Paso's most popular sports-radio program for decades to come. (Courtesy of Steve Kaplowitz.)

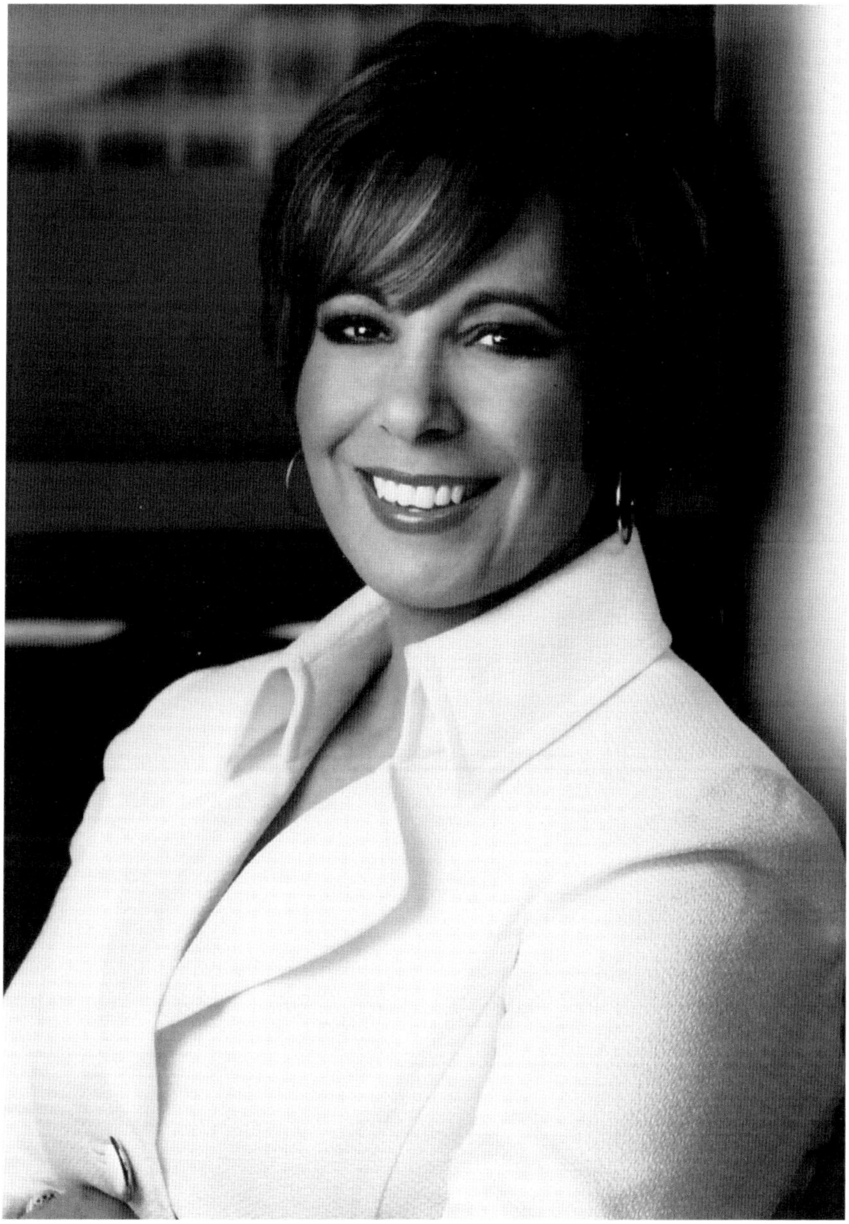

Estela Casas
Estela Casas is a first-generation El Pasoan who is widely seen as the face of television news in the El Paso region. Born in 1961, Casas came from humble beginnings with aspirations of becoming a pop singer. As that dream faded, new ones came into reality, and Casas has found herself in front of bright lights and cameras as El Pasoans turn on the television every night to watch her share the day's news.

Her career has seen her at a few local stations, with ABC affiliate KVIA being her home now for over 20 years. Casas is a strong advocate for health issues involving children and women in the region and helps with many events around the city. She did a live mammogram on television in 1993 and shared her story of battling thyroid cancer in 2008. Casas is married to her childhood sweetheart and has three children. (Courtesy of Estela Casas.)

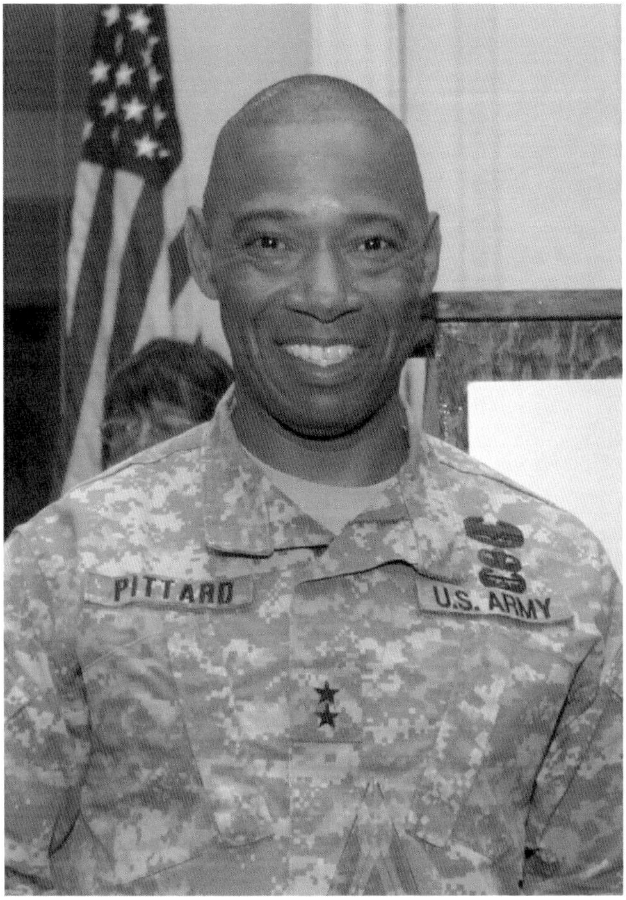

Gen. Dana Pittard

El Paso has been called home by many leaders throughout its existence. For Maj. Gen. Dana Pittard, El Paso is where a majority of his formative years were spent. Born in 1959 in Okinawa, Japan, to Robert and Jackie Pittard, the future major general moved to El Paso at eight months old. As with many who have found themselves in El Paso, the reason for the move was because of transfer orders to Fort Bliss. Pittard knew he wanted to join the military at a young age. "I decided that I wanted to go to West Point when I was 10 years old after looking at an article on Dwight D. Eisenhower in the July 1969 issue of *National Geographic*. I now always carry a copy of that July 1969 issue of *National Geographic* wherever I go to remind me of why I joined the military."

His career in the military has taken him to over 75 countries, and he hopes to have visited over 100 by the time his career is over. Through his travels, one of the biggest things he has learned is that even though cultures throughout the globe are different, people all have much more in common than they think. "I have learned that most people throughout the world desire some of the basic things in life—taking care of their families, security, freedom, and the ability to worship and live as they please."

In July 2010, a dream came true, and the former Eastwood High School graduate took over command of the 1st Armored Division and Fort Bliss. During his three years in command, Fort Bliss transformed with numerous construction projects and troops being reassigned to the post from overseas. Over the course of his career, he saw the Berlin Wall come down, spent time as the military aide in the White House to former president Bill Clinton, and led troops into combat four different times.

While much of his career has taken him around the world, El Paso is still near and dear to his heart. (Courtesy of El Paso Inc.)

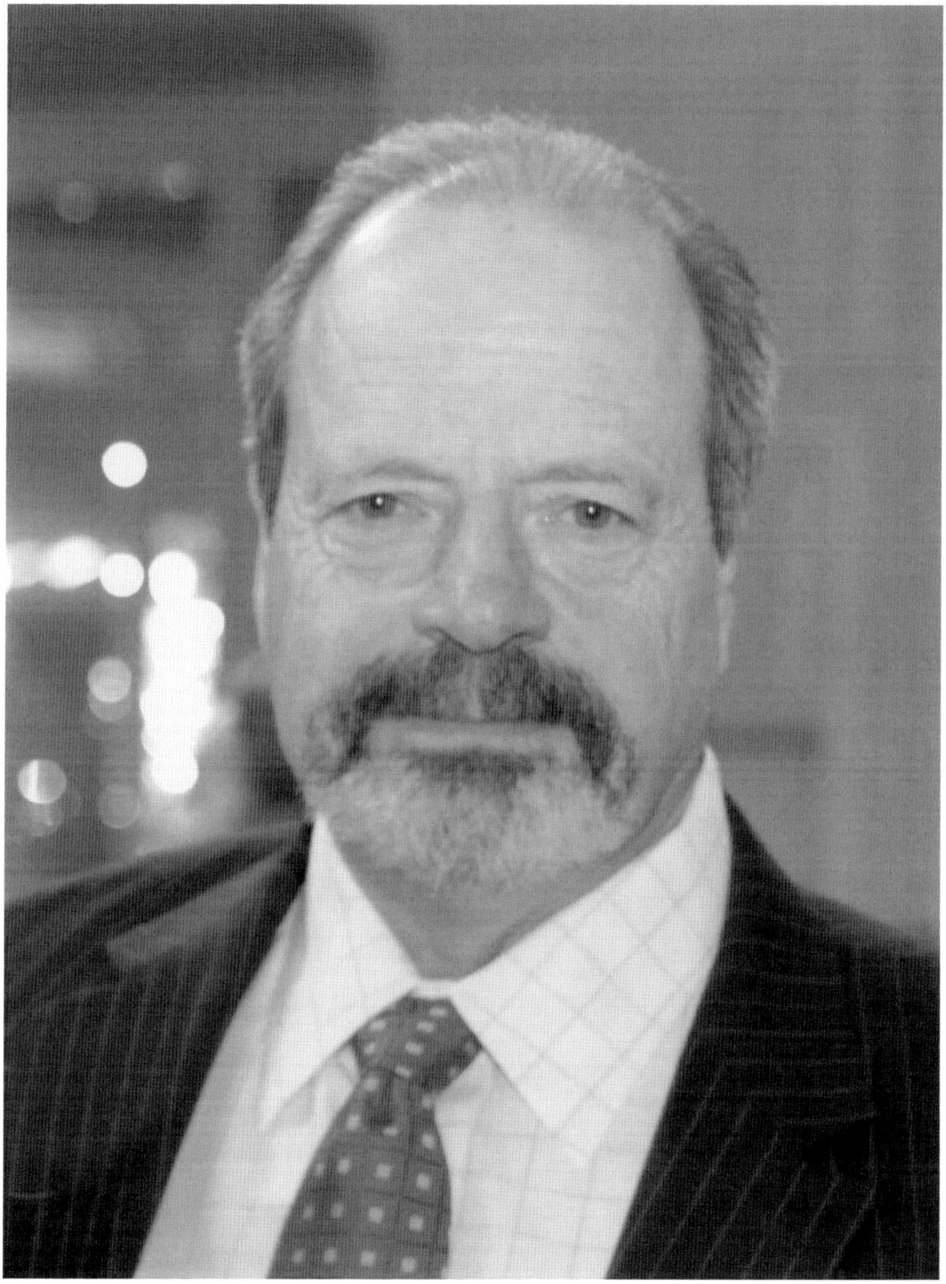

Oscar Leeser
Oscar Leeser was born in Chihuahua, Mexico, and moved to El Paso at the age of nine. A hard worker from early in life, he eventually became involved in the car business and opened up a very successful Hyundai dealership that has ranked in the top 10 of dealerships nationwide. Recently, he took his business acumen and ran for mayor of El Paso. After his victory, he announced that he and wife would be donating his city paycheck every month to a different charity. During his time in office he has helped create over 3,200 jobs in the city, and is actively pitching the benefits of setting up shop in El Paso to companies across the nation. (Courtesy of El Paso Inc.)

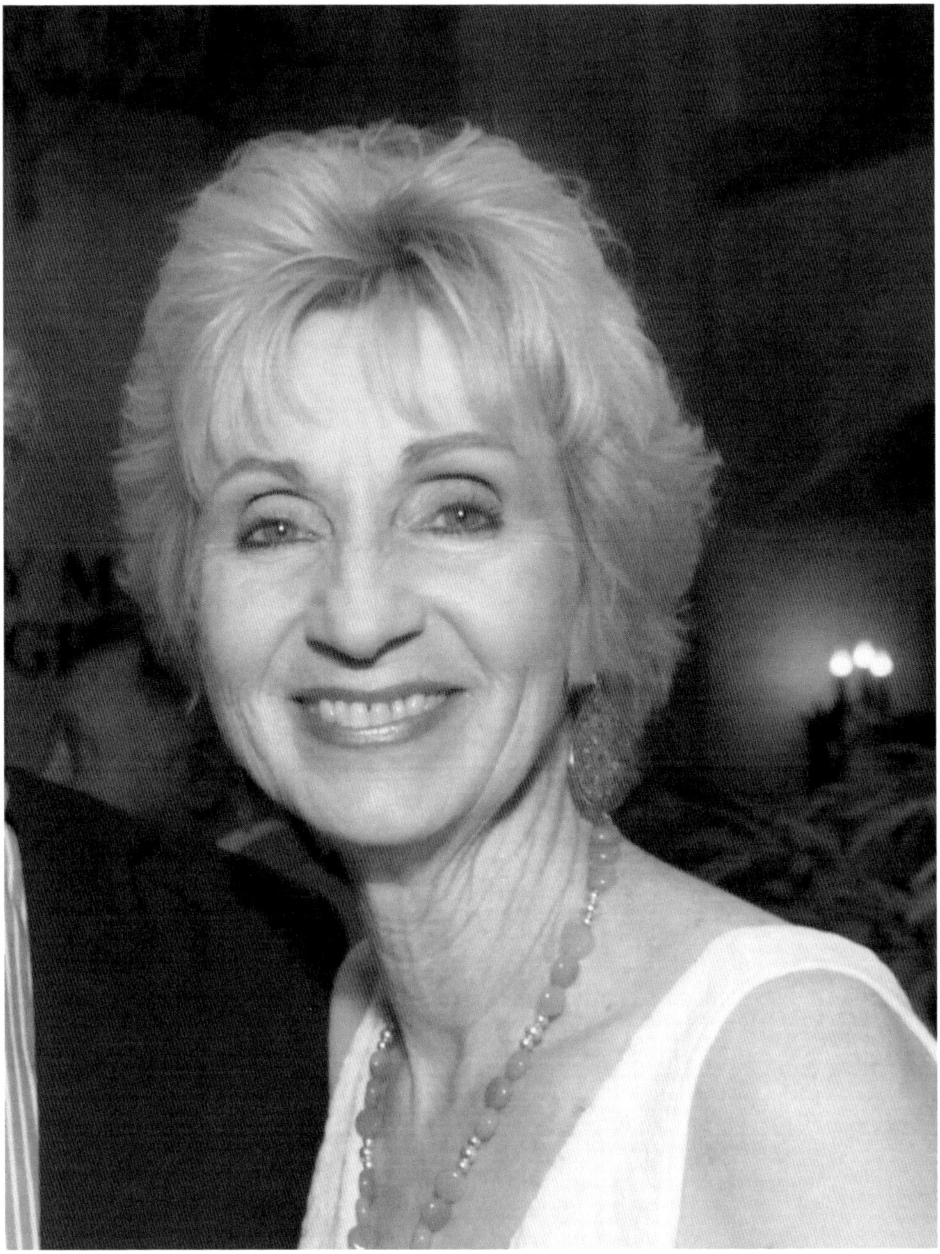

Joyce Wilson

In 2004, then-mayor Joe Wardy helped the city transition to a city manager form of government. That year, Joyce Wilson became the first person to hold the position, and her 10 years on the job were anything but boring. During her time, she helped manage and improve city departments, rehabilitate Sun Metro, and put together a number of bond projects that have improved the quality of life across the city. When city hall was demolished to make way for a new Triple-A baseball stadium, she was the recipient of a lot of criticism. Looking back at her time as city manager, Wilson helped improve the city and launch it into its next golden age. Wilson now serves as the president of Workforce Solutions: Upper Rio Grande. (Courtesy of El Paso Inc.)

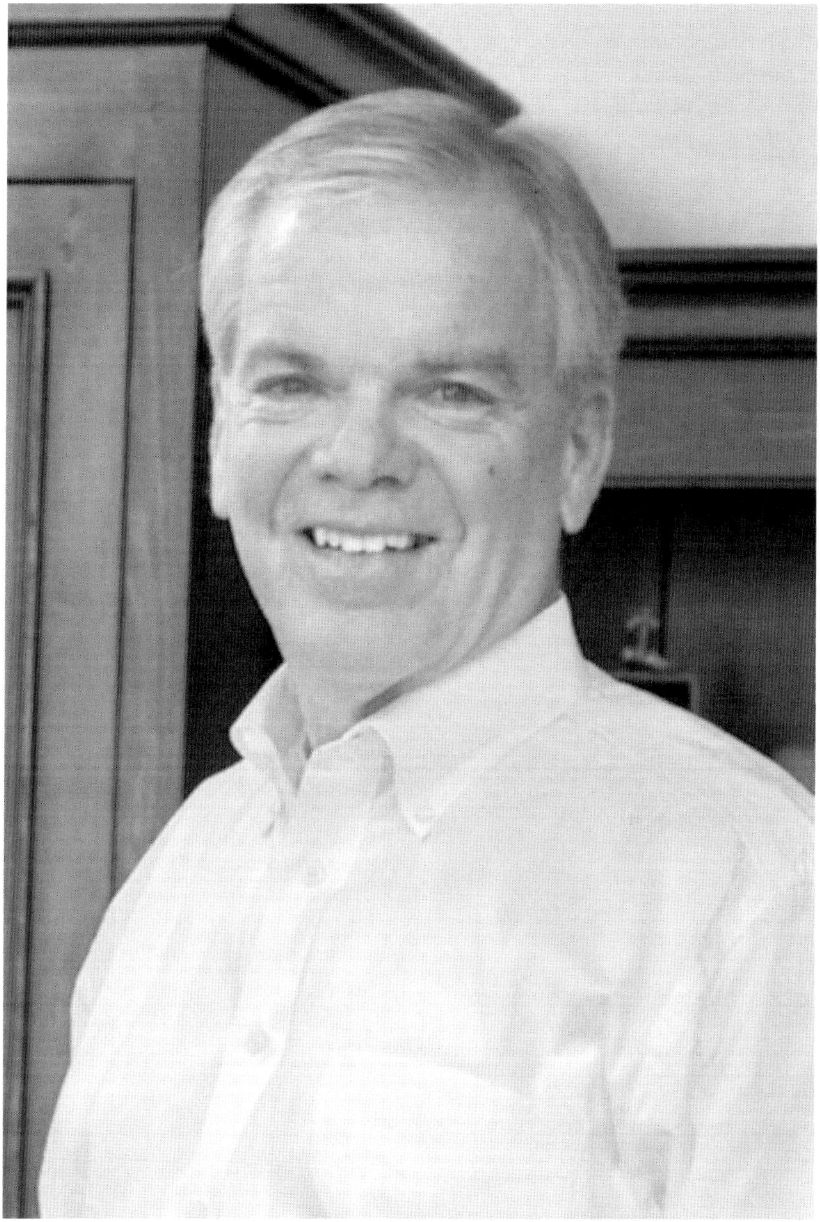

Ted Houghton

For over 11 years, El Paso has had representation on the Texas Transportation commission. Ted Hougton was born in El Paso, and the UTEP and NMSU graduate has helped represent El Paso on the commission since 2003, when he was appointed by Gov. Rick Perry. Houghton has said his reasons for wanting to volunteer and help the city are simple: "If you want to make a difference or change things, don't wait for someone else to do it."

During his time on the commission, they have worked with other planning organizations in the area, and the city and surrounding area have seen over $2 billion in road construction projects come to fruition. The 601 spur through Fort Bliss and the massive interchange at Loop 375 and I-10 are just a few of the projects that have taken place over the last decade. (Courtesy of El Paso Inc.)

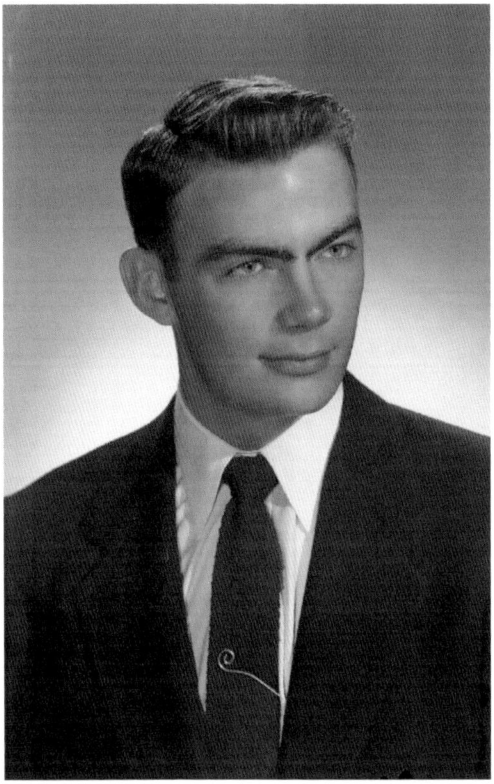

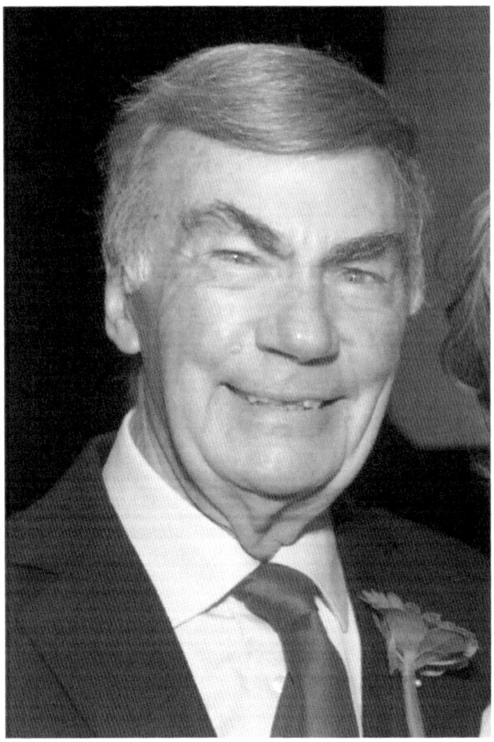

Sam Donaldson

Sam Donaldson was born in 1934 and raised on a farm in Chamborino, New Mexico. As a young boy, his mother drove him into El Paso every day to attend the Dudley School. After attending New Mexico Military Institute, Donaldson went on to attend Texas Western with an ROTC commission in 1955. He enjoyed his time while in college, and after school, he worked for a commercial radio station. "I played records and read the news. My program was Sam's Show." His radio program was a catalyst for his future media career.

Donaldson began working with ABC News in 1967 and has remained with the network ever since. During his time as a media correspondent he has covered many memorable events, but there are a few that particularly stand out in his mind, including the day Ronald Reagan was shot. Donaldson was feet away from the president when John Hinkley Jr. attempted to assassinate Reagan. Another time, he went to Argentina and tracked down a known Nazi war criminal who was deported to Italy, where he served a life sentence after the story aired. Donaldson now lives in New Mexico but still comes down to visit UTEP to give talks to students. Donaldson is not completely retired and can still be found on the speaking circuit and moderating political debates. (Top, courtesy of UTEP Special Collections; bottom, courtesy of El Paso Inc.)

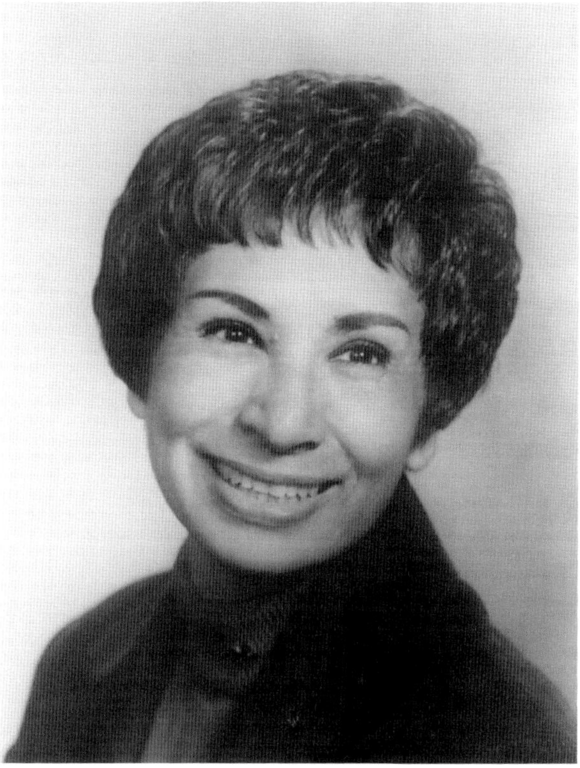

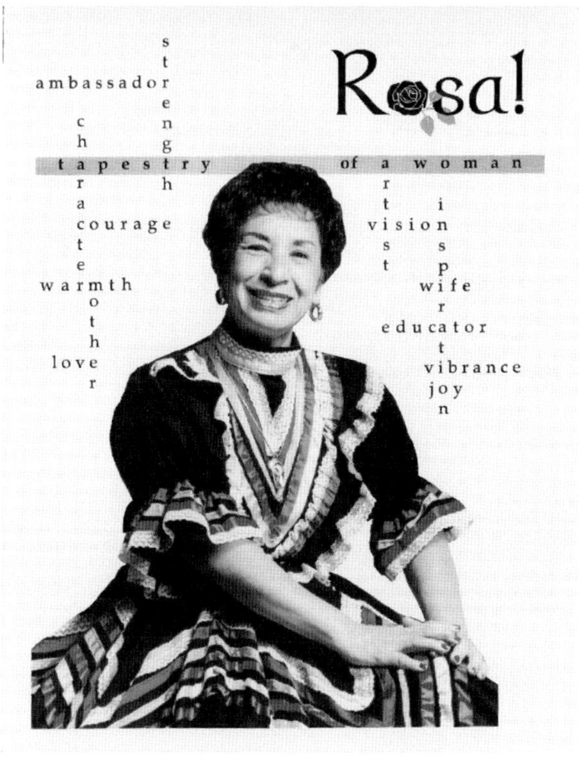

Rosa Guerrero

Born in 1934, Rosa Guerrero knew in third grade at Morehead Elementary that she wanted to be an educator. As the first from her family to obtain bachelor's and master's degrees, she held teaching positions at the El Paso Independent School District, EPCC, and UTEP. Her love of education and dance led her to form the International Folklórico Dance Group. The group performed for Pres. Ronald Reagan in 1983 and went on to perform in other cities across the country. Guerrero influenced others with her words as much as her dance. "Our Country is a multicultural tapestry, a mosaic of many people. Because of our differentness, we can all contribute something important to the fabric of the American life. Therefore, each person is special and unequalled." It is this message that Guerrero continues to spread to people young and old, and she has not lost a step when it comes to dancing. (Top, courtesy of the El Paso County Historical Society; bottom, courtesy of Rosa Guerrero.)

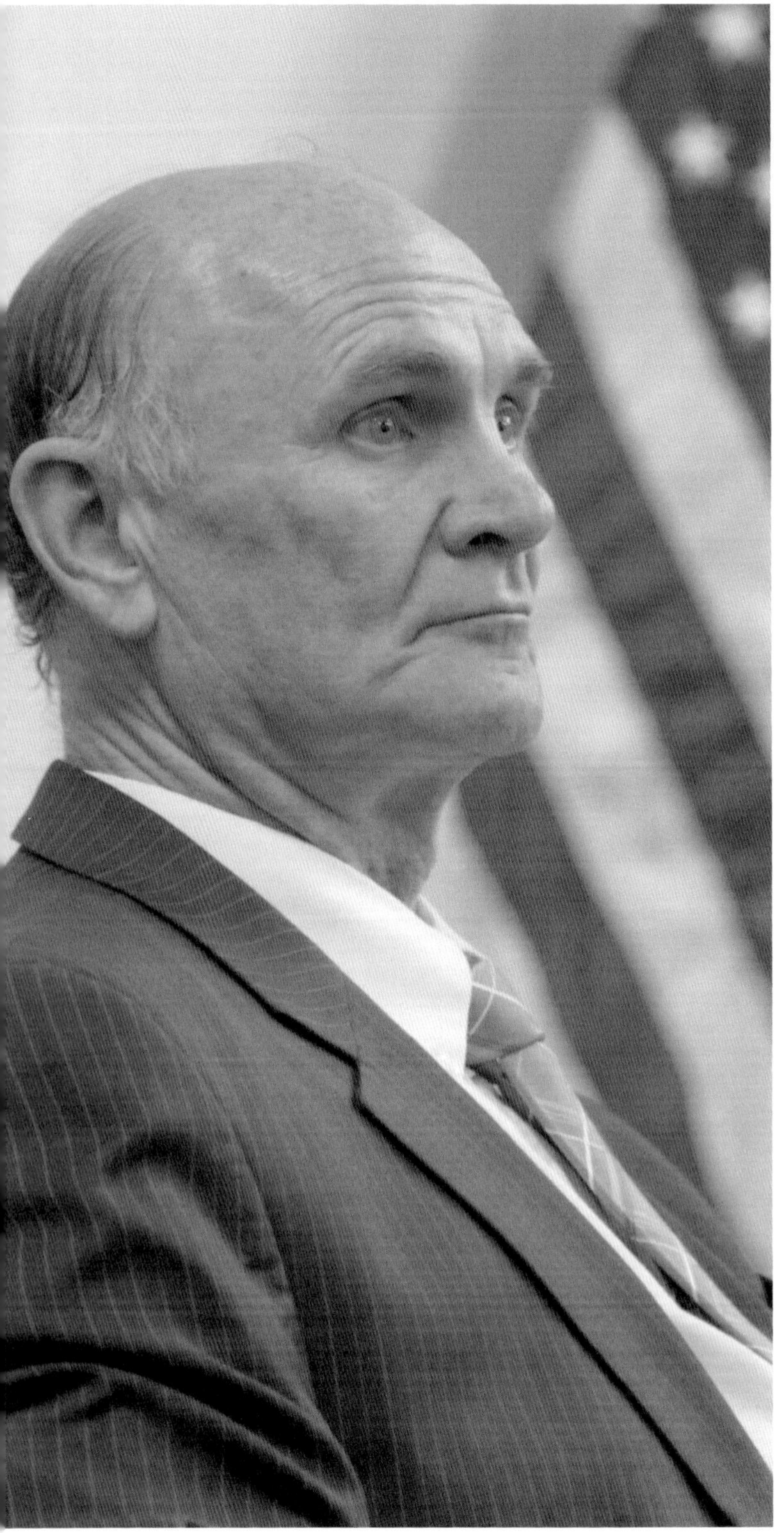

John Cook

Brooklyn-born John Cook made his way to El Paso through Fort Bliss, and in 1971, he made El Paso his permanent home. In 1999, Cook was elected to city council and served three terms. In 2005, he ran for mayor and went on to serve for eight years. Under Cook's leadership, the city saw an improved Sun Metro Transportation System and a $480-million quality of life bond passed by voters. His time in office was controversial, with the decision to allow the demolition of city hall where the current Chihuahuas stadium sits. The singing mayor always had an open-door policy and was willing to meet with all citizens. Cook is married to his wife, Tram, and has six children, 11 grandchildren, and two great grandchildren. (Courtesy of Steve Green.)

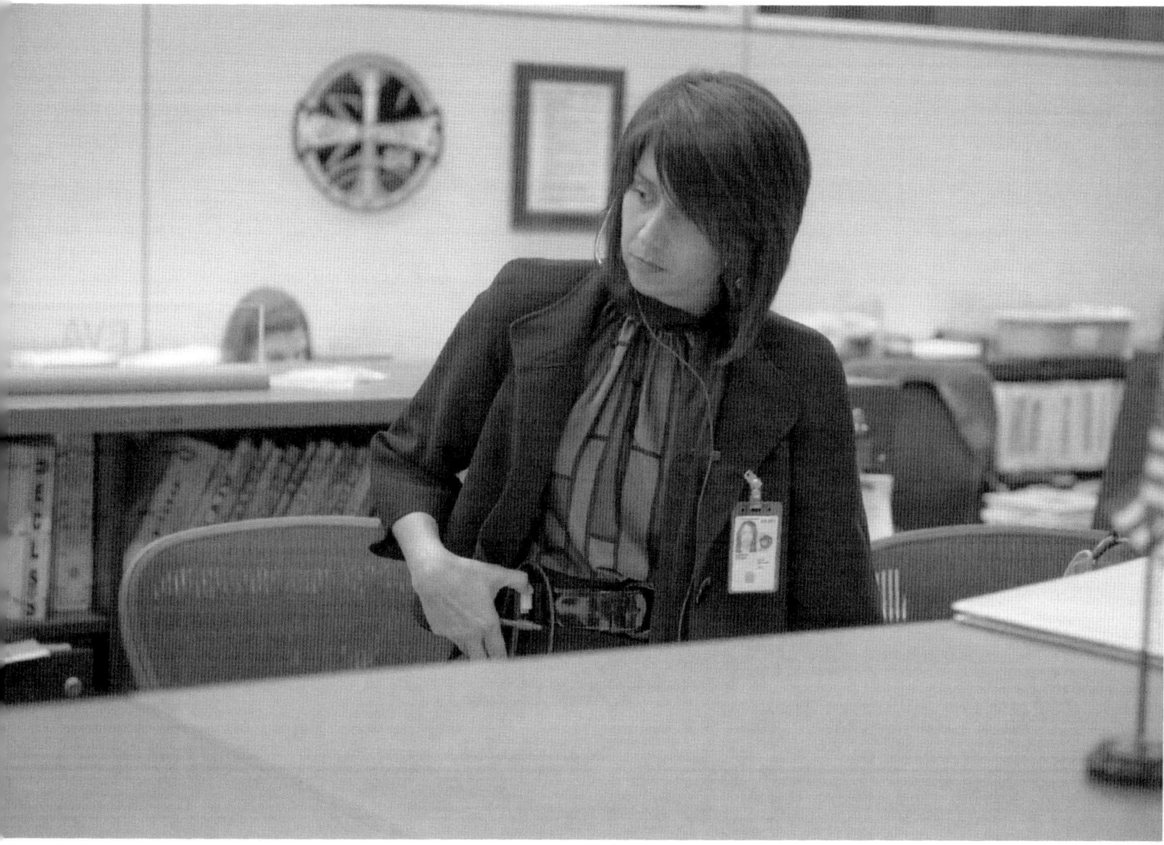

Ginger Kerrick

One day, on a weekly trip to the local El Paso library with her father, young Ginger Kerrick picked out a book about astronomy and astronauts. She did not know it at the time, but that book left a lasting impression on her and was the catalyst for what has been a very successful career at NASA. Kerrick has always been a hard worker and pushed herself every step of the way. After attending UTEP for a year, Kerrick transferred to Texas Tech, where NASA had a co-op program with the university. After school, Kerrick accepted a full-time position with the space agency. The young girl who had written to NASA as a child was living her dream after being asked to interview for the astronaut candidacy program. Unfortunately, a medical ailment disqualified her from moving forward, but in every darkness, there is a light. Kerrick moved into an instructor role in which she prepared astronauts going into space. Over her career, she has held positions as an ISS Life Support Systems Instructor, the first non-astronaut capsule communicator, and most recently, as flight director. In 2010, Kerrick was the commencement speaker for the December graduating class at Texas Tech. She did not get to where she is today on her own, and she credits her family and mentors who have supported her throughout her life. (Courtesy of Ginger Kerrick.)

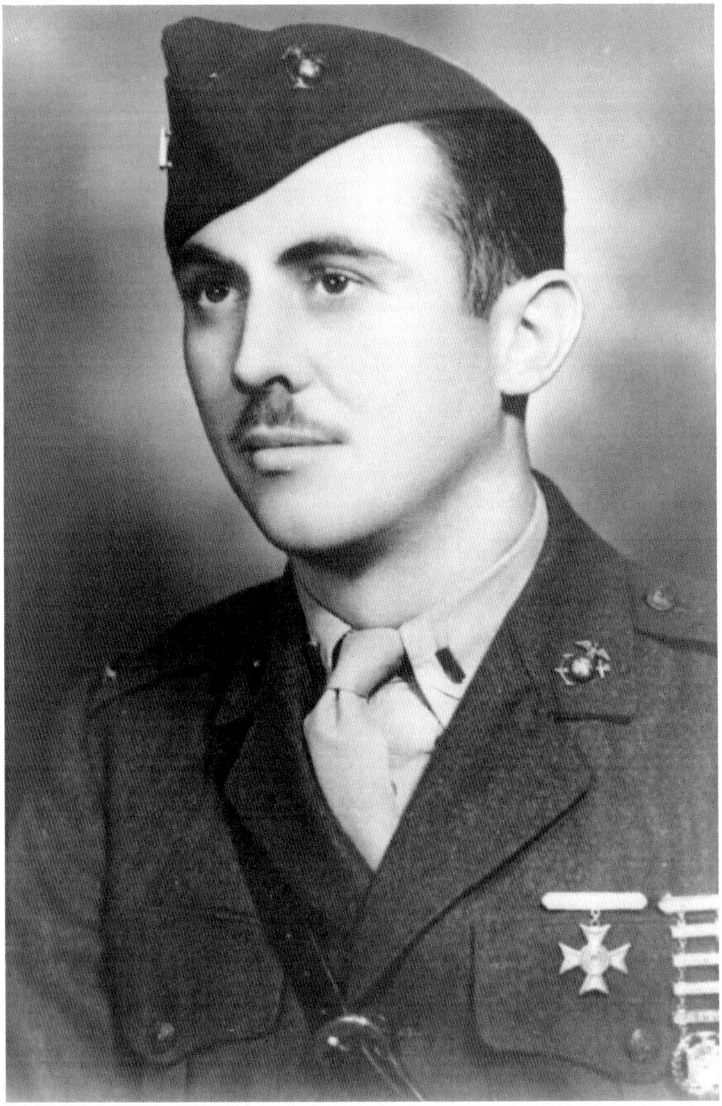

William D. Hawkins

World War II was full of heroes, many of whom sacrificed their lives for their country. One of those was an El Pasoan by the name of William Hawkins. Born in Fort Scott, Kansas, in 1914, his family moved to El Paso when he was a toddler. After attending El Paso High and then the Texas College of Mines (UTEP), Hawkins went on to hold a job as an engineer until 1942, when he enlisted in the Marines after the attack on Pearl Harbor. As a member of the 2nd Marines, 2nd Division, Hawkins was assigned to a scout sniper platoon.

After the Battle of Guadalcanal, he was promoted from sergeant to second lieutenant. In 1943, Hawkins led his platoon in the Battle of Tarawa while trying to take control of the beachhead. During the fight, he led his men in overtaking numerous fortified machine gun pillboxes while taking heavy fire. Hawkins continued to fight and lead his platoon even after being wounded. Lieutenant Hawkins was mortally wounded as he continued to advance his platoon in battle. For his actions and bravery, he was posthumously awarded the Medal of Honor, which his mother accepted from President Roosevelt in 1944 at a White House ceremony. (Courtesy of El Paso County Historical Society.)

CHAPTER SEVEN

Citizens and the Future

There is no written rule that one has to be a certain age to make a difference or influence another person's life. It is also not required to be well known in order to make a difference. Some of the people in the following chapter lead everyday lives, but they have all made a difference in the area. There are young entrepreneurs taking risks to better El Paso because they believe the benefits far outweigh the risks, and that is exciting for a city with an upward trajectory. While not as well known as some, these El Pasoans have all accomplished some amazing feats, and many are just getting started in their careers.

One educator spent his time sharing his love of music with countless students and found joy in each one's success. While Larry Phifer spends his days as a practicing attorney, his nights and free time are spent crafting children's books that have been nominated for several awards.

For most people, one marathon is a check off the bucket list. Flip Lyle has made over 330 of those checks and currently holds a seat in the Guinness Book of World Records for most triathlons completed by one athlete. Running aside, thousands upon thousands of concertgoers descend upon downtown as they take in the Neon Desert Music Festival. The annual festival was put together by four young El Pasoans who decided their hometown was the perfect place to put on a massive music festival, which has seen great success since its beginning. Not far from where the festival takes place, Carlo Mendo operates Loft Light Studio, which serves as a studio space that showcases local artists, photographers, and more. Life is filled with risk, but it is those who are willing to embrace the unknown who come out on top. The younger generation of El Paso has recognized that the city is in a key position of potential growth and prosperity, and it is that excitement that has caused many young people to take a chance and make their mark. Looking ahead, many hope good fortune awaits in the shadows and that El Paso will regain its standing as one of the top cities in the Southwest.

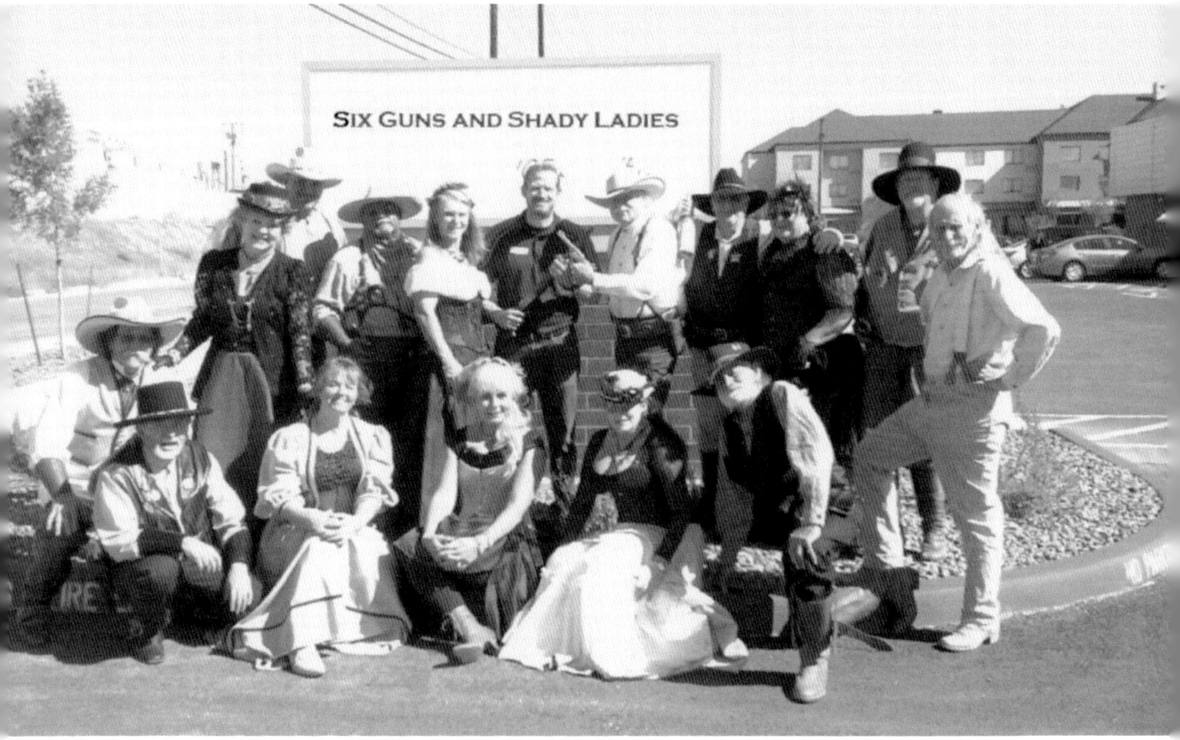

Six Guns and Shady Ladies

The Old West comes alive at least 40 times a year thanks to an award-winning group of citizens who recreate the events of El Paso and the Southwest area that existed from 1860 to 1910. Six Guns and Shady Ladies have been together since 1999, and their hard work has helped educate people young and old, from California to Texas, about the history that took place in this area. Their reenactments have been so good that Hollywood has called on the group to perform and help with productions. In the end, member Bernie Sargent says, "Our underlying mission is to educate the audiences of all ages on the history of the Southwest. Not only do we share the historical events as accurately as possible, we also make the safety of weapons handling a prominent part of our shows." (Courtesy of Bernie Sargent.)

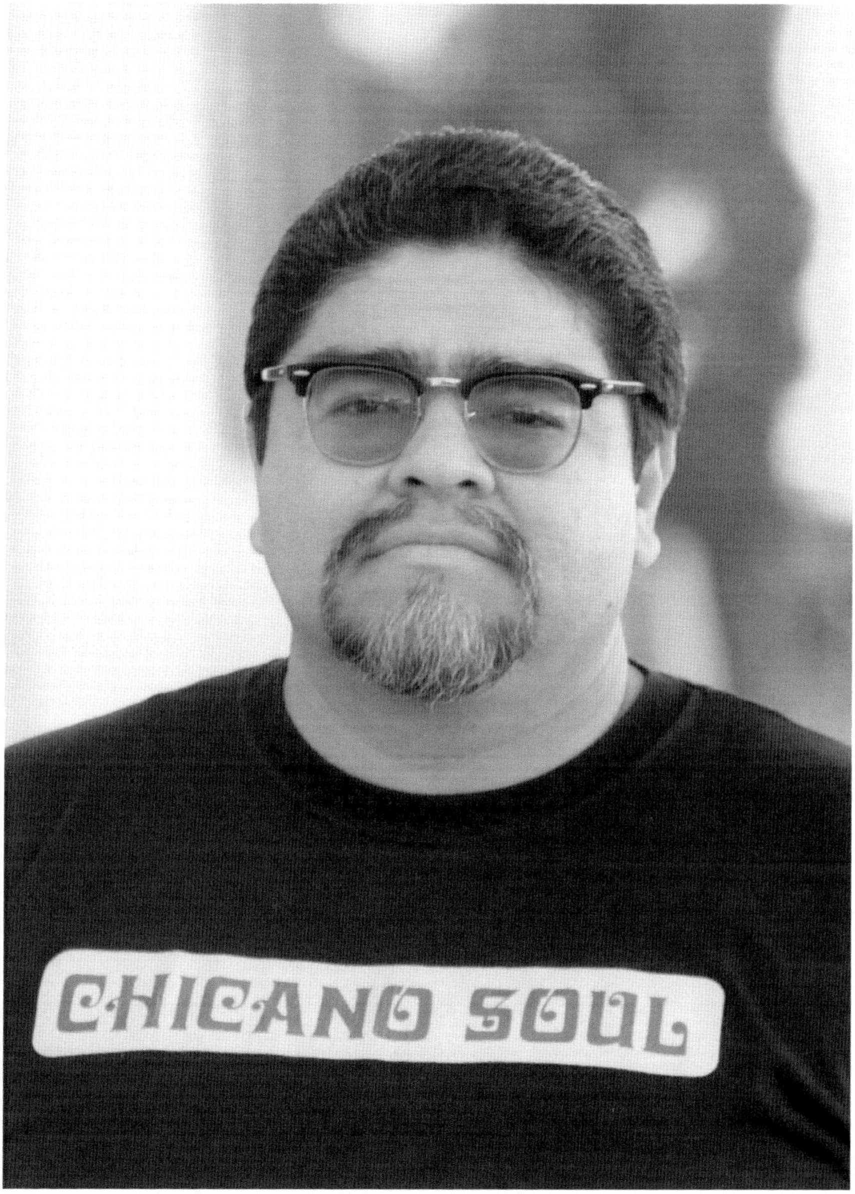

Osveldo Velez

Segundo Barrio is and always will be home for Osvaldo Velez. In 2014, Velez was featured in the PBS special *One Square Mile: Texas* and spoke about his experience of growing up and living in what used to be called El Paso's second ward. For Velez, much of his time as a child was spent at the events held at the recreation center. He now spends his days working as a janitor at Guillen Middle School, where, he says, his heart belongs. A few years ago, Velez recognized that the place he called home was in need of repair, and he got involved with the neighborhood association. He eventually became president of the organization and helped bring residents together to be more involved. Looking toward to the future, he hopes to see more affordable housing developed in the area to bring more people back to Segundo Barrio. The greatest life lesson he has learned is that in the end, "family, friends and neighbors are the most valuable things in life." (Courtesy of El Paso Inc.)

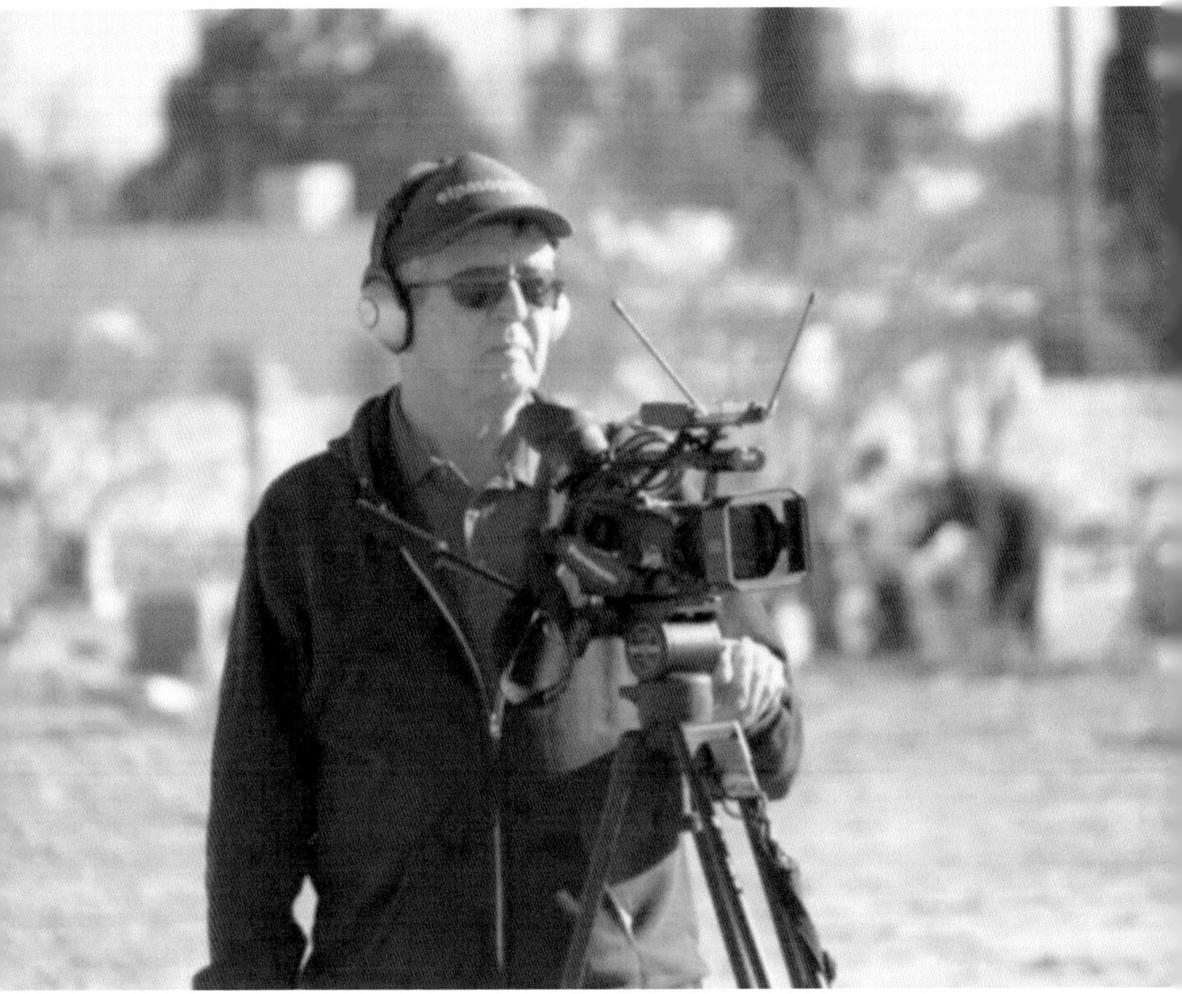

Jackson Polk

Preserving El Paso's history and telling those stories through film is a passion for local filmmaker and documentarian Jackson Polk. At 15, Polk got a job as a disc jockey in 1967 at the UTEP's KVOF. While he was not paid, he was a kid in high school working with a college radio program on Saturdays. Polk's first foray into television came when he went to work in Washington, DC, doing production for live television news. At 23, he did his first substantial documentary on the pyramids at Teotihuacan. Since then, Polk has gone on to produce many documentaries, with one of his latest capturing the final days of the ASARCO Smelter, which played a significant role in the lives of many El Pasoans. Looking toward the future, Polk hopes to continue to educate viewers on El Paso's history through television. (Courtesy of Jackson Polk.)

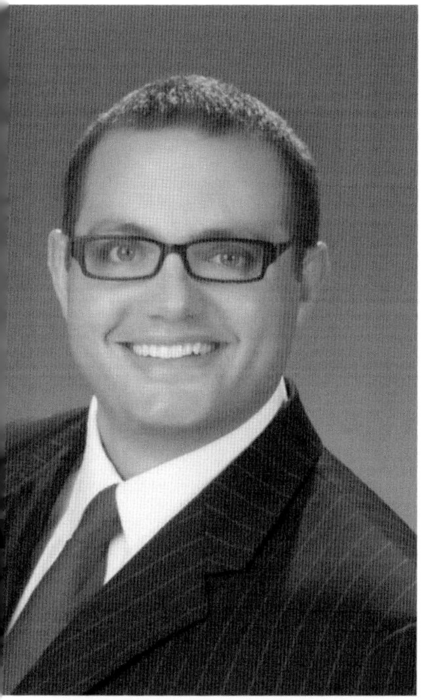

Larry Phifer

Larry Phifer is a board-certified practicing real estate attorney by day, and successful children's book author by night. For Phifer (born in 1976), writing has been a part of his life for as long as he can remember. His first children's book, *World on a String*, was published in 2013. It focuses on a boy named Charlie who deals with the loss of his best friend, a big red balloon. The underlying theme is geared toward helping children deal with the loss of a loved one. The book has already won the Silver Moonbeam Award for the best illustrator of the year, and is also up for the Bill Martin Jr. Picture Book Award. Larry resides in El Paso with his wife, Tiffany, and is already working on completing his second children's book with illustrator Danny Popovici. (Both, courtesy of Larry Phifer.)

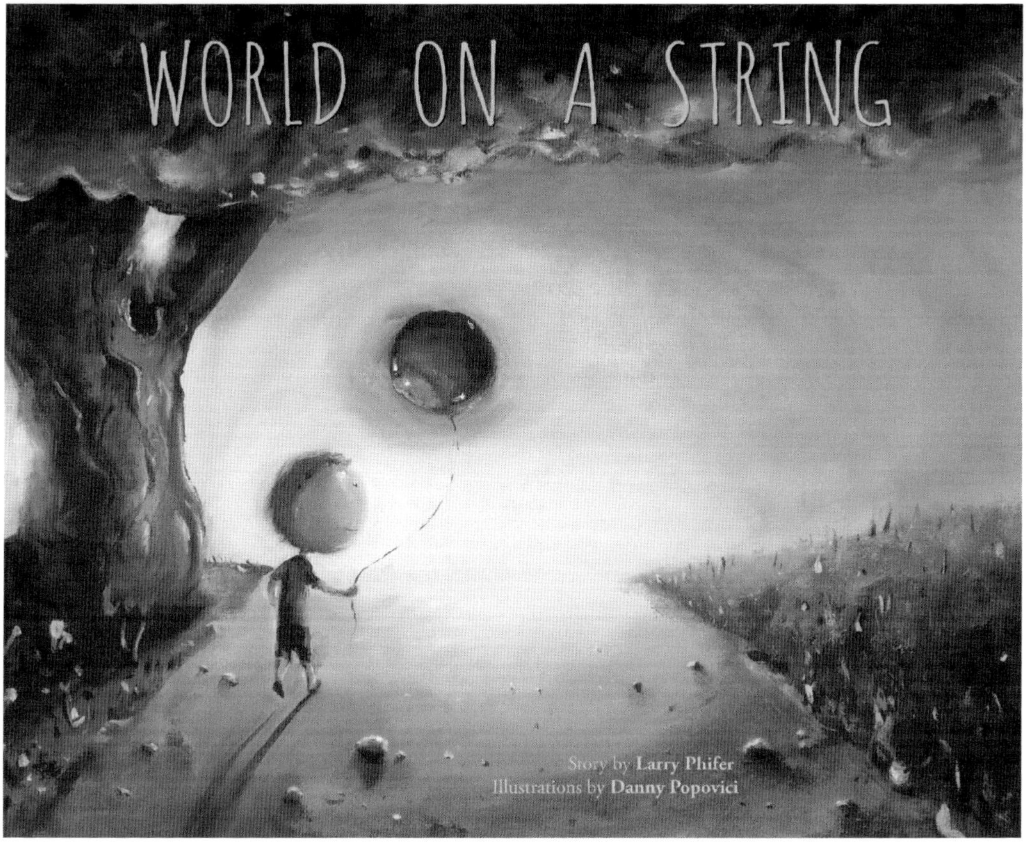

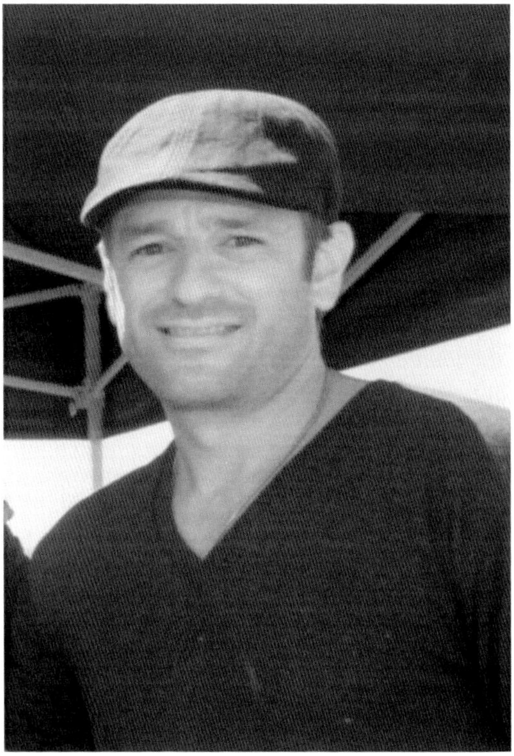

TJ Karam

Like many of the younger generation in El Paso, TJ Karam and his brothers saw opportunity in what El Paso had to offer and the bright future ahead. Time spent living outside of El Paso helped inspire Karam with ideas of what he could bring back to his hometown. He and his brothers wanted to see a vibrant downtown and decided to be some of the first to build new residential units there. Their reuse of the former furniture building resulted in nine residential lofts and ground retail space. The First Avenue Lofts were a beacon for El Paso's downtown revitalization, and since their development, many other projects have either been built or are under construction. Karam also opened Blackbird Cantina near the downtown ballpark, which has seen a flurry of development since it opened in 2014. (Left, courtesy of El Paso Inc.; below, author's collection.)

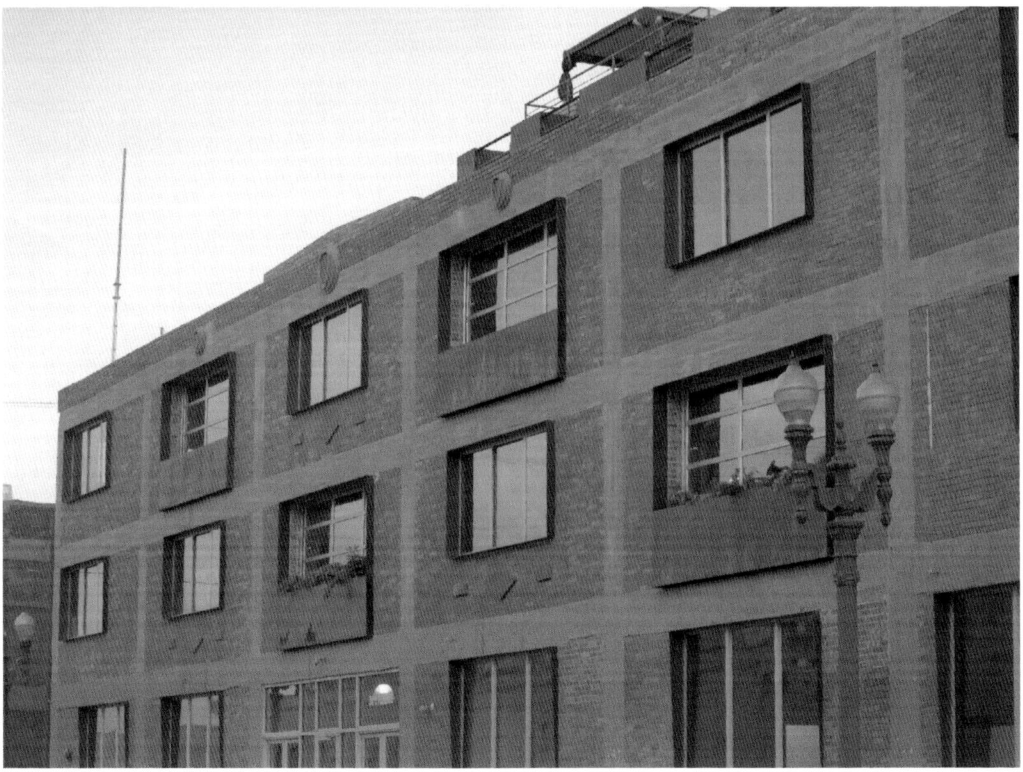

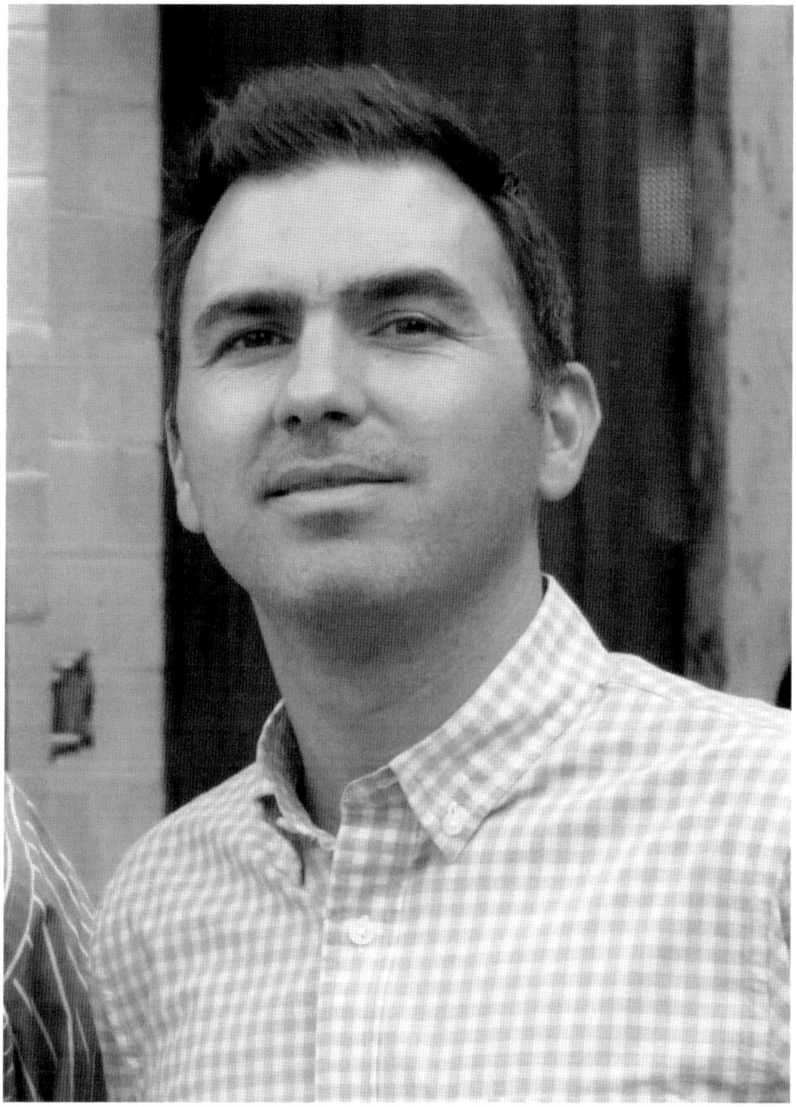

Octavio Gomez
When it comes to revitalization, somebody has to be the first one in to see if it is worth the investment. For Octavio Gomez, born in 1979, his goal was clear. He wanted to improve the quality of life in El Paso for everyone, but especially the younger generation. "I want to do my part to make the younger generation want to stay here and not move away for college or for work," he said. His first target for revitalization was the Union Plaza area. At that time, it was home to the train station and many derelict buildings. With a plan and a strong team, he was able to help transform it into what it is today—an area thriving with restaurants, lounges, apartments, and office space.

Gomez helped prove that downtown El Paso could be worth the time and effort, and since his initial entrance into the market, others have followed suit. Some of the current businesses that he is a part of are Independent Burger, Crave, The Garden, 1914 Lounge, and T.I.M.E at Monticello. The UTEP graduate has this to say for others looking to get into business: "Keep your head down and keep moving, there are a lot of people who would like to stop you and say things to hurt you and your business." (Courtesy of El Paso Inc.)

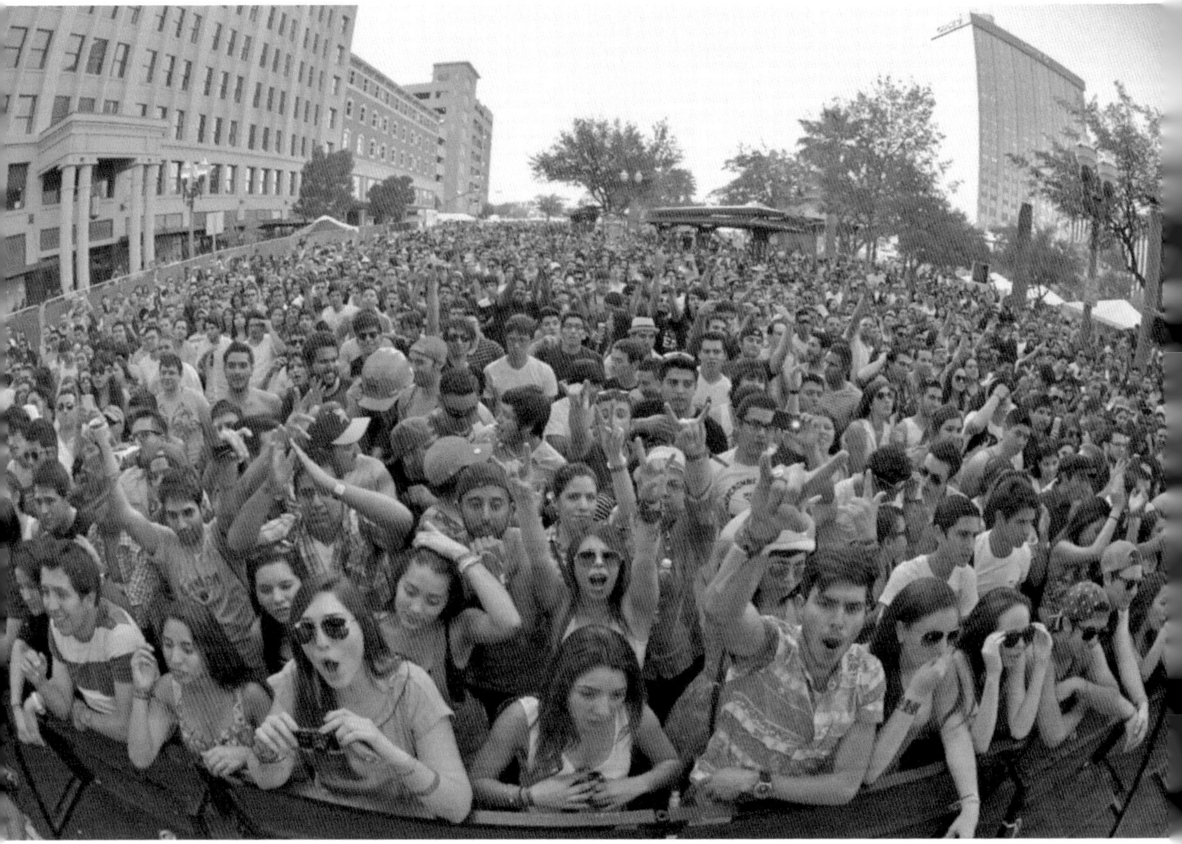

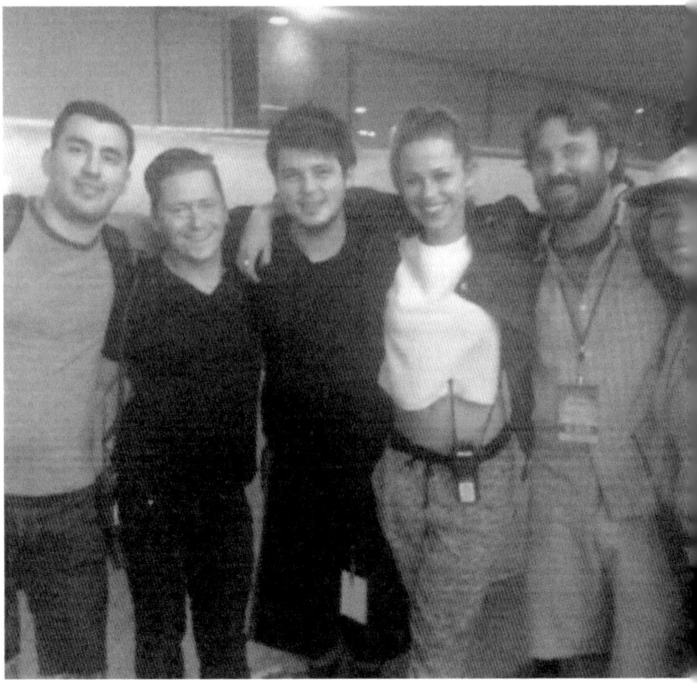

Neon Desert Music Festival Music echoed off buildings, and thousands of people moved and sang to the lyrics coming from the main stage as Los Amigos Invisibles took the crowd on a journey that helped kick off the inaugural Neon Desert Music Festival in 2011. Four El Pasoans are the brain trust behind the festival that takes place in downtown every year. Zach Paul, Gina Martinez, Brian Chavez, and Patrick McNeil started Sun City Productions, which is the company behind NDMF. The festival has grown every year and features performers such as Moby, MGMT, and Zedd. (Above, courtesy of NDMF; right, courtesy of Zach Paul.)

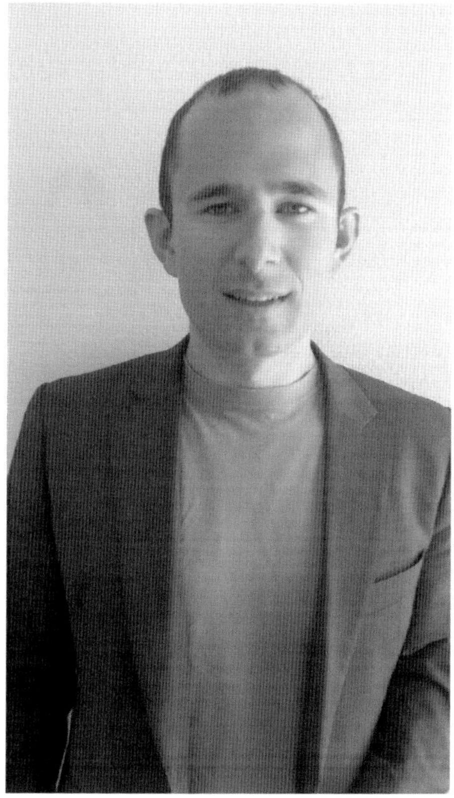

Lane Gaddy

El Paso is in the midst of downtown revitalization, and one of those leading the charge is a young entrepreneur by the name of Lane Gaddy. Born in Albuquerque, New Mexico, in 1983, Gaddy moved to El Paso after graduating from the University of Arizona. While working his way up to CEO of W. Silver Recycling, he and a group of investors have been active in purchasing properties throughout El Paso with a focus on downtown. In regards to downtown El Paso, Gaddy had this to say: "The renovation of our historic legacy in these buildings is symbolic of the progress we are making as a city." He and other young up-and-comers are helping shape the future of El Paso one day and one building at a time. (Courtesy of Lane Gaddy.)

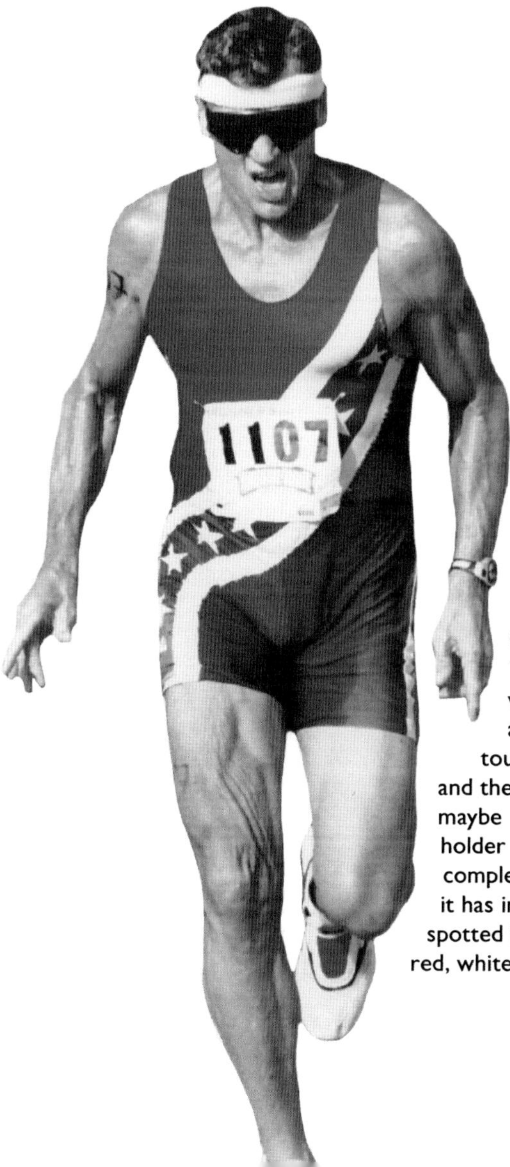

Flip Lyle

Swim, bike, run—James Arthur "Flip" Lyle has mastered the triathlon. He has competed in countless regional competitions and also the famed Ironman triathlons in Canada and Hawaii. The former Georgia Tech offensive guard made his way to El Paso when he entered into the service and was stationed at Fort Bliss. While he was on a tour in Korea, his passion for running was ignited, and the rest was history. His accolades are numerous, but maybe his greatest accomplishment is being the current holder of the Guinness World Record for most triathlons completed by one individual. That number was 250, and it has increased since that time in 2006. Lyle can be easily spotted in competition since he always wears his trademark red, white, and blue apparel. (Courtesy of Flip Lyle.)

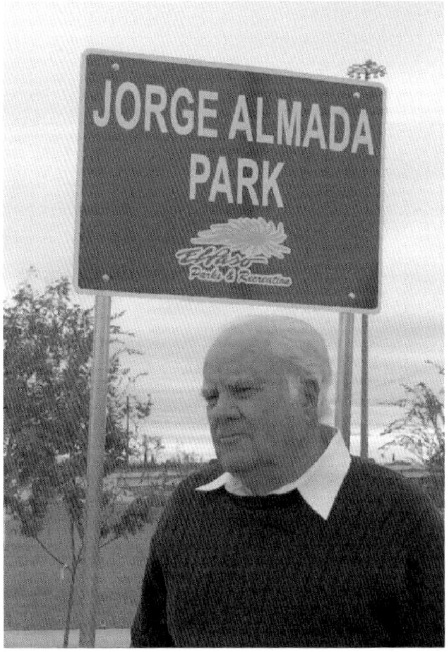

Jorge Almada

There are neighbors who take care of their home and yard to help keep the neighborhood looking nice, and then there is Jorge Almada. The World War II and Korean War veteran is a true champion for his central El Paso neighborhood. He sees his decision to get involved in the upkeep of his neighborhood as very simple: "It won't get fixed if you don't call. All I want to do is to improve the neighborhood the best I can." Improve it, he has. When he sees a pothole, he calls the city; when there is trash in an empty lot, a call to the city. He has been so effective at getting things done that neighbors now call him to report issues so he can let the city know. The Central Neighborhood Association president heads out to Pollard Park twice a day to raise and lower the American, Texas, and POW flags. Many times, people will ask him to fly one of the flags in honor of a loved one, and he obliges. In 2014, Pollard Park was renamed after him for his work and dedication to the community. (Both, courtesy of Jorge Almada and family.)

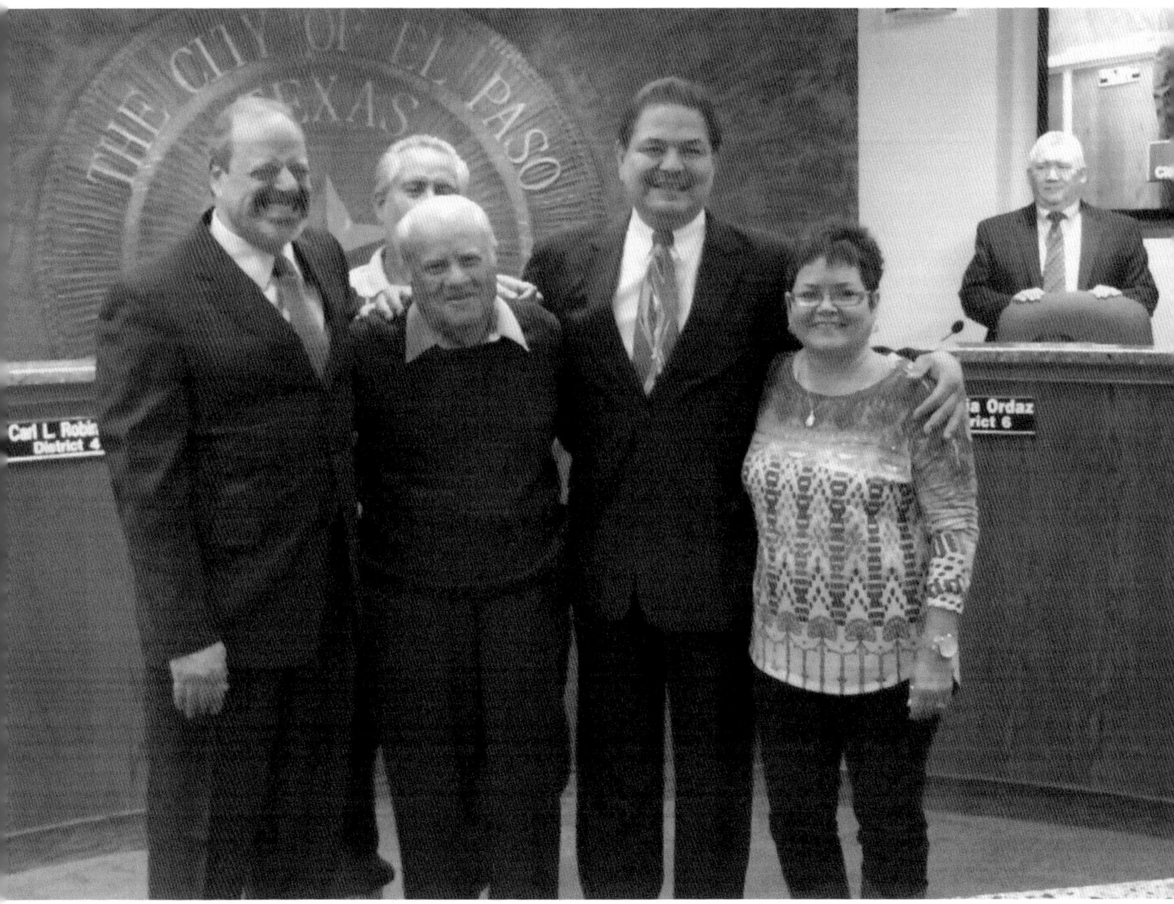

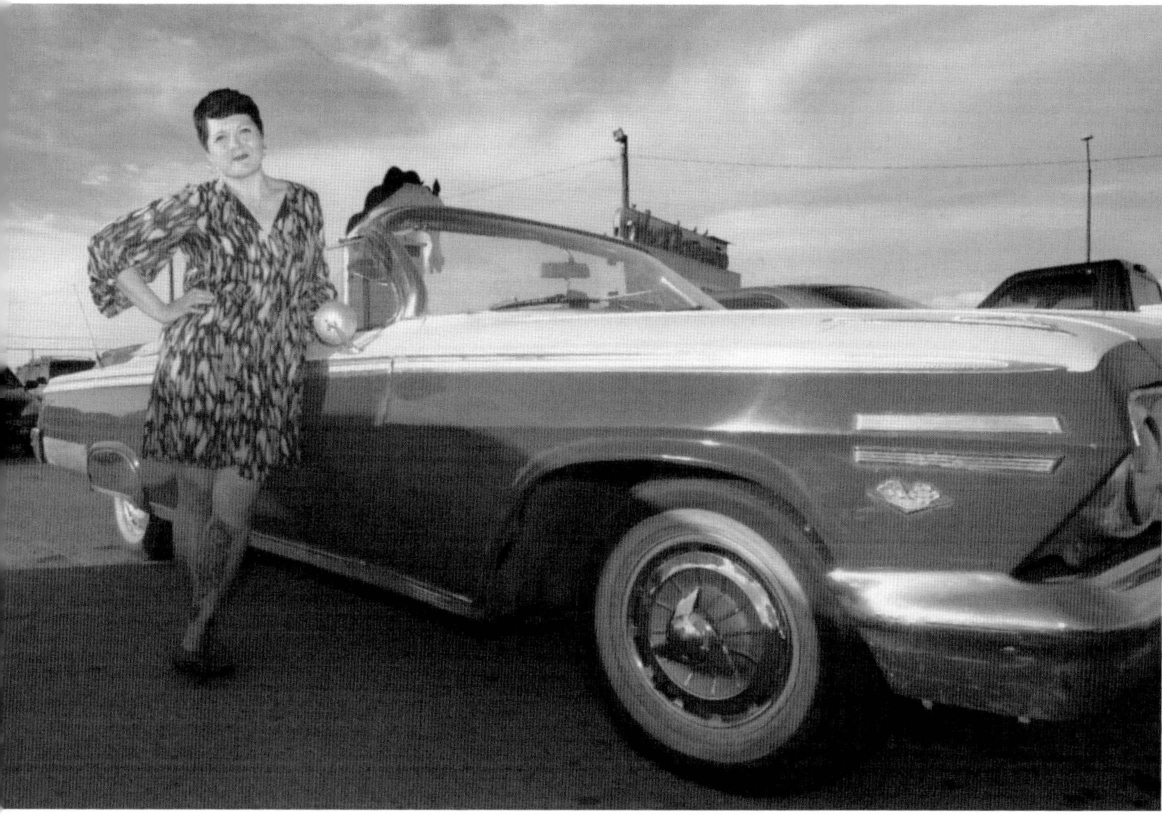

Marina Monsisvais

In 1977, Marina Monsisvais was born at the Neward Maternity Clinic in Segundo Barrio. Her family left shortly thereafter for California, but she moved back to El Paso while in middle school. The New Mexico State University graduate fondly remembers times visiting family in Juarez. "My grandmother owned a dress shop in downtown Juarez right by the cathedral so we'd spend lots of time weaving in and out of all the little shops stuffing our faces with Mexican candy and real Coca-Cola."

Holding jobs since she was 14 years old, Monsisvais has written for numerous publications, run promotions for Red Bull, and very recently, opened up her own business, Barracuda PR. Her love for El Paso and Juarez is deep, and it shows in her commitment to helping run community events such as the Mujer Festival and Chalk the Block. "I've had the honor of serving my community for a long time, community service is something that drives me, I need it as much as my community needs me. I love El Paso and I love to get fired up and do things that make an impact." (Courtesy of Marina Monsisvais.)

Ryan Piers Williams

While El Paso is known for its star on the mountain, one of its own is making a name for himself in the land of the stars. Born in 1981, Ryan Piers Williams grew up enjoying the beauty and mystery of the surrounding desert. His love for film started at Indian Ridge Middle School, and that spark propelled him to further his craft while at Hanks High School, UT Austin, and USC film school. To date, he has directed the films *X/Y* and *The Dry Land*. Williams married actress America Ferrera in 2011 and counts her as one of the many influences in his life in addition to his close family and his mentor, Stewart Stern. (Courtesy of Ryan Piers Williams.)

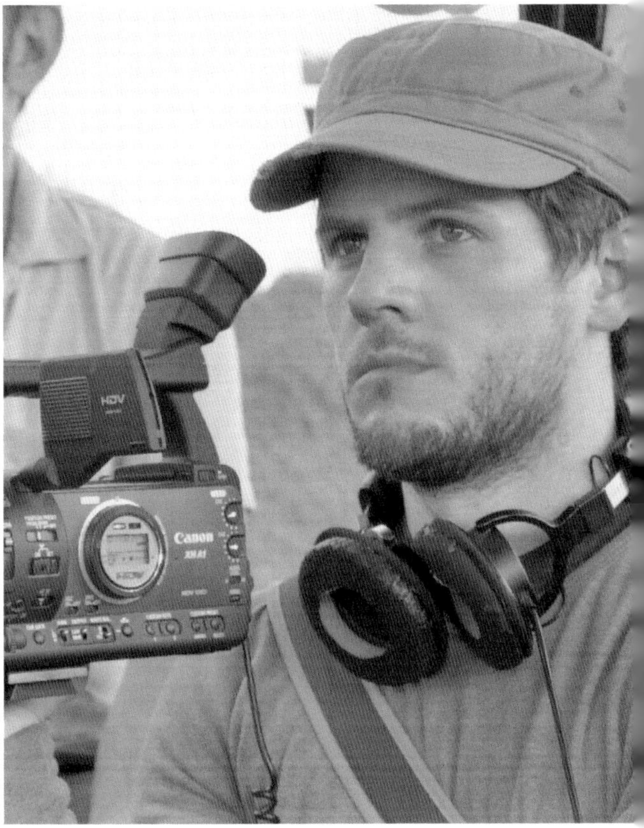

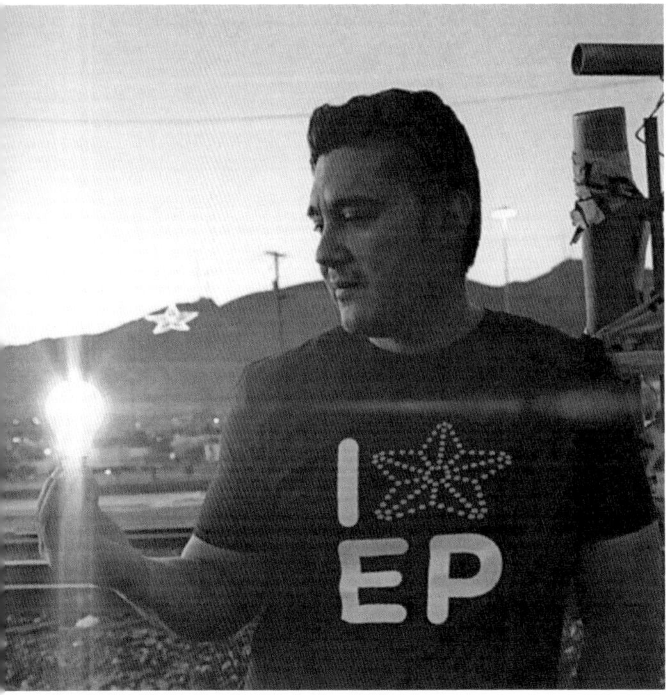

Carlo Mendo

The creative community found a place to showcase its work in downtown El Paso when Carlo Mendo opened Loft Light Studio. The young entrepreneur took a risk when he opened the studio, but his dreams and goals were far greater than failure. The studio has been a showcase for photographers, artists, and other creative types who are looking for a space to show their work. In addition to Loft Light, Mendo has taken an interest in permaculture and has helped start numerous community gardens, including Jardinez De La Fe and Valley Community Foundation. His hope is that through education of permaculture and sustainability, communities will adopt these methods and reduce their carbon footprint. Mendo is an important part of the younger generation of El Paso who have taken a keen interest in helping the city grow and thrive into the future. (Courtesy of Carlo Mendo.)

INDEX